México

0 100 200 300 400 Km.
0 100 200 300 400 Mi.

ESTADOS UNIDOS
Río Colorado
Río Gila
Río Misisipí
Tijuana
Mexicali
Nogales
Nogales
El Paso
Ciudad Juárez
Río Grande
Houston
San Antonio
Hermosillo
Chihuahua
Río Conchos
Río Bravo
BAJA CALIFORNIA
Golfo de California
SIERRA MADRE OCCIDENTAL
SIERRA MADRE ORIENTAL
Laredo
Nuevo Laredo
Brownsville
Reynosa
Matamoros
Torreón
Monterrey
Saltillo
Golfo de México
La Paz
Ciudad Victoria
Trópico de Cáncer
Mazatlán
Cabo San Lucas
Tula
Zacatecas
San Luis Potosí
Tampico
Aguascalientes
León
Guanajuato
Canal de Yucatán
Tizmín
Cancún
Mérida
Chichén Itzá
Cozumel
OCÉANO PACÍFICO
Puerto Vallarta
Guadalajara
Bahía de Campeche
Uxmal
Campeche
YUCATÁN
Teotihuacán
Morelia
México, D.F.
Jalapa
Veracruz
Toluca
Cuernavaca
Puebla
Uruapan
Orizaba
Islas Revillagigedo
Taxco
Río Balsas
Villahermosa
Acapulco
Tlapa
Oaxaca
ISTMO DE TEHUANTEPEC
Lago Petén Itzá
Belmopan
BELICE
Lago Isabel
GUATEMALA
San Pedro Sula
HONDURAS
Copán
Tegucigalpa
Guatemala
Golfo de Tehuantepec
San Salvador
EL SALVADOR

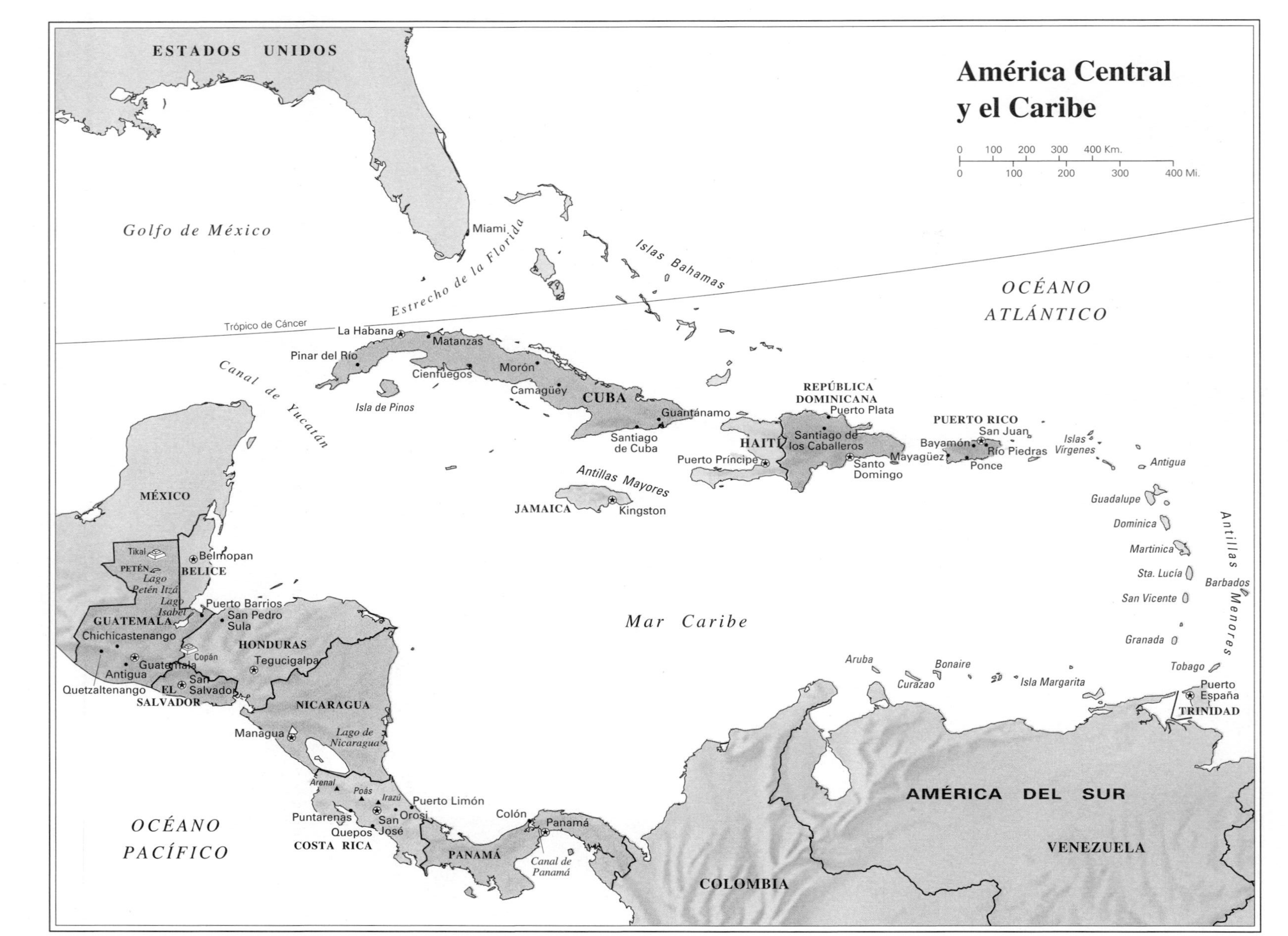

América Central
y el Caribe
0 100 200 300 400 Km.
0 100 200 300 400 Mi.
ESTADOS UNIDOS
Golfo de México
Miami
Estrecho de la Florida
Islas Bahamas
OCÉANO
ATLÁNTICO
Trópico de Cáncer
La Habana
Matanzas
Pinar del Río
Cienfuegos
Morón
Camagüey
CUBA
Isla de Pinos
Canal de Yucatán
Guantánamo
Santiago
de Cuba
REPÚBLICA
DOMINICANA
Puerto Plata
Santiago de
los Caballeros
HAITÍ
Puerto Príncipe
Santo
Domingo
PUERTO RICO
San Juan
Bayamón
Río Piedras
Mayagüez
Ponce
Islas
Vírgenes
Antigua
Antillas Mayores
JAMAICA
Kingston
Guadalupe
Dominica
Martinica
Sta. Lucía
Barbados
San Vicente
Antillas Menores
Granada
Tobago
Puerto
España
TRINIDAD
MÉXICO
Tikal
PETÉN
Lago
Petén Itzá
Belmopan
BELICE
Lago
Isabel
Puerto Barrios
San Pedro
Sula
GUATEMALA
Chichicastenango
HONDURAS
Copán
Tegucigalpa
Guatemala
Antigua
Quetzaltenango
EL
SALVADOR
San
Salvador
NICARAGUA
Mar Caribe
Aruba
Curazao
Bonaire
Isla Margarita
Managua
Lago de
Nicaragua
Arenal
Poás
Irazú
Puerto Limón
Puntarenas
San
José
Orosi
Quepos
COSTA RICA
Colón
Panamá
PANAMÁ
Canal de
Panamá
OCÉANO
PACÍFICO
COLOMBIA
AMÉRICA DEL SUR
VENEZUELA

THE BASIC SPANISH SERIES

BASIC SPANISH FOR LAW ENFORCEMENT

THE BASIC SPANISH SERIES

BASIC SPANISH FOR LAW ENFORCEMENT

ENHANCED SECOND EDITION

ANA C. JARVIS
Chandler-Gilbert Community College

LUIS LEBREDO

Australia • Brazil • Japan • Korea • Mexico • Singapore • Spain • United Kingdom • United States

Basic Spanish for Law Enforcement, Enhanced Second Edition
Ana C. Jarvis and Luis Lebredo

Product Director: Beth Kramer

Product Team Manager: Heather Bradley Cole

Product Manager: Mark Overstreet

Product Development Manager: Katie Wade

Associate Content Developer: Julie Allen

Marketing Director: Michelle Williams

Print Buyer: Betsy Donaghey

Cover Designer: Riezebos Holzbaur Design Group

Cover Image: istock

Art and Design Direction, Production Management, and Composition: Lumina Datamatics

© 2017, 2011, 2006 Cengage Learning

ALL RIGHTS RESERVED. No part of this work covered by the copyright herein may be reproduced, transmitted, stored, or used in any form or by any means graphic, electronic, or mechanical, including but not limited to photocopying, recording, scanning, digitizing, taping, Web distribution, information networks, or information storage and retrieval systems, except as permitted under Section 107 or 108 of the 1976 United States Copyright Act, without the prior written permission of the publisher.

For product information and technology assistance, contact us at **Cengage Learning Customer & Sales Support, 1-800-354-9706**

For permission to use material from this text or product, submit all requests online at **www.cengage.com/permissions.**
Further permissions questions can be emailed to
permissionrequest@cengage.com

Library of Congress Control Number: 2009944117

ISBN: 978-1-305-88603-2

Cengage Learning
20 Channel Center Street
Boston, MA 02210
USA

Cengage Learning is a leading provider of customized learning solutions with office locations around the globe, including Singapore, the United Kingdom, Australia, Mexico, Brazil, and Japan. Locate your local office at **international.cengage.com/region**

Cengage Learning products are represented in Canada by Nelson Education, Ltd.

For your course and learning solutions, visit **www.cengage.com.**

Purchase any of our products at your local college store or at our preferred online store **www.cengagebrain.com.**

Printed in the United States of America
Print Number: 01 Print Year: 2015

CONTENTS

PREFACE

Designed to fit multiple classroom styles, ***The Basic Spanish Series*** offers a flexible, concise introduction to Spanish grammar and communication with state-of-the-art online learning tools to better address the needs of today's students and professionals who need a working knowledge of Spanish.

Basic Spanish for Law Enforcement

As a component of *The Basic Spanish Series, Basic Spanish for Law Enforcement* is a career manual designed to serve those in the law enforcement professions who seek basic conversational skills in Spanish. Written for use in two-semester or three-quarter courses, it presents typical everyday situations that pre-professionals and professionals may encounter when dealing with Spanish speakers in the United States at work settings such as police stations, prisons, and on the street.

Basic Spanish for Law Enforcement introduces practical vocabulary, everyday on-the-job situations, and culture notes (*Notas culturales*) written from a cross-cultural perspective. It provides students with opportunities to apply, in a wide variety of practical contexts, the grammatical structures presented in the corresponding lessons of the *Basic Spanish* core text.

Organization of the Text

Basic Spanish for Law Enforcement contains one preliminary lesson (*Lección preliminar*), twenty regular lessons, four reading sections (*Lecturas*), and four review sections (*Repasos*).

Each lesson contains the following sections:

- A **lesson opener** consists of the lesson objectives divided into two categories: Structures practiced from *Basic Spanish* and Communication.
- A **Spanish dialogue** introduces and employs key vocabulary and grammatical structures in the context of the lesson theme. Divided into manageable segments, the dialogue features contexts specific to law enforcement. Audio recordings of the dialogues are available through the iLrn website in downloadable MP3 format. Translations of the dialogues can be found in the Instructor Resources folder on the iLrn website.
- The ***¡Escuchemos!*** activity and dialogue recording (available through iLrn) allow students to listen to the conversation and check their comprehension with true/false questions.
- The ***Vocabulario*** section summarizes new, active words and expressions presented in the dialogue, and categorizes them according to their parts of speech. The vocabulary highlights the most important communication tools needed in a variety of professional situations. A special subsection of cognates heads the vocabulary list so students can readily identify these terms. The *Vocabulario adicional* subsection supplies supplementary vocabulary related to the lesson theme.
- ***Notas culturales*** related to the lesson theme give students up-to-date information that highlights Hispanic customs and traditions.
- ***Dígame...*** questions check students' comprehension of the dialogue.
- The ***Hablemos*** section provides personalized questions spun off from the lesson theme, where students are encouraged to work in pairs, asking and answering each of the questions presented.
- ***Vamos a practicar*** activities review grammar topics that students need to know before proceeding in the lesson.

- ***Conversaciones breves*** activities practice the lesson's vocabulary.
- The ***En estas situaciones*** section develops students' communication skills through role-playing in pairs or small groups and encourages more interactive speaking practice.
- The ***Casos*** activity establishes professional situations such as conversations between a traffic officer and an accident witness, between a police officer and a burglary victim, or between a police officer and a suspect. The entire class participates in open-ended role-playing that re-creates and expands on the situations introduced in the dialogue and the *En estas situaciones* section.
- ***Un paso más*** features activities that practice the supplementary words and expressions in the *Vocabulario adicional* section, some through realia.
- Pair and group icons indicate pair and group activities.
- Audio icons show what is available either as downloadable In-Text Audio MP3s or in audio flashcards on the iLrn website.
- Quiz Quiz icons indicate available resources on the *Basic Spanish for Teachers* iLrn website.
- **Five maps** of the Spanish-speaking world are included in the front and back of the text.
- For easy reference and to aid in lesson planning, the table of contents lists the **grammar structures** presented in the corresponding *Basic Spanish* core text and practiced in *Basic Spanish for Law Enforcement,* plus the communication objective for each lesson.
- The text's grammatical sequence parallels the core text of the series, *Basic Spanish.*

Organization of the *Lecturas*

One short reading section appears after every five lessons:

- ***Lecturas*** deal with issues related to law enforcement, such as reporting suspicious activities and preventing a robbery.
- ***Dígame...*** activities check students' comprehension of the *Lectura.*

Organization of the *Repasos*

After every five lessons, a review section contains the following materials:

- ***Práctica de vocabulario*** exercises check students' cumulative knowledge and use of active vocabulary in a variety of formats: selecting the appropriate word to complete a sentence, identifying related words, matching, true/false, and puzzles.
- A ***Práctica oral*** section features questions that review key vocabulary and structures presented in the preceding five lessons. To develop students' aural and oral skills, the questions are available on the *Basic Spanish for Law Enforcement* iLrn Language Learning Center.

Appendixes

The appendixes of this book include the following:

- **Appendix A, Introduction to Spanish Sounds and the Alphabet,** presents the alphabet and briefly explains vowel sounds, consonant sounds, linking, rhythm, intonation, syllable formation, and accentuation.
- **Appendix B, Verbs,** presents charts of the three regular conjugations and of the **-ar, -er,** and **-ir** stem-changing verbs, as well as lists of orthographic-changing verbs and some common irregular verbs.
- **Appendix C, Useful Classroom Expressions,** consists of a list of the most common expressions and directions used in the introductory Spanish language class.
- **Appendix D, Weights and Measures,** features conversion formulas for temperature and metric weights and measures, as well as Spanish terms for U.S. weights and measures.

End Vocabularies

Comprehensive Spanish-English and English-Spanish vocabularies contain all words and expressions from the *Vocabulario* sections. Each term is followed by the lesson number where the active vocabulary is introduced. All passive vocabulary items found in the *Vocabulario adicional* sections, in marginal glosses to readings, and in glosses of direction lines or exercises are also included.

New to the Enhanced Second Edition

For this enhanced second edition, we are proud to offer an extensive technology program, which will give students easier access to required materials and give instructors the freedom to design their courses in the way that best meets their students' needs.

***Basic Spanish for Law Enforcement* iLrn Language Learning Center,** new to the enhanced second edition, allows students and instructors to access all the materials they need to prepare for class.

- Online, the core text *Basic Spanish* is transformed into a sophisticated, interactive eBook with built-in audio, note-taking features, and more.
- Students can **complete assignments** from *Basic Spanish for Law Enforcement* entirely online. Many activities can be graded automatically, giving students instant results and saving the instructor hours of correcting time.
- Results from completed activities flow into the instructor **gradebook**, a customizable tool that allows instructors to grade open-ended writing activities—**including communicative and role-playing activities**—and assign scores according to his/her own schema.
- **Diagnostic tests** appear in every chapter in iLrn, and automatically design an individualized review plan based on student responses.
- New ***Más práctica*** **grammar activities** provide plenty of extra practice outside of class, freeing up precious class time for more high-level discussion.
- All-new **video content from National Geographic™** along with corresponding activities introduce students to the cultures and landscapes of twenty-one different Spanish-speaking countries.

Assets

Available on ***The Basic Spanish for Law Enforcement*** **iLrn Language Learning Center**

For Students

- The **in-text audio** is available in downloadable MP3 format.
- Brief **grammar videos** feature a professor teaching specific grammar topics presented in the core text; Flash-based **grammar tutorials** help students learn and understand Spanish grammar through succinct, interactive explanations and quizzes.
- An *answer key* for *Basic Spanish for Law Enforcement* exercises is available to help students review for exams.
- Short **podcasts,** downloadable to a computer or MP3 device, review Spanish grammar and pronunciation for studying on-the-go.
- **Text glossaries** provide support for learning and practicing vocabulary.
- The downloadable **audio *Basic Spanish for Law Enforcement and Social Services Phrasebook*** provides vocabulary and phrases for real-life situations.
- The **iLrn website** includes access to additional quizzes, downloadable In-text Audio MP3s, audio-enabled flashcards, and Spanish pronunciation help.

For Instructors

- Instructors have access to **all iLrn content,** including resources for students. Instructor specific content is password protected and is not available to students.
- For instructors transitioning to *The Basic Spanish Series* from a different text, a **sample syllabus** offers suggestions for dividing the material evenly through the course of a typical semester.
- A series of **PowerPoint presentations** reviews Spanish grammar and correlates to each chapter of *Basic Spanish.* An additional set of PowerPoints presents Spanish vocabulary from each chapter of *Basic Spanish for Law Enforcement* and content from the *lecturas* as well.
- **Translations** for dialogues in *Basic Spanish for Law Enforcement* are available for download.
- **Answer keys** are provided for exercises in *Basic Spanish for Law Enforcement,* as well as for the self-directed tests.

Acknowledgments

We wish to thank our colleagues who have used previous editions of *Basic Spanish for Law Enforcement* for their many constructive comments and suggestions:

Melania Aguirre-Rabon, *Wake Technical College*
Vincent Como, *American InterContinental University*
Joan W. Delzangle, *Chaffee College*
Lance Hargitt, *Remington Colleges*
Hope Hernández, *Community College of Southern Nevada*
Dr. María R. Irizarry, Attorney, *Boston Public Schools, Boston, MA*
Lina Llerena, *Fullerton College*
Hugo Muñoz-Ballesteros, *Tarleton State University*
Michael Rice, *Remington Colleges*
Carmen Sobrino, *Wichita Friends University*
Alba Lucía Ulloa, *Pitt Community College*
Walter J. Weeks, *University of Massachusetts, Dartmouth*

We wish to recognize the contributions of Carlos Calvo and Sarah Link to this edition.

Finally, we extend our sincere appreciation to the World Languages team at Cengage Learning: Product Director, Beth Kramer; Product Team Manager, Heather Bradley Cole; Product Manager, Mark Overstreet; Product Development Manager, Katie Wade; and Associate Content Developer, Julie Allen.

Ana C. Jarvis
Luis Lebredo

CONVERSACIONES BREVES (*BRIEF CONVERSATIONS*)

OBJECTIVES

Structures

- Greetings and farewells
- The alphabet
- The definite and indefinite articles
- The present indicative of **ser**
- Cardinal numbers 0–39

Communication

- Greetings, farewells, and introductions in person and by telephone
- Asking for personal information

iLrn™

CONVERSACIONES BREVES

A. —Décima Estación de Policía, buenos días. ¿En qué puedo servirle?
—Buenos días. El[1] teniente Donoso, por favor.
—Un momento, por favor.

---

[1]When talking about a third person and giving that person a title, a definite article is used in Spanish: ***el* señor Pérez, *la* señora Robles.**

Nombre ______________________ **Sección** ____________ **Fecha** ____________

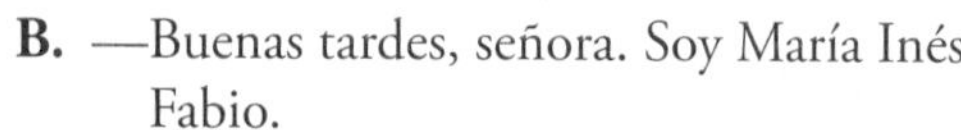

B. —Buenas tardes, señora. Soy María Inés Fabio.
—Buenas tardes, señorita Fabio. Pase y tome asiento, por favor. ¿Cómo está usted hoy?
—Bien, gracias. ¿Y usted[1]?
—Muy bien. ¿Qué se le ofrece?

C. —Buenas noches, sargento, y muchas gracias por la información.
—De nada, señora. Para servirle. Adiós.

D. —Hola, Mario. ¿Qué hay de nuevo?
—Nada, agente.
—Bueno, hasta luego.
—Hasta luego.

E. —¿Nombre y apellido[2]?
—Roberto Santacruz.
—¿Dirección?
—Avenida Magnolia, número treinta.[3]
—¿Número de teléfono?
—Cuatro, veintiocho, noventa y dos, sesenta y tres.
—¿Estado civil? ¿Es usted soltero, casado...?
—Soy divorciado.

---

[1]**Usted** and **ustedes** are abbreviated **Ud.** and **Uds.,** respectively.
[2]See ***Notas culturales*** on Spanish surnames in ***Lección 5.***
[3]In Spanish addresses, the name of the street precedes the number of the house.

© 2017 Cengage Learning

Nombre ______________________ Sección __________ Fecha __________

VOCABULARIO (*Vocabulary*)

Cognados (*Cognates*)

la avenida
la conversación
la información
el momento

Saludos y despedidas (*Greetings and farewells*)

Adiós *Good-bye*
Buenos días/Buen día *Good morning, Good day*
Buenas tardes *Good afternoon*
Buenas noches *Good evening, Good night*
¿Cómo está (usted)? *How are you?*
Hasta luego *So long, See you later*
Hasta mañana *See you tomorrow*
Hola *Hello, Hi*
¿Qué hay de nuevo? *What's new?*

Expresiones de cortesía (*Expressions of courtesy*)

De nada, No hay de qué *You're welcome, Don't mention it*
¿En qué puedo (podemos) servirle?, ¿Qué se le ofrece? *What can I (we) do for you?*
Gracias *Thank you*
Muchas gracias *Thank you very much*
para servirle *at your service*
por favor *please*

Títulos (*Titles*)

agente (Agte.) *officer*
sargento (Sgto.) *sergeant*
señor (Sr.) *Mr., sir, gentleman*
señora (Sra.) *Mrs., lady, Ma'am, Madam*
señorita (Srta.) *Miss, young lady*
teniente (Tte.) *lieutenant*

Nombres (*Nouns*)

el apellido *last name, surname*
el correo electrónico *e-mail*
la dirección, el domicilio *address*
la estación de policía, la jefatura de policía, la comisaría *police station*
el estado civil *marital status*
el nombre *name*
el número de teléfono (celular) *telephone (cell phone) number*

Verbo (*Verb*)

ser *to be*

Adjetivos (*Adjectives*)

breve(s) *brief*
casado(a)[1] *married*
décimo(a) *tenth*
divorciado(a) *divorced*
soltero(a) *single*

Otras palabras y expresiones (*Other words and expressions*)

Bien *Fine, Well*
bueno *okay*
con *with*
hoy *today*
muy *very*
nada *nothing*
Pase. *Come in.*
por *for*
Tome asiento. *Take a seat.*
y *and*

---

[1]**viudo(a):** *widower, widow*

© 2017 Cengage Learning

Nombre ______________________ Sección ______________ Fecha ______________

El español que usted ya conoce (*The Spanish you already know*)

Cognates (**Cognados**) are words that are similar in spelling in two languages. Some Spanish cognates are identical to English words. In other instances, the words differ only in minor or predictable ways. There are many Spanish cognates related to law enforcement, as illustrated in the following list. Learning to recognize and use cognates will help you to acquire vocabulary more rapidly and to read and speak Spanish more fluently.

el accidente
el adulto
la asociación
la autoridad
el banco
el caso
el cheque
la condición
el contrabando
la copia
la delincuencia
la división
el doctor
el documento
elegible
la familia
el homicidio
el hospital
el hotel
humano
la identificación
la información
legal
menor
la mercancía
la oficina
la opción
el paramédico
la persona
el plan
el problema
el programa
el (la) recepcionista
el (la) residente
el restaurante
el sargento
la sección
el teléfono
el transporte
la zona

Note: Many people who were born in the United States and whose ancestors came from Spanish-speaking countries use certain Spanish words that appear to be cognates. However, the traditional meanings of some of these words differ from one language to the other, sometimes slightly, but sometimes dramatically. This is one aspect of what is known as "Spanglish" (half Spanish, half English) or **espanglés.** For example, the word equivalent of *gang* is not **ganga,** but **pandilla.** The Spanish word **ganga** means *bargain. Officer* is an **agente de policía,** not an **oficial. Oficial** is used to designate any enlisted man ranking above a sergeant. *Felony* is not a **felonía,** but **delito grave** or **delito mayor. Felonía** means *treachery, disloyalty.* A *fatality* is not a **fatalidad** but a **muerto. Fatalidad** is the Spanish word for *ill luck* or *predetermined order of events.*

© 2017 Cengage Learning

Nombre ______________________ Sección ____________ Fecha ____________

Notas Culturales

- Personal interactions in the Spanish-speaking world are generally more formal than they are in the United States. Expressions of familiarity that often characterize friendly relations in this country—calling a person you just met by his or her first name right from the start, for example—may be interpreted in the Hispanic world as a lack of respect rather than a sign of friendship.
- The title of **señorita** is given only to a woman who has never been married. A woman who is married, a divorcée, or a widow is addressed or referred to as **señora.**

Actividades

Dígame... (*Tell me...*)

Write an appropriate response to the following statements.

1. Buenos días.

____

2. Buenas tardes. ¿Cómo está usted?

____

3. Pase y tome asiento, por favor.

____

4. ¿Nombre y apellido?

____

5. ¿Dirección?

____

6. ¿Número de teléfono celular?

____

7. ¿Estado civil?

____

8. Muchas gracias.

____

© 2017 Cengage Learning

Nombre ______________________ **Sección** ____________ **Fecha** ____________

9. ¿Dirección de correo electrónico?

____

10. Adiós.

____

11. ¿Qué hay de nuevo?

____

Quiz Vamos a practicar (*Let's practice*)

A You are a 911 dispatcher routing several telephone calls. Write in Spanish the name of the place and the telephone number (in words) you would call in each of the following situations. Since many of the words are cognates, guess at their meaning.

Garaje municipal 257-8493	Policía 112
Ambulancia 235-3001	Paramédicos 110
Clínica veterinaria 265-9267	

1. A distraught woman reports that her dog was run over by a car.

____

2. A bystander was shot at the scene of a drive-by shooting.

____

3. A husband says his wife is having a heart attack.

____

4. A caller reports a car with a flat tire on the highway.

____

5. A citizen calls in that a burglary is in progress at his/her neighbor's house.

____

© 2017 Cengage Learning

Nombre ______________________ **Sección** ____________ **Fecha** ____________

B You are responsible for logging all calls received at the police station today. In order to verify that you have written the following names correctly in the log book, spell each one aloud in Spanish.

1. Sandoval
2. Fuentes
3. Varela
4. Ugarte
5. Barrios
6. Zubizarreta

C Write the definite article before each word and then write the plural form.

1. ____________ comisaría ______________________
2. ____________ señorita ______________________
3. ____________ agente (*m.*) ______________________
4. ____________ señor ______________________
5. ____________ momento ______________________
6. ____________ información ______________________
7. ____________ calle ______________________
8. ____________ número ______________________

D Complete the following, using the present indicative of the verb **ser.**

1. —¿ ____________ usted casado, Sr. Arreola?

   —No, yo ____________ soltero.

   —¿Y Adela?

   —Ella ____________ divorciada.

2. —¿Ustedes ____________ tenientes?

   —No, nosotros ____________ sargentos.

3. —¿Tú ____________ de (*from*) México?

   —No, ____________ de Guatemala. Jorge ____________ de México.

© 2017 Cengage Learning

Nombre ______________________ Sección ____________ Fecha ____________

En estas situaciones (*In these situations*) With a partner, act out the following situations in Spanish.

1. You greet a colleague in the morning and ask how he/she is.
2. Someone knocks on the door of your office.
3. You thank someone for giving you information.
4. You receive a telephone call and ask what you can do for the caller.
5. You say "good night" to a colleague.
6. You ask someone whether he is single or married.

© 2017 Cengage Learning

En una estación de policía

Objectives

Structures

- Subject pronouns
- The present indicative of regular -**ar** verbs
- Interrogative and negative sentences
- Possession with **de**
- Cardinal numbers 40–299 and 300–1,000
- Forms and position of adjectives
- Telling time

Communication

- On the telephone: giving and receiving simple information; reporting an accident or a robbery
- Spelling; indicating addresses and telephone numbers

iLrn™

En una estación de policía

Son las dos de la tarde. El señor Pérez llama por teléfono para notificar un accidente.

Señor Pérez —Yo no hablo inglés, pero deseo avisar de un accidente.
Telefonista —¿Dónde? Yo hablo un poco de español.
Señor Pérez —Aquí, frente a mi casa, en la calle Central, entre Florida y Terracina.
Telefonista —Despacio, por favor.
Señor Pérez —Calle Central, entre Florida y Terracina. (*Deletrea.*) Te-e-erre-a-ce-i-ene-a.
Telefonista —Muy bien, gracias. ¿Hay personas heridas?
Señor Pérez —Sí, hay dos heridas graves: una mujer anciana y una niña pequeña.
Telefonista —Bien. Ahora necesito sus datos personales. ¿Quién habla? Necesito su nombre y apellido, por favor.
Señor Pérez —José Antonio Pérez.
Telefonista —¿Domicilio?
Señor Pérez —Calle Central, mil quinientos cuarenta y seis, apartamento siete.
Telefonista —¿Número de teléfono?
Señor Pérez —Siete, setenta y tres, cincuenta y nueve, cero, ocho.
Telefonista —Enseguida mando para allá a los paramédicos y un carro patrullero. Muchas gracias por su información.
Señor Pérez —De nada.

En persona, la señora Vera denuncia un robo.

Señora Vera —Yo no hablo inglés, pero necesito ayuda. Deseo hablar con un policía.
Recepcionista —¿Habla español? Un momento.
Agente López —Buenos días, señora. ¿Qué desea usted?
Señora Vera —Deseo denunciar un robo.
Agente López —Un momento. Usted necesita hablar con el sargento Viñas, de la Sección de Robos, pero primero necesita llenar un informe de robo.

La señora Vera llena el reporte de robo.

¡Escuchemos!

While listening to the dialogue, circle **V (verdadero)** if the statement is true and **F (falso)** if it is false.

1.	El Sr. Pérez habla inglés.	V	F
2.	La telefonista habla un poco de español.	V	F
3.	El Sr. Pérez desea avisar de un robo.	V	F
4.	El Sr. Pérez deletrea en español.	V	F
5.	No hay heridos graves en el accidente.	V	F
6.	La telefonista necesita los datos personales del Sr. Pérez.	V	F
7.	El nombre del Sr. Pérez es José Antonio.	V	F
8.	La Sra. Vera desea hablar con un paramédico.	V	F
9.	La Sra. Vera desea denunciar un accidente.	V	F
10.	Ella necesita hablar con el sargento Viñas.	V	F

© 2017 Cengage Learning

Nombre ______________________ Sección ____________ Fecha ____________

VOCABULARIO

Cognados

el accidente
el apartamento
central
el (la) paramédico(a)
la persona
la policía
el (la) policía
el reporte
la sección, la división
el teléfono

Nombres (*Nouns*)

la ayuda *help*
la calle *street*
el carro patrullero *patrol car*
la casa *house, home*
el dato personal *personal data, information*
el español *Spanish (language)*
el (la) herido(a) *injured person*
el informe *report*
el inglés *English (language)*
la mujer *woman*
la niña *child, girl*
el niño *child, boy*
el robo *robbery, burglary*
la tarde[1] *afternoon*
el (la) telefonista, el (la) operador(a) *telephone operator, dispatcher*

Verbos (*Verbs*)

avisar de, notificar *to inform, to give notice, to report*
deletrear *to spell*
denunciar *to report (a crime)*
desear *to want, to wish*
hablar *to speak, to talk*
llamar *to call*
llenar *to fill out*
mandar, enviar[2] *to send*
necesitar *to need*

Adjetivos (*Adjectives*)

anciano(a) *old*
grave *serious*
herido(a) *hurt, injured*
mi *my*
muerto(a) *dead*
pequeño(a) *little, small*
su *your*

Otras palabras y expresiones (*Other words and expressions*)

ahora *now*
aquí *here*
de *of*
despacio *slowly*
¿dónde? *where?*
en *in, on, at*
en persona *personally, in person*
enseguida *right away*
entre *between*
frente a *in front of*
hay *there is, there are*
para *for*
para allá *there, over there*
pero *but*
por teléfono *on the telephone, by telephone*
primero *first*
¿qué? *what?*
¿quién?, ¿quiénes? *who?, whom?*
sí *yes*
un poco de *a little*

---

[1]**la mañana:** *morning;* **la noche:** *evening*
[2]Irregular forms: **envío, envías, envía, enviamos, envían**

© 2017 Cengage Learning

Nombre ______________________ Sección ____________ Fecha ____________

VOCABULARIO ADICIONAL (*Additional vocabulary*)

Actividades delictivas (*Criminal activities*)

asaltar *to assault, to mug, to hijack*
el asalto *assault, mugging, holdup, hijacking*
asesinar *to murder*
el (la) asesino(a) *murderer*
el asesinato *murder*
el chantaje *blackmail*
el (la) chantajista *blackmailer*
chantajear *to blackmail*
contrabandear *to smuggle*
el (la) contrabandista *smuggler*
el contrabando *contraband, smuggling*
la estafa *swindle, fraud*
estafar *to swindle*
la falsificación *falsification, counterfeit, forgery*
el (la) falsificador(a) *forger*
falsificar *to falsify, to counterfeit, to forge*
el fuego intencional, el incendio intencional *arson*
el (la) homicida *murderer*
el homicidio *homicide, manslaughter*
la infracción de tránsito *traffic violation*
incendiar *to set on fire*
el (la) secuestrador(a) *kidnapper*
secuestrar *to kidnap*
el secuestro *kidnapping*
la violación *rape*
el (la) violador(a) *rapist*
violar *to rape*

Notas Culturales

- Most Spanish-speaking people usually say their telephone numbers in Spanish using a sequence other than the one used in English. For example, 549-2732 would be said as **cinco-cuarenta y nueve-veintisiete-treinta y dos** (5–49–27–32). The telephone number 890-1106 would be said as **ocho-noventa-once-cero-seis** (8–90–11–0–6). Puerto Ricans are an exception to this rule, as they generally say their telephone numbers one digit at a time. Notice that Spanish speakers say **cero** and not "o," as is frequent in English.
- Different words are used to answer the telephone in different Spanish-speaking countries: in Mexico, **bueno** or **mande;** in Puerto Rico, **hola, diga,** or **aló;** in Cuba, **hola, oigo,** or **diga;** in Spain, **diga** or **¿sí?**

Actividades

Dígame... Answer the following questions, basing your answers on the dialogues.

1. ¿Qué hora es cuando (*when*) el señor Pérez llama por teléfono?

____

2. ¿Habla inglés el señor Pérez?

____

© 2017 Cengage Learning

3. Y la telefonista, ¿habla español?

____

4. ¿Qué desea el señor Pérez?

____

5. ¿Hay heridos?

____

6. ¿Quiénes son las personas heridas?

____

7. ¿Cuál es (*What is*) el número de teléfono del señor Pérez?

____

8. ¿Qué necesita la señora Vera?

____

9. ¿Con quiénes habla la señora Vera?

____

10. ¿Qué desea la señora Vera?

____

11. ¿Con quién necesita hablar la señora Vera?

____

12. ¿Qué necesita llenar?

____

Hablemos (*Let's talk*)

Interview a classmate, using the following questions. When you have finished, switch roles.

1. ¿Nombre y apellido, por favor?
2. ¿Domicilio?
3. ¿Número de teléfono?
4. ¿Necesita un carro patrullero?
5. ¿Habla español?
6. ¿Con quién desea hablar?
7. ¿Necesita ayuda?

© 2017 Cengage Learning

Nombre ______________________ Sección ____________ Fecha ____________

Quiz

Vamos a practicar

A Write affirmative sentences using the subjects and verbs given. Then rewrite them in the negative form.

Modelo yo / desear
Yo deseo hablar con un policía.
Yo no deseo hablar con un policía.

1. usted / necesitar

____

____

2. yo / llenar

____

____

3. la telefonista / mandar

____

____

4. la señora / desear

____

____

5. nosotras / denunciar

____

____

6. el señor Pérez / hablar

____

____

© 2017 Cengage Learning

7. tú / notificar

______

______

8. ustedes / llamar

______

______

B Write appropriate questions that would elicit the following answers.

1. ¿______?

Sí, la señora Vera denuncia un robo.

2. ¿______?

No, la señora Vera no necesita llenar un informe de robo ahora.

3. ¿______?

Sí, ellos mandan un carro patrullero enseguida.

4. ¿______?

No, no hay muertos; sólo heridos.

C Give the Spanish equivalent of the following expressions. Remember to use the preposition **de** in each answer.

Modelo police station
estación de policía

1. telephone number

______

2. robbery division

______

3. accident report

______

4. police officer

______

© 2017 Cengage Learning

Nombre ______________________ Sección ______________ Fecha ______________

D Write the following numbers in Spanish.

1. 596 ______________________
2. 358 ______________________
3. 715 ______________________
4. 969 ______________________
5. 1.670 ______________________

E Change each adjective according to the new nouns.

1. señor anciano

   mujeres ______________________

2. niña muerta

   niños ______________________

3. señora divorciada

   señores ______________________

F ¿Qué hora es? (*What time is it?*)

1. ______________________ 2. ______________________ 3. ______________________

Conversaciones breves

Complete the following dialogues, using your imagination and the vocabulary from this lesson.

Al teléfono:

Telefonista —Estación de policía, buenos días.

Señor Soto —______________________

© 2017 Cengage Learning

Nombre ______________________ **Sección** ____________ **Fecha** ____________

Telefonista —¿Quién habla?

Señor Soto —________________________________

Telefonista —¿Domicilio, por favor?

Señor Soto —________________________________

Telefonista —¿Número de teléfono, por favor?

Señor Soto —________________________________

Telefonista —En seguida mando un carro patrullero, señor Soto.

Señor Soto —________________________________

Telefonista —________________________________

Un accidente:

Señora Mesa —Necesito ayuda.

Telefonista —________________________________

Señora Mesa —Un accidente de tráfico (*traffic*) en la calle Magnolia.

Telefonista —________________________________

Señora Mesa —¿El agente Muñoz...?

Telefonista —________________________________

En estas situaciones

With a partner, act out the following situations in Spanish.

1. You are a sergeant in the Traffic Division. Someone calls to report an accident in front of his/her house. Get the person's name, address, and telephone number. Thank the person for the information.
2. While patrolling a neighborhood you come across an elderly Hispanic American who has fallen down and needs help. Tell the person you don't speak Spanish very well; ask if he/she speaks English. Ask the person to talk slowly.
3. You are the switchboard operator at the police station. Someone calls to report a robbery. Refer the caller to Officer Rojas of the Robbery Division.

Casos (*Cases*)

With you and a partner playing the roles, work through the following scenarios.

1. You are a traffic officer helping a witness complete the standard accident report form.
2. Imagine yourself to be an excited witness reporting an accident to an officer.
3. You are a police officer talking to someone who has come to the station to report a robbery.

© 2017 Cengage Learning

Nombre ______________________ Sección ______________ Fecha ______________

Un paso más (*One step further*)

A Review the **Vocabulario adicional** in this lesson and match the terms in column **A** with their English equivalents in column **B.**

A	B
1. ________ el homicidio	a. assault
2. ________ el asesinato	b. kidnapping
3. ________ la infracción de tránsito	c. forgery
4. ________ la falsificación	d. swindle
5. ________ el asalto	e. blackmail
6. ________ el contrabando	f. rape
7. ________ el secuestro	g. homicide
8. ________ el chantaje	h. smuggling
9. ________ la estafa	i. murder
10. ________ la violación	j. traffic violation

B List each verb under the appropriate categories.

asaltar
asesinar
contrabandear
chantajear
estafar
falsificar
incendiar
secuestrar
violar

Crimes that involve money	Crimes that involve physical assault	Crimes that involve fire
________	________	________
________	________	________
________	________	________
________	________	________

© 2017 Cengage Learning

CON UN AGENTE HISPANO, EN UNA CALLE DE LA CIUDAD

OBJECTIVES

Structures

- The present indicative of regular **-er** and **-ir** verbs
- Possession with **de**
- Possessive adjectives

Communication

- Police work in the streets: requesting and giving directions; enforcing the use of a helmet; questioning a child walking alone
- Identifying places and geographical locations

iLrn™

CON UN AGENTE HISPANO, EN UNA CALLE DE LA CIUDAD

Una señora solicita información.

Señora —Ud. habla español, ¿verdad?
Agente —Sí, señora. ¿En qué puedo servirle?
Señora —Por favor, ¿dónde queda el Banco de América?
Agente —En la calle Magnolia, entre las avenidas Roma y París.
Señora —¿Cómo llego allá?
Agente —Debe seguir derecho hasta llegar a la calle Magnolia. Allí dobla a la izquierda.
Señora —¿Cuántas cuadras debo caminar por Magnolia?
Agente —Unas cinco o seis cuadras.
Señora —Muchas gracias por la información.
Agente —Para servirle, señora.

El agente habla con un muchacho en bicicleta.

Agente —Un momento, por favor. ¿Por qué no llevas puesto el casco de seguridad?
Muchacho —El casco es muy incómodo, señor.
Agente —En este estado la ley exige el uso del casco y, además, los cascos salvan muchas vidas. ¿Dónde vives?
Muchacho —Vivo a una cuadra de aquí, en la calle Madison.
Agente —Bien, debes regresar a tu casa a pie y buscar el casco.

Muchacho —¿Debo dejar mi bicicleta aquí?
Agente —No, debes caminar y llevar tu bicicleta de la mano.

El agente ve a una niña que anda sola por la calle y habla con ella.

Agente —Niña, ¿por qué andas sola?
Niña —Yo ya soy grande...
Agente —No, todavía eres muy pequeña para andar sola por la calle.
Niña —No es muy tarde...
Agente —Sí, es tarde. ¿Dónde vives?
Niña —Vivo en la calle California, número doscientos sesenta y siete, apartamento dieciocho.
Agente —Bien, vamos. Yo necesito hablar con tu mamá.

Más tarde el agente habla con la mamá de la niña.

Madre —¡Ay, Dios mío! ¿Qué sucede? ¿Qué pasa con la niña?
Agente —Nada, señora, pero su hija es muy pequeña para andar sola por la calle.
Madre —Desde luego, pero no me hace caso.

¡Escuchemos!

While listening to the dialogue circle **V (verdadero)** if the statement is true and **F (falso)** if it is false.

1.	El Banco de América queda en la calle Magnolia.	V	F
2.	El banco queda entre las avenidas París y Roma.	V	F
3.	La señora debe doblar a la izquierda en la calle Magnolia.	V	F
4.	La señora debe caminar una cuadra por Magnolia.	V	F
5.	El agente habla con un muchacho en bicicleta.	V	F
6.	El muchacho lleva puesto el casco.	V	F
7.	El muchacho debe regresar a su casa en bicicleta.	V	F
8.	El agente habla con una niña que anda sola por la calle.	V	F
9.	La niña vive en un apartamento en la calle Roma.	V	F
10.	La niña no le hace caso a su madre.	V	F

© 2017 Cengage Learning

Nombre ______________________ Sección ____________ Fecha ____________

VOCABULARIO

Cognados

el banco
la bicicleta
hispano(a)
el uso

Nombres

el casco de seguridad *safety (bike) helmet*
la ciudad *city*
la cuadra *block*
el estado *state*
la hija *daughter*
el hijo *son*
la ley *law*
la mamá, la madre *mom, mother*
el (la) muchacho(a) *boy, girl*
la vida *life*

Verbos

andar, caminar *to walk*
buscar *to look for*
deber *must, should*
dejar *to leave (behind)*
doblar, voltear (*Méx.*) *to turn*
exigir[1] *to demand*
llegar (a) *to arrive (at), to reach*
llevar *to take; to carry; to wear*
quedar *to be located*
regresar *to return*
salvar *to save*
solicitar *to ask for*
suceder, pasar *to happen*
ver[2] *to see*
vivir *to live*

Adjetivos

este(a) *this*
grande *big, large*
incómodo(a) *uncomfortable*
muchos(as) *many*
solo(a) *alone*
tu *your*
unos(as) *about, around*

Otras palabras y expresiones

a *to, at, on*
a la izquierda, a la derecha *to the left, to the right*
a pie *on foot*
a una cuadra de aquí *a block from here*
a veces *sometimes*
además *besides*
allá, allí *there*
¡Ay, Dios mío! *Oh, goodness gracious!*
¿cómo? *how?*
¿cuántos(as)? *how many?*
de la mano *hand in hand*
desde luego *of course*
en bicicleta *on a bike*
hasta *until*
llevar puesto(a) *to wear*
más tarde *later*
No me hace caso. *He/She doesn't pay attention to me.*
por *on (by way of), through*
¿por qué? *why?*
que *who, that*
¿qué? *what?, which?*
seguir derecho *to go straight ahead*
tarde *late*
temprano *early*
todavía *still, yet*
Vamos. *Let's go.*
¿verdad? *right?, true?*
ya *already*

---

[1]First person singular: **yo exijo**
[2]First person singular: **yo veo**

© 2017 Cengage Learning

Nombre ______________________ Sección ______________ Fecha ______________

VOCABULARIO ADICIONAL

En la ciudad

el centro comercial *shopping mall*
el cine *movie theater*
la escuela *school*
la estación de bomberos *fire department*
la estatua, el monumento *statue, monument*
la farmacia, la botica *drugstore*
la gasolinera, la estación de servicio *gas station*
el hospital *hospital*
el hotel *hotel*
la iglesia *church*
el mercado, el supermercado *market, supermarket*
el mercado al aire libre, el tianguis (*Méx.*) *open-air market*
la oficina de correos, el correo *post office*

PUNTOS CARDINALES
(CARDINAL POINTS)

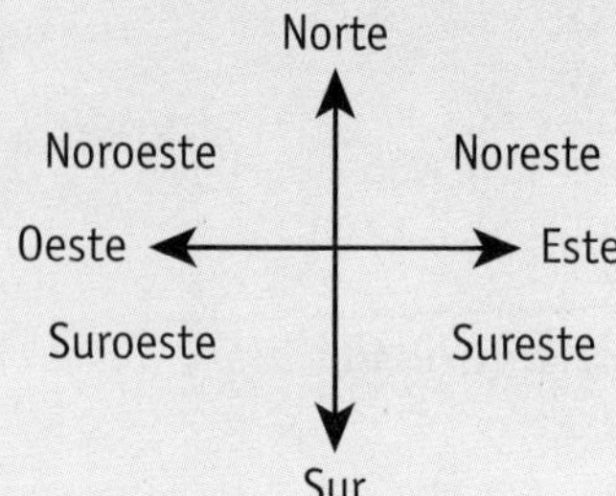

la oficina de turismo *tourist office*
la parada de autobuses (ómnibus), la parada de guaguas (*Cuba y Puerto Rico*), **la parada de camiones** (*Méx.*) *bus stop*
el parque *park*
el restaurante *restaurant*
el teatro *theater*

Notas Culturales

- The word *Hispanic* should be used to refer to someone whose language and culture derive from Spain or Spanish America. It does not refer to race. A Hispanic person can be Caucasian, Black, Asian, or Native American. When we speak of **Latinoamérica** (Latin America), we are including Brazil (colonized by Portugal) and Haiti and other countries colonized by France. When we speak of **Hispanoamérica** (Hispanic America), we are not including those countries.
- Many Spanish-speaking immigrants in the United States come from countries in which the police force is a repressive institution that often fails to respect the rights of citizens. As a result, many Latinos become frightened when they see a police officer arrive at their home. They also often prefer not to ask questions of police officers.

© 2017 Cengage Learning

Nombre ____________________ Sección ____________ Fecha ____________

Actividades

Dígame... Answer the following questions, basing your answers on the dialogues.

1. ¿En qué calle queda el Banco de América?

   ____

2. ¿Entre qué avenidas queda el banco?

   ____

3. ¿Cuántas cuadras debe seguir derecho la señora?

   ____

4. ¿Por qué no lleva puesto el muchacho el casco de seguridad?

   ____

5. ¿Qué exige la ley? ¿Por qué?

   ____

6. ¿Dónde vive el muchacho?

   ____

7. ¿El muchacho debe dejar su bicicleta en la calle?

   ____

8. ¿Es grande o (*or*) pequeña la niña que anda sola?

   ____

9. ¿Dónde vive ella?

   ____

10. ¿Con quién habla el agente?

    ____

© 2017 Cengage Learning

Nombre ______________________________ Sección ______________ Fecha ______________

Hablemos Interview a classmate, using the following questions. When you have finished, switch roles.

1. ¿Dónde queda la estación de policía en esta ciudad?
2. ¿Vive Ud. en una casa o en un apartamento? ¿Es grande o pequeño(a)? ¿Dónde queda?
3. ¿A veces regresa a su casa a pie?
4. ¿A cuántas cuadras de su casa está el parque?
5. ¿Regresa Ud. a su casa tarde? ¿A qué hora?

Vamos a practicar

Quiz

A Write sentences using the subjects and verbs provided. Add words from the dialogues, as needed.

1. Ud. / deber

   ____

2. nosotras / vivir

   ____

3. el agente Smith / exigir

   ____

4. yo / vivir

   ____

5. tú / deber

   ____

6. yo / ver

   ____

B Complete the following sentences with the Spanish equivalent of the words in parentheses.

1. Nosotros no vemos ______________________ los domingos. (*Mrs. Carreras's daughter*)
2. Yo debo llevar ______________________ a la estación de policía. (*my mother*)
3. ______________________ no andan ______________________ por la calle. (*Our daughters / alone*)

© 2017 Cengage Learning

Nombre ____________________ Sección ____________ Fecha ____________

4. Hay ____________________ aquí. (*many small children*)

5. Hay ____________________ en esta calle. (*a shopping mall*)

Conversaciones breves

Complete the following dialogues, using your imagination and the vocabulary from this lesson.

El agente Varela habla con un niño.

Niño —____________________

Agente Varela —¿El Restaurante Azteca? Queda en la calle Magnolia.

Niño —____________________

Agente Varela —Debes caminar cinco cuadras y doblar a la izquierda en la calle Magnolia. ¿Dónde vives?

Niño —____________________

El agente Varela llega a la casa de la Sra. Vega.

Sra. Vega —Buenas tardes, señor.

Agente Varela —____________________

Sra. Vega —Pase, por favor.

Agente Varela —____________________

Sra. Vega —¿Qué pasa con mi hijo?

Agente Varela —____________________

En estas situaciones

With a partner, act out the following situations in Spanish.

1. You are on traffic duty. Someone asks if you speak Spanish and wants to know where the bank is. Tell the person to go straight ahead to Seventh Street. There he/she should turn left and walk about three blocks.
2. Two teenagers are riding their bikes without helmets. Ask them why. Explain the law to them and point out that helmets save lives. Tell them they must wear their helmets.
3. You find a little girl who is apparently lost. Find out where she lives. Tell her she shouldn't walk in the street alone. Say that you need to speak with her mom.

Casos

With you and a partner playing the roles, work through the following scenarios.

1. You are a lost tourist who asks a police officer how to get to a famous landmark.
2. You are a police officer speaking to a lost child.
3. You have been asked to explain to a class of first-graders why bike helmets must be worn.

© 2017 Cengage Learning

Nombre ______________________ Sección ____________ Fecha ____________

Un paso más

A Review the **Vocabulario adicional** in this lesson and write the place that you would go to in each situation.

MODELO You want to visit a sick friend. **el hospital**

1. You want to go out to dinner. ______________________
2. You want to attend a wedding. ______________________
3. You need to buy groceries. ______________________
4. You need to take a bus. ______________________
5. You want to see a play. ______________________
6. You need to buy medicine. ______________________
7. You need to mail a package. ______________________
8. You need gas for your car. ______________________
9. You need lodging. ______________________
10. You want to see a movie. ______________________

B Say where the following states are.

MODELO Arizona **en el suroeste**

1. Rhode Island ______________________
2. California ______________________
3. Florida ______________________
4. Washington ______________________
5. Wisconsin ______________________

© 2017 Cengage Learning

CON EL AGENTE SMITH

OBJECTIVES

Structures

- The irregular verbs **ir, dar,** and **estar**
- **Ir a** + infinitive
- Uses of the verbs **ser** and **estar**
- Contractions

Communication

- Police work in the streets: dealing with gang members; arresting a thief
- Recognizing family relationships

iLrn™

CON EL AGENTE SMITH

El agente Smith habla con dos miembros de una pandilla.

Agente Smith —(*Al mayor de ellos*) ¿Qué hacen Uds. en la calle a esta hora?
José —Nada. ¿Por qué?
Agente Smith —Porque hay un toque de queda para las personas menores de edad, y Uds. deben estar en su casa antes de la medianoche.
Mario —Nosotros siempre estamos en esta esquina con nuestros amigos.
Agente Smith —Vamos a la comisaría. Voy a llamar a sus padres.

Los muchachos protestan, pero suben al carro patrullero del agente sin problema.

A las seis de la mañana, el agente Smith habla con un hombre que está en el patio de una casa desocupada.

Agente Smith —Buenos días, señor. ¿Por qué está Ud. en el patio de una casa desocupada?
Hombre —Soy el jardinero del Sr. Rodríguez. El dueño va a vender la casa.
Agente Smith —Su identificación, por favor.
Hombre —Mi tarjeta verde, ¿está bien?
Agente Smith —Necesito una identificación con su fotografía.

Nombre ______________________ Sección ______________ Fecha ______________

Hombre —Bien, aquí está mi licencia de conducir.
Agente Smith —Muy bien, muchas gracias por su cooperación.
Hombre —A sus órdenes, agente.

El agente Smith arresta a un ladrón.

Agente Smith —¡Policía! ¡Alto! ¡Alto o disparo! ¡Quieto!

¡Escuchemos!

While listening to the dialogue, circle **V (verdadero)** if the statement is true and **F (falso)** if it is false.

1. El agente Smith habla con dos miembros de una pandilla. V F
2. El mayor de los dos muchachos es Antonio. V F
3. Hay un toque de queda para las personas menores de edad. V F
4. El agente no va a llamar a los padres de los muchachos. V F
5. Los muchachos no suben al carro patrullero. V F
6. Hay un hombre en el patio de una casa desocupada. V F
7. El hombre que está en el patio de la casa desocupada es un policía. V F
8. El Sr. Rodríguez es un policía. V F
9. El agente necesita ver la licencia de conducir del jardinero. V F
10. El agente Smith arresta a un ladrón. V F

VOCABULARIO

Cognados

la cooperación
la fotografía
la identificación
el problema

Nombres

el (la) amigo(a) *friend*
el documento de identidad *ID*
el (la) dueño(a) *owner*
la esquina *(street) corner*
el hombre *man*
la hora *time, hour*
el (la) jardinero(a) *gardener*
el ladrón, la ladrona *thief, burglar*
la licencia de conducir, la licencia para manejar, el carné de conducir *driver's license*

© 2017 Cengage Learning

Nombre ______________________ Sección ____________ Fecha ____________

la medianoche *midnight*
el (la) menor de edad *minor*
el (la) miembro[1] *member*
los padres *parents*
la pandilla *gang*
el patio *yard*
la tarjeta verde *green card*
el toque de queda *curfew*

Verbos

arrestar, prender *to arrest*
dar[2] *to give*
disparar *to shoot*
estar[3] *to be*
hacer[4] *to do, to make*
ir[5] *to go*
protestar *to complain, to protest*
subir *to get in (a car, etc.)*
vender *to sell*

Adjetivos

desocupado(a) *vacant, empty*
mayor *older, oldest*

Otras palabras y expresiones

a esta hora *at this time, at this hour*
a sus órdenes *at your service, any time*
al *to the*
¡Alto! *Halt!, Stop!*
antes de *before*
del *of the, from the*
¿Está bien? *Is that okay?*
o *or*
porque *because*
¡Quieto(a)! *Freeze!*
siempre *always*
sin *without*

VOCABULARIO ADICIONAL

La familia hispánica

la abuela *grandmother*
el abuelo *grandfather*
la esposa, la mujer *wife*
el esposo, el marido *husband*
la hermana *sister*
el hermano *brother*
los hijos[6] *children*
la nieta *granddaughter*
el nieto *grandson*
el padre *father*
los parientes *relatives*
el (la) primo(a) *cousin*
la sobrina *niece*
el sobrino *nephew*
la tía *aunt*
el tío *uncle*

Los parientes políticos (*The in-laws*)

la cuñada *sister-in-law*
el cuñado *brother-in-law*
la nuera *daughter-in-law*
la suegra *mother-in-law*
el suegro *father-in-law*
el yerno *son-in-law*

---

[1]The feminine form **miembra** is rarely used.
[2]Irregular first person present indicative: **yo doy**
[3]Irregular first person present indicative: **yo estoy**
[4]Irregular first person present indicative: **yo hago**
[5]**Ir** is irregular in the present indicative: **voy, vas, va, vamos, van**
[6]The plural form **hijos** may mean *sons*, or it may mean *children* if it refers to son(s) and daughter(s).

© 2017 Cengage Learning

Nombre ______________________ Sección ______________ Fecha ______________

Otros miembros de la familia
(*Other members of the family*)

la hermanastra *stepsister*
el hermanastro *stepbrother*
la hijastra *stepdaughter*
el hijastro *stepson*
la madrastra *stepmother*
el padrastro *stepfather*

Otros tipos de relaciones
(*Other types of relationships*)

la ahijada *goddaughter*
el ahijado *godson*
la madrina[1] *godmother*
la novia *girlfriend*
el novio *boyfriend*
los padres de crianza / adoptivos *foster parents*
el padrino[1] *godfather*
la prometida *fiancée*
el prometido *fiancé*

Notas Culturales

- In many Spanish-speaking countries, adults must always carry an official identification card, and the police can ask anyone to show his/her identification document. Because of this, Spanish-speaking immigrants generally cooperate with the police when asked to identify themselves.
- It is important to remember that Latinos in the United States and Canada do not constitute a homogeneous ethnic group. They have significant cultural, racial, and ethnic differences resulting from various combinations of Spanish, indigenous, African, European, and **mestizo** traditions. They have different immigration stories, even within a single national group. The term "Mexican American," for example, may identify both recent immigrants and persons whose families have lived in what is now the United States since the sixteenth century. Nevertheless, certain underlying cultural traditions and values prevail; familiarity with them may provide law enforcement professionals with insights into the behaviors and attitudes of Hispanic Americans with whom they interact.

Actividades

Dígame... Answer the following questions, basing your answers on the dialogues.

1. ¿Con quiénes habla el agente Smith?

   ____

2. ¿Por qué deben estar los muchachos en su casa antes de la medianoche?

   ____

3. ¿Adónde van el agente Smith y los muchachos? ¿Por qué?

   ____

[1]**La comadre** and **el compadre** are the names by which the parents of a child and the godparents address each other.

© 2017 Cengage Learning

Nombre ______________________ Sección ____________ Fecha ____________

4. ¿Dan los muchachos problemas antes de subir al carro patrullero?

____

5. ¿Es inmigrante el jardinero?

____

6. ¿Quién es el dueño de la casa donde está el jardinero?

____

7. ¿Qué identificación desea el agente Smith?

____

8. ¿Qué tiene (*has*) el jardinero?

____

9. ¿A quién arresta el agente Smith?

____

Hablemos Interview a classmate, using the following questions. When you have finished, switch roles.

1. ¿Está Ud. solo(a) ahora?
2. ¿Es Ud. menor de edad?
3. ¿Está Ud. siempre con sus amigos(as) por la noche (*at night*)?
4. ¿Cómo se llaman sus padres?
5. ¿Va a vender Ud. su casa?

Quiz

Vamos a practicar

A Complete the following exchanges, using the present indicative of **estar, ir,** or **dar.**

Modelo Yo __________ a la estación de policía.
Yo ____**voy**____ a la estación de policía.

1. —¿Dónde __________ Uds.?

—Nosotros __________ en la calle Quinta.

© 2017 Cengage Learning

2. —¿Adónde __________ Ud.?

   —__________ a la casa de mi hija.

3. —¿Tú __________ tu número de teléfono?

   —No, yo no __________ mi número de teléfono.

4. —¿Tú __________ herido?

   —No, no __________ herido.

B Complete each sentence with the correct forms of **ser** or **estar,** as needed.

1. Ellas __________ agentes de policía.
2. ¿Dónde __________ el carro?
3. ¿ __________ Ud. herido(a)?
4. Él y ella __________ en el patio.
5. Yo no __________ la mamá de Roberto.
6. El sargento Viñas __________ agente de policía.
7. Él __________ en la estación de policía.
8. Tú __________ menor de edad.
9. ¿Dónde __________ tus padres?
10. Mi papá __________ en el patio. Mi mamá __________ en casa.
11. A esta hora debes __________ en casa.
12. ¿ __________ Ud. el amigo de Roberto?

C Give the Spanish equivalent of the words in parentheses.

1. Necesito ver ______________________. (*Mr. Lima's green card*)
2. El agente Morales ______________________. (*is going to arrest the thief*)
3. ______________________ es Jorge Rodríguez. (*The owner's name*)
4. ______________________ la hija de Amanda ______________________.
   (*I'm going to take / to the hospital*)

© 2017 Cengage Learning

Nombre ______________________ Sección ____________ Fecha ____________

Conversaciones breves

Complete the following dialogues, using your imagination and the vocabulary from this lesson.

El agente Robles habla con el papá adoptivo de María Soto.

Agente Robles —______________________________

Sr. Soto —Sí, señor. Soy el papá de crianza de María Soto. ¿Qué pasa?

Agente Robles —______________________________

Sr. Soto —¿En la esquina? ¿Con quiénes?

Agente Robles —______________________________

El agente Robles habla con la Srta. Roca.

Agente Robles —______________________________

Srta. Roca —Mariana Roca, señor.

Agente Robles —______________________________

Srta. Roca —Aquí está mi tarjeta verde.

Agente Robles —______________________________

En estas situaciones

With a partner, act out the following situations in Spanish.

1. You see a fifteen-year-old girl walking on the street late at night. Ask her why she's not home and where her parents are. Tell her she is a minor and she must be home before midnight.
2. Tell someone you need to see an ID with a photograph. Thank the person for cooperating.
3. You want a suspect to stop. Tell him to halt or you'll shoot. Another man appears. Tell him to freeze.

Casos

With you and a partner playing the roles, work through the following scenarios.

1. Stop a suspect who is attempting to flee the scene of a crime.
2. While working the graveyard shift, you see a minor walking alone. Find out why he/she is on the street alone at this time of night.

Un paso más

Review the **Vocabulario adicional** in this lesson and complete the following definitions.

1. La esposa de mi hermano es mi ______________________.
2. El esposo de mi hermana es mi ______________________.

© 2017 Cengage Learning

Nombre ______________________ Sección ______________ Fecha ______________

3. La mamá de mi esposa(o) es mi ______________________.

4. El papá de mi esposa(o) es mi ______________________.

5. El hermano de mi mamá es mi ______________________.

6. La hija de mi tía es mi ______________________.

7. El hijo de mi hermana es mi ______________________.

8. La mamá de mi papá es mi ______________________.

9. La esposa de mi hijo es mi ______________________.

10. El hijo de mi hija es mi ______________________.

11. La hija de mi hermano es mi ______________________.

12. Yo soy el nieto (la nieta) de mi ______________________.

13. El hijo de mi tío es mi ______________________.

14. El esposo de mi hija es mi ______________________.

15. Es la esposa de mi papá, pero no es mi mamá. Es mi ______________.

16. Es el esposo de mi mamá, pero no es mi papá. Es mi ______________.

17. Mis tíos, primos, abuelos, etcétera, son mis ______________.

18. Mi mamá y mi papá son mis______________________.

19. No es mi hijo; es el hijo de mi esposa(o). Es mi ______________.

20. Ella es mi madrina y él es mi ______________________.

21. El hijo de mi madrastra es mi ______________________.

22. Adela va a ser la esposa de Sergio. Ella es su ______________.

© 2017 Cengage Learning

LLAMADAS TELEFÓNICAS

OBJECTIVES

Structures

- The irregular verbs **tener** and **venir**
- Expressions with **tener**
- Comparative forms
- Irregular comparative forms

Communication

- 911 calls: receiving emergency calls; describing people
- Describing clothes

iLrn™

LLAMADAS TELEFÓNICAS

La telefonista de la Comisaría Cuarta recibe una llamada de emergencia.

Telefonista —Departamento de Policía, buenas noches.
Señora —¡Por favor! ¡Necesito ayuda urgente!
Telefonista —¿Qué sucede, señora?
Señora —Hay un hombre extraño en el patio de mi casa y estoy sola con mis hijos. Tengo mucho miedo.
Telefonista —Bien. ¿Cuál es su dirección?
Señora —Avenida Tercera, número setecientos nueve, entre las calles Once y Trece. A dos cuadras del hospital.
Telefonista —Enseguida mando un carro patrullero. Si el hombre trata de entrar, debe prender la luz.
Señora —¡Tiene que mandar a alguien pronto! Mi esposo tiene un revólver en la casa...
Telefonista —¿Está Ud. entrenada en el uso de armas de fuego?
Señora —No, señora.
Telefonista —Entonces, usar el revólver es más peligroso para Ud. que para él. ¿Cómo es el hombre? ¿Es alto o bajo?

Señora —Es alto y creo que es blanco.
Telefonista —¿Cómo está vestido?
Señora —Con ropa oscura. El pantalón es azul o negro y la camisa es azul... no tan oscura como el pantalón.
Telefonista —¿Lleva sombrero?
Señora —Una gorra roja. ¿Cuándo vienen los agentes?
Telefonista —Ya están en camino.

La telefonista recibe otra llamada.

Señor —Llamo para avisar que hay un hombre y una mujer en la casa de mis vecinos y ellos están de vacaciones y no vienen hasta la semana próxima.
Telefonista —El hombre y la mujer, ¿están dentro o fuera de la casa?
Señor —Dentro. La casa está oscura, pero ellos tienen una linterna.
Telefonista —¿Cómo son ellos?
Señor —El hombre es de estatura mediana y la muchacha es un poco más bajita que él.
Telefonista —¿Son jóvenes?
Señor —Sí, pero ella parece mucho menor que él. Ella debe tener menos de veinte años.
Telefonista —Muy bien. Ahora necesito la dirección de la casa de sus vecinos.

¡Escuchemos! While listening to the dialogue, circle **V (verdadero)** if the statement is true and **F (falso)** if it is false.

1. La telefonista recibe una llamada de emergencia de una señora. V F
2. La señora necesita ayuda urgente porque hay un accidente en el patio de su casa. V F
3. La señora no tiene miedo porque tiene un revólver. V F
4. La señora está sola con sus hijos. V F
5. La señora está entrenada en el uso de armas de fuego. V F
6. Usar el revólver es más peligroso para la señora que para el ladrón. V F
7. El hombre y la mujer que están dentro de la casa tienen una linterna. V F
8. La muchacha es más alta que el hombre. V F
9. Ella parece mucho mayor que él. V F
10. Ella debe tener menos de veinte años. V F

© 2017 Cengage Learning

Nombre ______________________ Sección ____________ Fecha ____________

VOCABULARIO

Cognados

el departamento
la emergencia
el hospital
mucho
la pistola
el revólver
urgente

Nombres

el arma de fuego *firearm*
la camisa *shirt*
el esposo, el marido *husband*
la gorra *cap*
los hijos *children*
la linterna *flashlight*
la llamada *call*
la luz *light*
el pantalón, los pantalones *trousers, pants*
la ropa *clothes, clothing*
la semana *week*
el sombrero *hat*
el (la) vecino(a) *neighbor*

Verbos

creer *to believe, to think*
entrar (en) *to go in*
parecer[1] *to seem*
prender *to turn on (a light)*
recibir *to receive*
tener[2] *to have*
tratar (de) *to try (to)*
usar *to use*
venir[3] *to come*

Adjetivos

alto(a) *tall*
azul *blue*
bajo(a), bajito(a) (*Cuba*), **chaparro(a)** (*Méx.*) *short*
blanco(a) *white*
cuarto(a) *fourth*
entrenado(a) *trained*
extraño(a) *strange*
joven[4] *young*
menor *younger*
negro(a) *black*
oscuro(a) *dark*
otro(a) *other, another*
peligroso(a) *dangerous*
próximo(a) *next*
rojo(a) *red*
telefónico(a) *telephone*
vestido(a) *dressed*

Otras palabras y expresiones

alguien *someone*
¿Cómo es? *What does/do he/she/you look like?*
¿cuál? *which?, what?*
¿cuándo? *when?*
de estatura mediana *of medium height*
de vacaciones[5] *on vacation*
dentro *inside*
entonces *then*
fuera *outside*
más... que (de)[6] *more . . . than*
menos que (de)[6] *less than, fewer than*
pronto *soon*
si *if*

---

[1]Irregular first person present indicative: **yo parezco**
[2]**Tener** is irregular in the present indicative: **tengo, tienes, tiene, tenemos, tienen**
[3]**Venir** is irregular in the present indicative: **vengo, vienes, viene, venimos, vienen**
[4]The plural of **joven** is **jóvenes.**
[5]**Vacación** (*f.*) is rarely used in the singular.
[6]**De** is used with numbers: **más de ochenta pesos.**

© 2017 Cengage Learning

Nombre ______________________ **Sección** __________ **Fecha** __________

tan... como *as . . . as*
tener... años[1] *to be . . . years old*
tener (mucho) miedo *to be (very) scared*
tener que (+ *inf.*) *to have to (do something)*
Ya están en camino *They are on their way.*

Notas Culturales

Generally, Latino families interact socially with their neighbors more than do other North American families. They tend to make and receive unannounced visits and to do small favors for each other with some frequency. In addition, in many neighborhoods in Spanish-speaking countries, the local grocery store often becomes a sort of mini social center at which people gather to chat and exchange community information.

VOCABULARIO ADICIONAL

La ropa

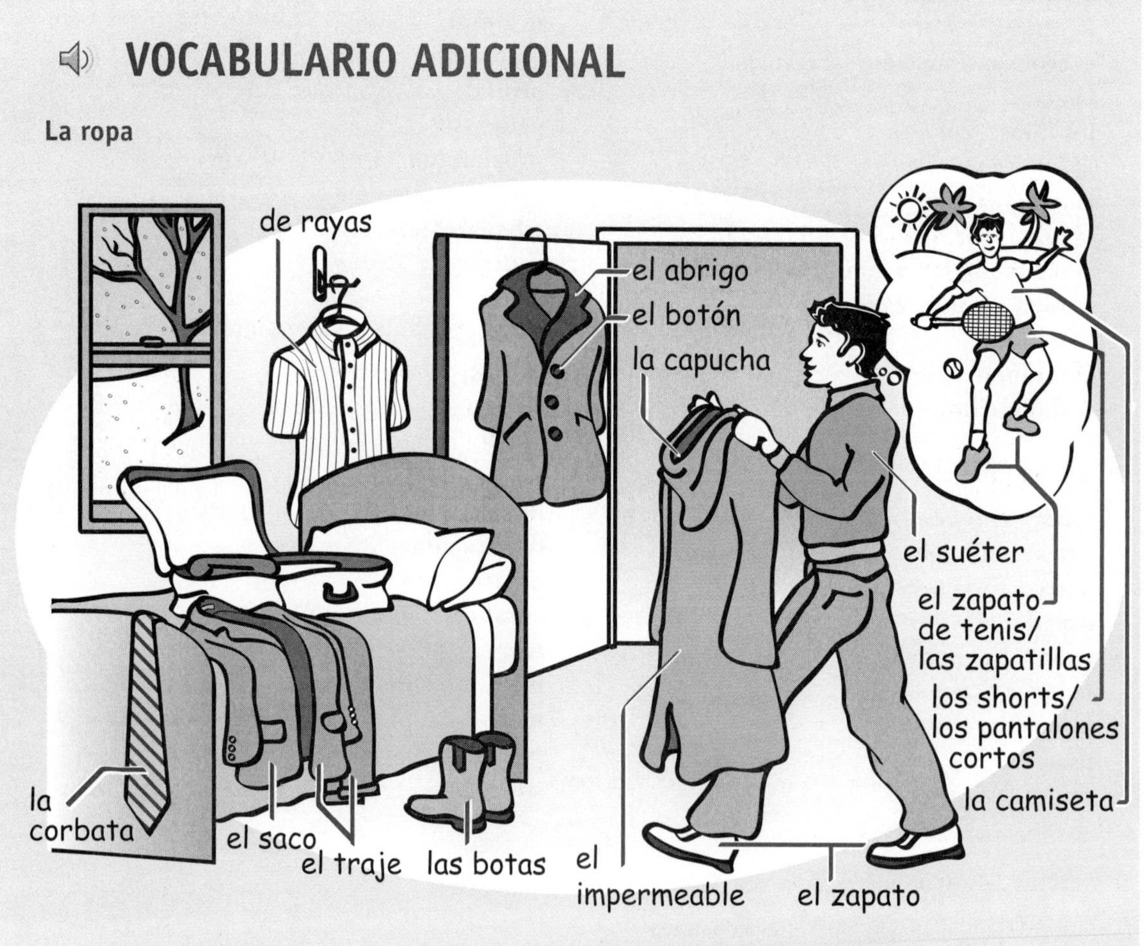

[1]To ask how old a person is, use: **¿Cuántos años tiene(s)?**

© 2017 Cengage Learning

Nombre ______________________ Sección ____________ Fecha ____________

Actividades

Dígame... Answer the following questions, basing your answers on the dialogues.

1. ¿Por qué llama la señora a la comisaría? ¿Tiene miedo?

____

2. ¿Cuál es la dirección de la señora?

____

3. ¿Debe usar el revólver de su esposo la señora? ¿Por qué?

____

4. ¿Cómo es el hombre que está en el patio?

____

5. ¿Qué ropa lleva puesta el hombre?

____

© 2017 Cengage Learning

Nombre ______________________ **Sección** ____________ **Fecha** ____________

6. ¿Qué tiene que mandar enseguida la telefonista?

____

7. ¿Por qué llama el señor a la comisaría?

____

8. ¿Dónde están los vecinos del señor?

____

9. ¿Dónde están el hombre y la mujer? ¿Dentro o fuera de la casa?

____

10. ¿Qué tienen ellos? ¿Por qué?

____

11. ¿El hombre es alto o bajo? ¿Quién es más alto, el hombre o la mujer?

____

12. ¿Quién parece menor, el hombre o la muchacha?

____

Hablemos Interview a classmate, using the following questions. When you have finished, switch roles.

1. ¿Cómo es Ud.? ¿Alto(a)? ¿Bajo(a)? ¿De estatura mediana?
2. ¿Tiene un revólver en su casa?
3. Si una persona desea usar un revólver, ¿debe estar entrenada? ¿Por qué?
4. ¿Manda Ud. un carro patrullero enseguida si hay una emergencia?
5. ¿Qué tiene que hacer hoy?
6. ¿Cuántos años tiene Ud.?
7. ¿Es Ud. mayor o menor que su mejor (*best*) amigo(a)?
8. ¿Quién es más alto(a), Ud. o su mamá?

© 2017 Cengage Learning

Nombre ______________________ Sección ____________ Fecha ____________

Vamos a practicar

Quiz

A Write sentences using the elements given.

1. yo / tener / un pantalón azul oscuro

____

2. ella / tener / una pistola

____

3. nosotros / no tener / armas de fuego en la casa

____

4. yo / venir / vestido(a) con ropa oscura

____

5. Ud. / venir / con mi esposo(a)

____

6. nosotras / venir / la semana próxima

____

B Express comparisons by giving the Spanish equivalent of the words in parentheses.

1. Los pantalones son ______________________ (*darker than*) la camisa.
2. El revólver es ______________________ (*more dangerous*) para Ud. que para el ladrón.
3. Este accidente no es ______________________ (*as serious as*) el otro.
4. Ud. tiene que mandar ______________________ (*as many patrol cars as*) yo.
5. Esta gorra no es ______________________ (*as big as*) mi sombrero.
6. Mi casa es ______________________ (*the smallest on*) la calle.
7. Ella es ______________________ (*younger than*) Uds.
8. ¿Es este hospital ______________________ (*the best in*) la ciudad?
9. Mi hermana es ______________________ (*much taller than*) yo.
10. Yo ______________________ (*am as afraid as*) tú.

© 2017 Cengage Learning

Nombre ______________________ **Sección** __________ **Fecha** __________

Conversaciones breves

Complete the following dialogue, using your imagination and the vocabulary from this lesson.

La telefonista y la Sra. Díaz:

Telefonista —____

Sra. Díaz —Necesito ayuda. Hay un hombre extraño en el patio de mi casa.

Telefonista —____

Sra. Díaz —Estoy con mi hijo de seis años, pero mi esposo no está.

Telefonista —____

Sra. Díaz —De estatura mediana.

Telefonista —____

Sra. Díaz —Creo que lleva puesto un pantalón verde o azul. No tiene camisa.

Telefonista —____

Sra. Díaz —Calle Quinta, número seiscientos treinta y dos.

Telefonista —____

En estas situaciones

With a partner, act out the following situations in Spanish.

1. You are a police dispatcher, and a child calls to report a strange man in the yard. Ask if the child is alone, find out the address, including the cross streets, and get a description of the intruder.
2. You receive an emergency call from someone who says a strange man with a gun is trying to enter his/her apartment. He/She says you have to send a patrol car right away.
3. Someone calls to report a robbery at a bank. The caller says a woman and a man with guns are in the bank. You ask for a description, and the caller says the man is white and the woman is Hispanic; both are dressed in dark clothes and wearing caps. You get the address of the bank and thank the caller.

Casos

With you and a partner playing the roles, work through the following scenarios.

1. You are a police dispatcher taking a call about an intruder in someone's yard.
2. While working the night shift as a police dispatcher, you receive a call from a person reporting that someone with a gun is trying to enter his/her house.

© 2017 Cengage Learning

Nombre ____________________ Sección ____________ Fecha ____________

Un paso más

A Review the **Vocabulario adicional** in this lesson and name the following articles of clothing and other clothing-related terms.

1. ____________________
2. ____________________
3. ____________________
4. ____________________
5. ____________________
6. ____________________
7. ____________________
8. ____________________
9. ____________________
10. ____________________
11. ____________________
12. ____________________
13. ____________________
14. ____________________
15. ____________________
16. ____________________
17. ____________________

© 2017 Cengage Learning

Nombre ______________________ **Sección** ____________ **Fecha** ____________

B Identify the articles of clothing and other clothing-related terms in the spaces provided.

1. ____________	10. ____________
2. ____________	11. ____________
3. ____________	12. ____________
4. ____________	13. ____________
5. ____________	14. ____________
6. ____________	15. ____________
7. ____________	16. ____________
8. ____________	17. ____________
9. ____________	18. ____________

© 2017 Cengage Learning

BUENOS VECINOS

OBJECTIVES

Structures

- Stem-changing verbs (**e:ie**)
- The present progressive
- Some uses of the definite article

Communication

- Neighborhood policing: helping to implement a neighborhood watch program
- Describing parts of the house

iLrn™

BUENOS VECINOS

Los lunes y miércoles, el agente Martí ayuda a establecer programas especiales. Hoy está hablando con un grupo de vecinos que quieren organizar un programa de vigilancia en el barrio.

Agente Martí —¿Quieren saber la mejor manera de prevenir los robos, los secuestros y otros delitos? ¡Tener un vecindario unido!

Sr. Lima —El problema es que casi todos estamos mucho tiempo fuera de la casa.

Agente Martí —Entonces tenemos que comenzar por identificar a las personas que generalmente están en su casa durante el día.

Sra. Paz —Mi mamá, por ejemplo, está en casa cuidando a los niños mientras yo trabajo.

Agente Martí —Su mamá y las demás personas que no trabajan deben tratar de observar cualquier actividad no usual en el barrio. Si notan algo sospechoso deben llamar a la policía inmediatamente.

Sr. Vega —¿Al nueve, uno, uno?

Agente Martí —No, ese número es sólo para emergencias. Deben tener, en un lugar visible, el número de la estación de policía más cercana.

Sr. Alba —También tenemos que tomar otras medidas para evitar los robos.

Agente Martí —Lo primero es cerrar las puertas con llave y no dejar ventanas abiertas. Es una buena idea instalar cerrojos de seguridad en las puertas.

Sr. Lima —Nosotros siempre encendemos la luz del portal por la noche.

Nombre ______________________ Sección ____________ Fecha ____________

Agente Martí —Buena idea, y la puerta de la calle debe tener un agujerito para mirar quién está tocando el timbre.

Sra. Paz —¡Y si es un extraño, no entra en la casa!

Sra. Caso —Yo pienso que lo más importante es proteger a los niños...

Agente Martí —En primer lugar, los niños no deben estar solos en su casa y, cuando regresan de la escuela, deben tener un lugar adonde ir si hay problemas. ¡Ah! Son las seis. Es la hora de la cena. Regreso el próximo lunes.

Sra. Caso —Si es posible, nosotros preferimos tener la próxima reunión el miércoles.

¡Escuchemos!

While listening to the dialogue, circle **V (verdadero)** if the statement is true and **F (falso)** if it is false.

1. El agente Martí ayuda a establecer programas especiales. V F
2. Los vecinos quieren saber la manera de prevenir accidentes. V F
3. Hay que comenzar por identificar a los vecinos que generalmente están en su casa durante el día. V F
4. La mamá de la Sra. Paz cuida a los niños. V F
5. Si las personas que no trabajan ven algo sospechoso, deben llamar al nueve, uno, uno. V F
6. Ellas deben tener el número de teléfono de la estación de policía más cercana en un lugar visible. V F
7. No debemos cerrar la puerta de la calle con llave. V F
8. No es una buena idea instalar cerrojos de seguridad en las puertas. V F
9. Los niños no deben estar solos cuando regresan de la escuela. V F
10. Los vecinos prefieren tener la próxima reunión el lunes. V F

© 2017 Cengage Learning

Nombre ______________________ Sección ____________ Fecha ____________

VOCABULARIO

Cognados

la actividad
especial
generalmente
el grupo
la idea
importante
inmediatamente
posible
el programa
usual
visible

Nombres

el agujerito *peephole*
la cena *dinner*
el cerrojo de seguridad *deadbolt*
el delito *crime*
el delito mayor (grave) *felony*
el delito menor (leve) *misdemeanor*
el (la) extraño(a) *stranger*
el lugar *place*
la manera, el modo *way*
el número *number*
el portal *porch*
la puerta *door*
la puerta de la calle *front door*
la reunión, la junta (*Méx.*) *meeting*
el secuestro *kidnapping*
el tiempo *time*
el vecindario, el barrio *neighborhood*
el (la) vecino(a) *neighbor*
la ventana *window*

Verbos

ayudar *to help*
cerrar (e:ie) *to close*
comenzar (e:ie), empezar (e:ie) *to begin*
cuidar *to take care of*
encender (e:ie), prender *to turn on (i.e. the light)*
establecer[1] *to establish*
evitar *to avoid*
identificar *to identify*
instalar *to install*
mirar *to look at, to watch*
notar *to notice*
observar *to observe*
organizar *to organize*
pensar (e:ie) *to think*
preferir (e:ie) *to prefer*
prevenir[2] *to prevent*
proteger[3] *to protect*
querer (e:ie) *to want, to wish*
saber[4] *to know*

Adjetivos

abierto(a) *open*
cercano(a) *close, nearby*
cualquier *any*
ese, esa *that*
primero(a) *first*
sospechoso(a) *suspicious*
todos(as) *all, everybody*
unido(a) *united*

---

[1]Irregular first person present indicative: **yo establezco**
[2]**yo prevengo**
[3]**yo protejo**
[4]Irregular first person present indicative: **yo sé**

© 2017 Cengage Learning

Nombre ______________________ Sección ____________ Fecha ____________

Otras palabras y expresiones

a donde, adonde *where (to)*
algo *something*
casi *almost*
cerrar (e:ie) con llave *to lock*
cuando *when*
durante *during*
en casa *at home*
en primer lugar *in the first place*
lo más importante *the most important thing*
lo primero *the first thing*
los (las) demás *the others*
mientras *while*
no usual *unusual*
para *to, in order to*
por ejemplo *for example*
sólo, solamente *only*
también *also, too*
tocar el timbre *to ring the doorbell*
tomar medidas *to take measures*
la vigilancia del barrio *neighborhood watch*

VOCABULARIO ADICIONAL

La casa

el baño, el escusado[1] (*Méx.*) *bathroom*
el comedor *dining room*
el cuarto, la habitación *room*
el dormitorio, la recámara (*Méx.*) *bedroom*
la entrada *entrance*
el garaje *garage*
el jardín *garden*
la pared *wall*
el pasillo *hall*
la sala *living room*
la sala de estar *family room*
el sótano *basement*
el techo (de tejas) (*tile*) *roof*
la terraza *terrace*

Algunas palabras relacionadas con la seguridad (*Some words related to safety*)

la alarma *alarm*
el (la) bombero *firefighter*
cortar el césped *to mow the lawn*
dejar encendido(a), dejar prendido(a) *to leave turned on*
podar arbustos (árboles) *to trim bushes (trees)*
la puerta blindada *armored door*
¡Socorro!, ¡Auxilio! *Help!*
suspender la entrega *to stop delivery*
  ... de la correspondencia *of the mail*
  ... del periódico *of the newspaper*
la ventana con rejas *window with bars*

---

[1]Also **excusado**

© 2017 Cengage Learning

Nombre ______________________ Sección ____________ Fecha ____________

Notas Culturales

- In Spanish-speaking countries, people generally have two surnames: the father's surname and the mother's maiden name. For example, the children of María *Rivas* and Juan *Pérez* would use the surnames *Pérez Rivas*. In this country, this custom may cause some confusion when completing forms, making appointments, or filing records. In addition, many Spanish surnames include **de, del, de la(s),** or **de los.** When this happens, these words are placed after the name. The proper order for alphabetizing Spanish names is to list people according to the father's surname.

  Alba, Antonio de
  Casas, Juan Carlos de las
  Cerros, Andrés de los
  Nodal Ortiz, Fernando
  Orta Sánchez, Josefina
  Peña Aguilar, Rosa María
  Peña Gómez, Ricardo
  Peña Gómez, Tomás
  Torre, Margarita de la
  Valle, Fernando del

- In Spanish-speaking countries a woman doesn't change her last name when she marries, but she may add her husband's last name after her own, preceded by **de:** i.e., if Teresa Gómez marries Juan Pérez she may sign *Teresa Gómez de Pérez.* Many Hispanic American women living in the U.S., however, do use their husband's last name.

Actividades

Dígame... Answer the following questions, basing your answers on the dialogue.

1. ¿Qué hace el agente Martí los lunes y miércoles?

   ____

2. ¿Con quiénes está hablando hoy?

   ____

3. ¿Cuál es la mejor manera de prevenir los robos y otros delitos?

   ____

4. ¿Qué es lo primero que tienen que hacer?

   ____

5. ¿Qué hace la mamá de la Sra. Paz mientras ella trabaja?

   ____

6. ¿Qué deben hacer las personas que no trabajan durante el día?

   ____

© 2017 Cengage Learning

Nombre ______________________ Sección ____________ Fecha ____________

7. ¿Qué deben hacer si notan algo sospechoso?

____

8. ¿Qué deben tener las personas en un lugar visible?

____

9. ¿Qué hacen siempre la Sra. Lima y su esposo?

____

10. ¿Qué es lo más importante según (*according to*) la Sra. Caso?

____

Hablemos Interview a classmate, using the following questions. When you have finished, switch roles.

1. ¿Hay un programa de vigilancia en su barrio?
2. ¿Qué medidas debemos tomar para prevenir los robos?
3. ¿Pasa Ud. mucho tiempo fuera de su casa?
4. ¿Qué hace Ud. si nota algo sospechoso?
5. ¿Qué números de teléfono tiene Ud. en un lugar visible?
6. ¿Tiene Ud. un cerrojo de seguridad en la puerta de la calle?
7. ¿Enciende Ud. la luz del portal por la noche?
8. Cuando tocan a la puerta, ¿mira Ud. por el agujerito?

Quiz

Vamos a practicar

A Complete the following exchanges, using the present indicative of the verbs given.

1. pensar —¿Qué ______________ Uds. que es lo más importante?
   —Nosotros ______________ que lo más importante es estar unidos.
2. querer —¿Tú ______________ organizar el programa?
   —Sí, y también ______________ hablar con el teniente.
3. encender —¿Teresa va a ______________ la luz?
   —No, ella no ______________ la luz durante el día.

© 2017 Cengage Learning

Nombre ______________________ Sección ____________ Fecha ____________

4. empezar —¿A qué hora ______________ la reunión?

—______________ a las dos.

5. cerrar —¿Tú ______________ las puertas con llave?

—Sí, y también ______________ las ventanas.

B Complete the following sentences, using the present progressive of the verbs given to indicate that the action is taking place right now.

1. El agente ______________ (ayudar) a los vecinos.
2. Ellos ______________ (encender) las luces.
3. Yo ______________ (proteger) a los niños.
4. Nosotros ______________ (instalar) una puerta blindada.
5. ¿Qué ______________ (hacer) tú?

C Complete the following sentences with the Spanish equivalent of the words in parentheses.

1. Ella viene ______________ (*on Tuesdays*).
2. Son ______________ (*two-thirty*).
3. Los niños van ______________ (*to school*).
4. Ellos regresan ______________ (*next week*).
5. ______________ (*Children*) necesitan mucho amor (*love*).

Conversaciones breves

Complete the following dialogues, using your imagination and the vocabulary from this lesson.

En una reunión para organizar un programa de vigilancia del barrio.

Sr. Cota —______________

Agente —Identificar a las personas que no trabajan.

Sr. Cota —______________

Agente —Entonces, su mamá debe ayudar a vigilar el barrio.

Sr. Cota —______________

Agente —Debe llamar a la policía.

Sr. Cota —______________

Agente —No, no debe llamar a ese número.

© 2017 Cengage Learning

Nombre _______________ Sección _______________ Fecha _______________

Sr. Cota —_______________

Agente —Debe llamar al teléfono de la estación de policía más cercana.

Sr. Cota —_______________

Agente —En un lugar visible.

Sr. Cota —_______________

Agente —Lo mejor es tener ventanas con rejas.

Sr. Cota —_______________

Agente —Deben mirar por el agujerito de la puerta.

Sr. Cota —_______________

Agente —Si es posible, prefiero tener la reunión mañana.

En estas situaciones

With a partner, act out the following situations in Spanish.

1. You tell a neighbor that you are going to organize a neighborhood watch. Tell him/her the meeting starts at seven-thirty.
2. You tell a friend that you spend a lot of time outside the house and that you are not at home during the day.
3. You ask a friend if he/she wants to install a deadbolt on his/her door. Ask him/her also if he/she always turns the porch lights on.

Casos

With you and a partner playing the roles, work through the following scenarios.

1. You and a neighbor are discussing security measures to prevent burglaries.
2. You and a friend are discussing measures to keep the neighborhood children safe.

© 2017 Cengage Learning

Nombre ______________________________ Sección ____________ Fecha ____________

Un paso más

A Review the **Vocabulario adicional** in this lesson and then draw a floor plan of your dream house in which you label each part and room of the house.

© 2017 Cengage Learning

Nombre ______________________ Sección ______________ Fecha ______________

B Review the vocabulary related to safety measures in the **Vocabulario adicional.** What words or phrases come to mind when you think of the following?

You are going on vacation.	You are screaming for help.
______________________	______________________
______________________	______________________
______________________	______________________
There is a fire next door.	**Someone breaks into a house.**
______________________	______________________
______________________	______________________
______________________	______________________

© 2017 Cengage Learning

LECTURA 1 DENUNCIANDO ACTIVIDADES SOSPECHOSAS

Read the information in the following pamphlet about reporting suspicious activities. Try to guess the meaning of all cognates.

DENUNCIANDO ACTIVIDADES SOSPECHOSAS[1]

¡La policía necesita la ayuda de todos los miembros de la comunidad! Cuando[2] Ud. ayuda a la policía, también se ayuda a sí mismo.[3] Si Ud. toma responsabilidad, puede evitar[4] ser víctima de un crimen. ¡La atención de la comunidad es la mejor prevención!

Recuerde[5]:

1. Si Ud. ve[6] alguna[7] actividad criminal, llame a la policía enseguida. Describa con exactitud lo que vio.[8]
2. No deje de[9] llamar a la policía si Ud. sospecha[10] algo.[11] No importa si es una falsa alarma.
3. En cuanto pueda,[12] anote[13] lo que recuerde.
4. Guarde[14] una copia de los siguientes[15] formularios[16]. Es posible que Ud. las necesite[17] en el futuro.

© Cengage Learning

[1] *Reporting suspicious activities*
[2] *When*
[3] **sí...** *yourself*
[4] *avoid*
[5] *Remember*
[6] *see*
[7] *any*
[8] **lo...** *what you saw*
[9] **No...** *Don't fail to*
[10] *suspect*
[11] *something*
[12] **En...** *As soon as you can*
[13] *write down*
[14] *Keep*
[15] *following*
[16] *forms*
[17] **Ud...** *you may need them*

Dígame...

1. Which of the following points does the brochure recommend? Si Ud. ve alguna actividad criminal...

_____ **a.** debe esperar (*wait*) hasta mañana para llamar a la policía.

_____ **b.** Ud. necesita guardar una copia de la descripción de la persona y de la descripción del vehículo.

_____ **c.** primero debe hablar con los vecinos.

_____ **d.** debe anotar una descripción exacta de lo que vio.

© 2017 Cengage Learning

Nombre ______________________ **Sección** ____________ **Fecha** ____________

2. Interview a classmate who reports some suspicious activity. Complete the description. When you have finished, switch roles.

DESCRIPCIÓN DE LA PERSONA	DESCRIPCIÓN DEL VEHÍCULO
Sexo ____________	2 puertas[12] ______ 4 puertas ______
Raza ____________	Convertible/camión[13] ____________
Edad ____________	Carro deportivo[14] ____________
Estatura ____________	Motocicleta ____________
Peso[1] ____________	Otro ____________
Cabello[2] ____________	Marca[15] ____________
Ojos[3] ____________	Modelo ____________ Año ______
Armas ____________	Color ____________
Ropa ____________	Nº de placa[16] ____________
Complexión[4] (delgado,[5] grueso,[6] mediano[7]) ____________	Estado ____________
	N.º de personas en el vehículo ______
Características (lentes,[8] bigote,[9] cicatrices,[10] etc.) ____________	Hombre(s) ______ Mujer(es) ______
____________	¿Dónde fue visto últimamente?
¿Dónde fue visto últimamente[11]?	____________
____________	____________
____________	____________
Dirección en que se fue ____________	Dirección en que se fue[17] ____________
____________	____________
	____________

[1] *Weight*
[2] *Hair*
[3] *Eyes*
[4] *Build*
[5] *thin*
[6] *fat*
[7] *average*
[8] *glasses*
[9] *moustache*
[10] *scars*
[11] **fue...** *was he/she last seen?*
[12] *doors*
[13] *truck*
[14] **Carro...** *Sports car*
[15] *Make*
[16] *License plate number*
[17] **se...** *he/she went*

© 2017 Cengage Learning

Nombre ______________________ Sección ____________ Fecha ____________

REPASO

Práctica de vocabulario

A Circle the word or phrase that does not belong in each group.

1. rojo extraño blanco
2. notar observar dejar
3. padres delito hijos
4. instalar cuidar ayudar
5. establecer evitar organizar
6. cena mañana tarde
7. lugar cercano a una cuadra de aquí enseguida
8. llegar doblar voltear
9. sucede denuncia pasa
10. ¡Alto! ¡Siempre! ¡Quieto!

B Circle the word or phrase that best completes each sentence.

1. La señora necesita (robo / ayuda / estado).
2. La casa (queda / deletrea / llena) en la calle Campbell.
3. Es un hombre (solo / incómodo / anciano). Tiene noventa años.
4. Hablan (pero / por / muy) teléfono.
5. ¿Tienes el (herido / lugar / casco) de seguridad?
6. Arizona es (un estado / una ciudad / un barrio).
7. Ellos (deben / salvan / andan) solos por la calle.
8. Debe seguir derecho hasta (llevar / llegar / quedar) a la calle Estrella.

© 2017 Cengage Learning

Nombre ______________________ Sección ____________ Fecha ____________

9. Vivo en la calle Heather, (como / entre / ya) Arroyo y Puente.
10. La ley (sucede / dobla / exige) el uso del casco.
11. Los cascos salvan muchas (cuadras / gorras / vidas).
12. Necesito mi licencia para (manejar / chantajear / arrestar).
13. Hay un (patio / toque / padre) de queda para las personas menores de 18 años.
14. Ella es de México, pero tiene su (pandilla / licencia / tarjeta) verde.
15. El dueño va a (disparar / vender / protestar) la casa.
16. Es una mujer muy (joven / cuarta / azul). Tiene veintidós años.
17. ¿Está Ud. (alta / extraña / entrenada) en el uso de armas?
18. ¿(Cómo / Cuál / Cuánto) es ella? ¿Alta o baja?

C Match the questions in column **A** with the answers in column **B.**

A		B	
1.	_____ ¿Cuál es el mejor modo de prevenir robos?	a.	El próximo viernes.
2.	_____ ¿Quién cuida a los niños?	b.	A las tres y media.
3.	_____ ¿Notan algo sospechoso?	c.	Calle Sexta, número 589.
4.	_____ ¿A qué hora regresa de la escuela?	d.	Sí, pero no graves.
5.	_____ ¿Cierran las puertas?	e.	Mi mamá.
6.	_____ ¿Qué van a instalar?	f.	Sí, son las siete.
7.	_____ ¿Cuándo tenemos la reunión?	g.	Sí, de la Sección de Robos.
8.	_____ ¿La puerta tiene un agujerito?	h.	Un cerrojo de seguridad.
9.	_____ ¿Es la hora de la cena?	i.	Tener un vecindario unido.
10.	_____ ¿Cuál es su domicilio?	j.	Sí, con llave.
11.	_____ ¿Es Ud. el sargento Villa?	k.	Sí, vamos a llamar a la policía.
12.	_____ ¿Hay heridos?	l.	Sí, para mirar quién está tocando el timbre.

© 2017 Cengage Learning

Nombre ______________________ Sección ____________ Fecha ____________

D Crucigrama

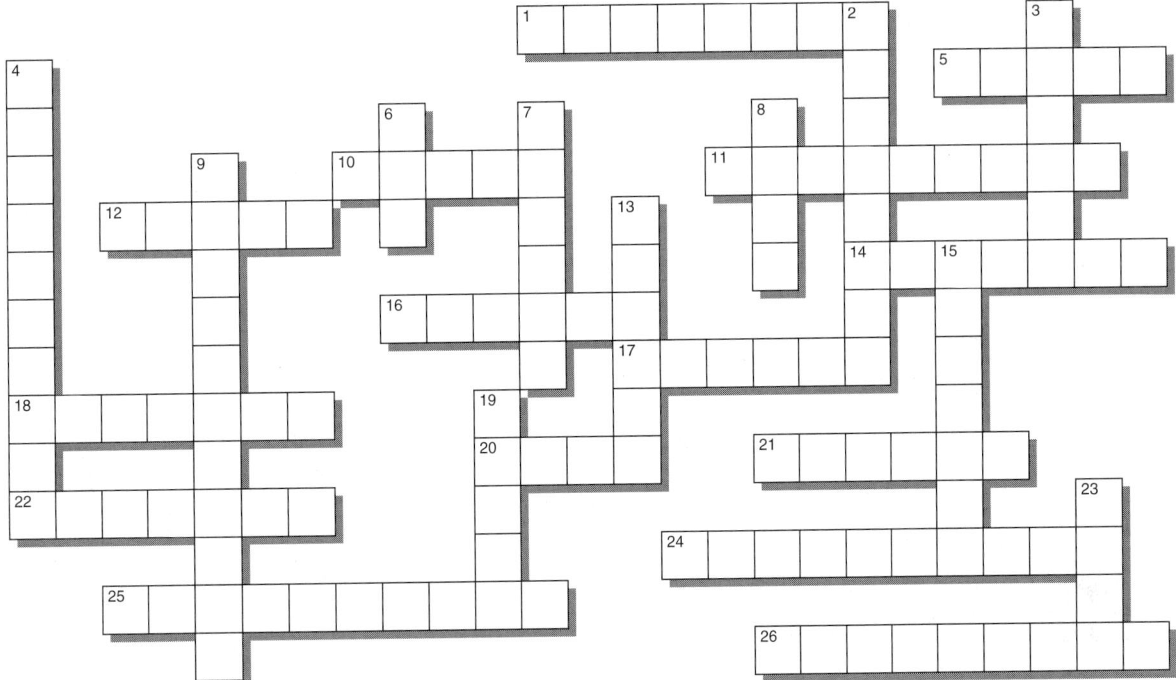

Horizontales

1. prende
5. opuesto de "dentro"
10. Tienen muchas armas de ____________.
11. avisar de
12. La casa es de ella; ella es la ____________.
14. Es de estatura ____________.
16. desear
17. En Washington hablan ____________.
18. Van a instalar un ____________ de seguridad.
20. opuesto de "bajo"
21. opuesto de "negro"
22. Está en la ____________ de las calles Quinta y Magnolia.
24. barrio
25. Van a enviar un carro ____________.
26. empiezan

Verticales

2. mandamos
3. siete días
4. las doce de la noche
6. Voy a encender la ____________.
7. ¿Es una mujer o un ____________?
8. manera
9. operador(a)
13. esposo
15. opuesto de "izquierda"
19. opuesto de "menor"
23. *clothes,* en español

© 2017 Cengage Learning

Nombre ______________________ Sección ______________ Fecha ______________

Práctica oral

Listen to the following exercise on the audio program. The speaker will ask you some questions. Answer the questions using the cues provided. The speaker will confirm the correct answer. Repeat the correct answer.

1. ¿En qué calle vive Ud.? (en la calle París)
2. ¿Vive Ud. en una casa o en un apartamento? (en una casa)
3. ¿Tiene Ud. jardinero? (no)
4. ¿Está Ud. con sus amigos ahora? (no)
5. ¿Ud. habla español o inglés con sus amigos? (inglés)
6. ¿Habla Ud. español rápido o despacio? (despacio)
7. ¿Con quién desea salir Ud. ahora? (con mi amiga)
8. ¿Es Ud. menor que su amiga? (no)
9. ¿Tiene Ud. mis datos personales? (sí)
10. ¿Dónde queda la comisaría? (en la calle Roma)
11. Para llegar a la comisaría, ¿tengo que seguir derecho o doblar? (doblar)
12. ¿Hay muchas pandillas en su ciudad? (sí)
13. ¿A qué hora debe estar en su casa una persona menor de edad? (antes de la medianoche)
14. ¿Qué arma de fuego tiene Ud. en su casa? (una pistola)
15. ¿Qué debe tener siempre una identificación? (una fotografía)
16. ¿Tiene Ud. fotografías de sus padres? (sí, muchas)
17. ¿Su mamá es alta, baja o de estatura mediana? (de estatura mediana)
18. ¿Su mamá es más baja o más alta que su papá? (un poco más baja)
19. ¿Hay un programa de vigilancia en su barrio? (sí)
20. ¿Cuándo está Ud. en su casa durante el día? (los sábados)
21. Si Ud. nota algo sospechoso, ¿a quién llama? (a la policía)
22. ¿Qué es lo más importante? (proteger a los niños)
23. ¿Cierra Ud. la puerta con llave? (sí)
24. ¿Qué luz enciende Ud. por la noche? (la luz del portal)
25. ¿Qué necesita instalar Ud. en la puerta de la calle? (un cerrojo de seguridad)

© 2017 Cengage Learning

El agente Chávez lee la advertencia Miranda

Objectives

Structures

- Stem-changing verbs (**o:ue**)
- Affirmative and negative expressions
- Direct object pronouns

Communication

- Detaining suspects: reading the Miranda warning; traffic violations and DUI

iLrn™

El agente Chávez lee la advertencia Miranda

El agente detiene a dos jóvenes que están escribiendo en la pared de un edificio.

Agente Chávez —¡Policía! ¡Alto! ¡No se muevan! ¡Están detenidos!
Joven 1 —¿Por qué? No estamos haciendo nada malo.
Agente Chávez —Están cometiendo un delito de vandalismo. Está prohibido escribir en la pared de un edificio.

El agente saca una tarjeta de su bolsillo y lee la advertencia Miranda.

LA ADVERTENCIA MIRANDA

1. Ud. tiene el derecho de permanecer callado.
2. Si decide hablar con nosotros, cualquier cosa que diga puede usarse y se usará en contra de Ud. en el juicio.
3. Ud. tiene el derecho de hablar con un abogado, y de tenerlo presente durante el interrogatorio.
4. Si Ud. no puede pagar un abogado, se le nombrará uno para que lo represente antes de que lo interroguen, si Ud. lo desea.

Agente Chávez —¿Entienden Uds. cada uno de estos derechos?

Joven 1 —Sí, los entendemos. ¿Y qué? ¿Nos va a llevar presos?

Joven 2 —Conmigo pierde su tiempo. Yo tengo menos de quince años; dentro de unas horas estoy en mi casa otra vez.

Agente Chávez —Ahora van a la estación de policía conmigo. Yo no decido lo demás.

Horas después, el agente detiene al chofer de un automóvil que comete una infracción de tránsito. Cuando habla con él, nota que el hombre está endrogado.

Agente Chávez —Buenos días. Su licencia de manejar y el registro del carro, por favor.

Chofer —¿Me va a arrestar? ¿Por qué? No estoy borracho. Además, yo manejo mejor que nunca cuando tomo un par de tragos.

El agente nota marcas de aguja en el brazo y en la mano del hombre. Las marcas son nuevas.

Agente Chávez —A ver el brazo. ¿Tiene diabetes?

Chofer —No.

Agente Chávez —¿Da Ud. sangre a menudo?

Chofer —Sí, doy sangre a veces.

Agente Chávez —¿Dónde está el banco de sangre?

Chofer —En... No recuerdo ahora.

Agente Chávez —Mire aquí, por favor. Debe tratar de no parpadear.

Chofer —No puedo dejar de parpadear. Tengo mucho sueño... No duermo bien últimamente.

Agente Chávez —Lo siento, pero tiene que ir conmigo. Ud. no está en condiciones de manejar.

Chofer —¡Pero tengo que volver a mi casa! ¿Por qué estoy detenido? ¿Cuál es mi delito?

Agente Chávez —Conducir bajo los efectos de alguna droga. (*El agente lee la advertencia Miranda.*)

¡Escuchemos!

While listening to the dialogue, circle **V (verdadero)** if the statement is true and **F (falso)** if it is false.

1. Está prohibido escribir en la pared de un edificio.
2. Los dos jóvenes no están haciendo nada malo.
3. El vandalismo no es un delito.
4. El agente saca una tarjeta de su bolsillo.
5. Ud. no tiene derecho a permanecer callado.
6. Ud. no tiene derecho a hablar con un abogado antes de hablar con la policía.
7. Los muchachos entienden sus derechos.
8. El joven 2 tiene menos de quince años.

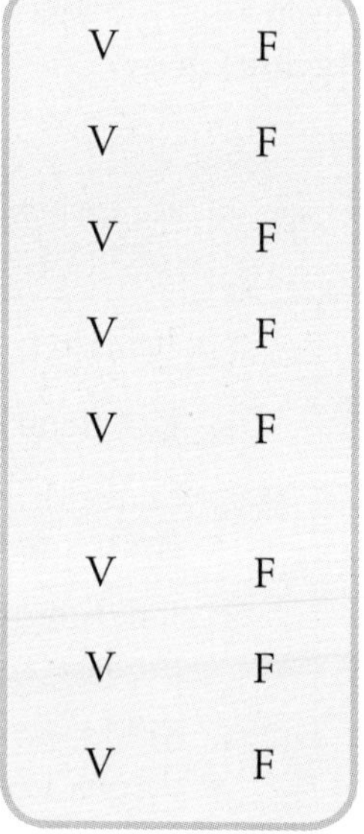

© 2017 Cengage Learning

Nombre ______________________ Sección ____________ Fecha ____________

9. Un chofer maneja mejor que nunca cuando toma un par de tragos. V F

10. El agente nota que el chofer está endrogado. V F

VOCABULARIO

Cognados

el automóvil
el caso
la condición
la diabetes
la droga
el interrogatorio
la marca
presente
el vandalismo

Nombres

el (la) abogado(a) *lawyer*
la aguja *needle*
el banco de sangre *blood bank*
el bolsillo *pocket*
el brazo *arm*
el carro, el coche, la máquina (*Cuba*) *car*
el (la) chofer *driver*
la cosa *thing*
el derecho *right*
el edificio *building*
la infracción de tránsito *traffic violation*
el (la) joven *young man, young woman*
el juicio *trial*
la mano *hand*
la pared *wall*
el registro *registration*
el trago *drink*

Verbos

cometer *to commit, to perpetrate*
decidir *to decide*
detener[1] *to detain, to stop*
dormir (o:ue) *to sleep*
entender (e:ie) *to understand*
escribir *to write*
interrogar *to question, to interrogate*
leer *to read*
manejar, conducir[2] *to drive*
mover (o:ue) *to move*
negarse (e:ie) *to refuse*
pagar *to pay (for)*
parpadear *to blink*
perder (e:ie) *to waste, to lose*
permanecer[3] *to stay, to remain*
poder (o:ue) *can, to be able*
recordar (o:ue) *to remember*
sacar *to take out*
tomar *to drink; to take*
volver (o:ue) *to return, to come back*

Adjetivos

algún, alguno(a) *some, any*
borracho(a) *drunk*
cada *each, every*
callado(a) *silent, quiet*
detenido(a), arrestado(a), preso(a) *arrested*

---

[1]**Detener** is irregular in the present indicative: **detengo, detienes, detiene, detenemos, detienen**
[2]Irregular first person present indicative: **yo conduzco**
[3]Irregular first person present indicative: **yo permanezco**

© 2017 Cengage Learning

Nombre ______________________________ Sección ______________ Fecha ______________

endrogado(a) (*Cuba, Ven.*) *on drugs, drugged*
estos(as) *these*
malo(a) *bad*
nuevo(a) *new, fresh*
prohibido(a) *forbidden*

Otras palabras y expresiones

a menudo *often*
a ver *let's see*
la advertencia Miranda *Miranda warning*
antes de que lo interroguen *before they question you*
bajo los efectos (de) *under the influence (of)*
con él *with him*
conmigo *with me*
cualquier cosa que diga *anything you say*
dejar de (+ *inf.*) *to stop (doing something)*
dentro de *in, within*
después *later*
en contra de *against*
estar en condiciones de (+ *inf.*) *to be in a condition to (do something)*
lo *you, him, it*
lo demás *the rest*
Lo siento *I'm sorry*
mejor que nunca *better than ever*
Mire *Look*
negarse a hablar *to refuse to speak*
¡No se muevan![1] *Don't move!, Freeze!*
¿Nos va a llevar presos? *Are you going to arrest us?*
nunca *never*
otra vez *again, once again*
para que lo represente *to represent you*
puede usarse *can be used*
se le nombrará uno *one will be appointed for you*
se usará *will be used*
si Ud. lo desea *if you wish*
tener el derecho de (tenerlo presente) *to have the right to (have him present)*
tener (mucho) sueño *to be (very) sleepy*
últimamente *lately, these days*
un par de *a couple of*
¿Y qué? *So what?*

VOCABULARIO ADICIONAL

bajo juramento *under oath*
el (la) compañero(a) *pal, peer*
la declaración falsa *false statement*
el (la) delincuente juvenil *juvenile delinquent*
el (la) drogadicto(a) *drug addict*
el grafiti *graffiti*
el juramento *oath*
jurar *to take an oath, to swear*
el juzgado, la corte *court (of law)*
la mentira *lie*
la pregunta *question*
la respuesta, la contestación *answer*
el (la) traficante *drug pusher*
la verdad *truth*

[1]When speaking to only one person, use **¡No se mueva!**

© 2017 Cengage Learning

Nombre ____________________ Sección ____________ Fecha ____________

Notas Culturales

- Alcoholism and cirrhosis are important health issues that affect the Latino population in North America. The incidence rate is particularly high among Mexican Americans and Puerto Ricans. In addition, Hispanic Americans have a disproportionate number of deaths due to narcotic addictions. In a recent Hispanic Health and Nutrition Survey done in the United States, 21.5% of Puerto Ricans reported having used cocaine, while the figure was 11.1% for Mexican Americans and 9.2% for Cuban Americans.
- In Spanish, the word **droga** does not mean *medicine* as in English. Latinos use this term to refer to narcotics and other illegal drugs.

Actividades

Dígame... Answer the following questions, basing your answers on the dialogues.

1. ¿A quiénes detiene el agente Chávez?

____

2. ¿Qué están haciendo?

____

3. ¿Cuál es el delito que están cometiendo?

____

4. ¿Qué lee el agente Chávez?

____

5. Según (*According to*) el joven 2, ¿por qué pierde el agente Chávez su tiempo con él?

____

6. ¿Adónde van los tres?

____

7. ¿Qué comete el chofer de un automóvil?

____

8. Cuando el agente Chávez habla con el chofer, ¿qué nota? ¿Qué tiene en el brazo y en la mano?

____

© 2017 Cengage Learning

Nombre ______________________ Sección ______________ Fecha ______________

9. ¿Por qué cree Ud. que el chofer no recuerda dónde está el banco de sangre?

____

10. ¿Por qué tiene que ir el chofer con el agente Chávez a la estación de policía? ¿Cuál es su delito?

____

Hablemos

Interview a classmate, using the following questions. When you have finished, switch roles.

1. ¿Puede Ud. escribir en las paredes de los edificios? ¿Por qué?
2. ¿Da Ud. sangre a veces?
3. ¿Siempre toma un par de tragos antes de manejar?
4. ¿Está Ud. en condiciones de manejar ahora? ¿Por qué?
5. ¿Puede venir a la estación de policía conmigo?
6. ¿Lee Ud. la advertencia Miranda a veces?

Quiz

Vamos a practicar

A Rewrite the following sentences using the new subjects and making all necessary changes.

1. No podemos arrestar al chofer. (yo)

____

2. Volvemos al edificio con ella. (ellos)

____

3. No recordamos nada. (Ud.)

____

4. Nosotros dormimos en la estación de policía. (ellos)

____

5. Podemos leer la advertencia ahora. (Ud.)

____

B Answer the following questions in the negative, using one of the following words in your answer.

nada	nunca
nadie	tampoco

1. ¿Alguna persona de su familia es traficante?

____

© 2017 Cengage Learning

Nombre ____________________ Sección ____________ Fecha ____________

2. ¿Tiene que hacer algo (*something*) hoy?

____

3. ¿Siempre toma un trago cuando maneja?

____

4. ¿Hay alguien en su carro ahora?

____

5. Yo no escribo en las paredes de los edificios. ¿Y Ud.?

____

C Answer the following questions in the affirmative, using the appropriate object pronouns to replace the underlined words.

MODELO ¿Tienes el casco de seguridad?
Sí, **lo** tengo.

1. ¿Vas a leer la advertencia Miranda?

____

2. ¿El policía arresta a los jóvenes?

____

3. ¿Necesitas estas linternas?

____

4. ¿Puedes llevarme en tu coche?

____

5. ¿Tus amigos te recuerdan?

____

Conversaciones breves

Complete the following dialogue, using your imagination and the vocabulary from this lesson.

El agente Mora detiene a un chofer.

Agente Mora —____

Chofer —Tengo marcas de aguja en el brazo porque doy sangre muy a menudo.

© 2017 Cengage Learning

Nombre ______________________ **Sección** ____________ **Fecha** ____________

Agente Mora —______________________________

Chofer —No recuerdo en este momento. Además, las marcas de aguja no son nuevas...

Agente Mora —______________________________

Chofer —Trato de no parpadear, pero tengo mucho sueño...

Agente Mora —______________________________

Chofer —No, no uso drogas nunca.

Agente Mora —______________________________

Chofer —¿Yo? ¿Detenido? Pero, ¿cómo puede ser?

Agente Mora —______________________________

En estas situaciones

With a partner, act out the following situations in Spanish.

1. You catch three teenagers vandalizing cars. Identify yourself as a police officer and tell them to halt. They say they're not afraid because they are minors. Inform them that they are under arrest and that they are going to the police station with you.
2. You see someone trying to break into a bank. Tell the person to halt and not to move, or you'll shoot and arrest him/her. The suspect says he/she isn't doing anything. Read the Miranda warning to him/her.
3. You stop a driver and ask to see a driver's license and car registration. Say that you think that he/she is drunk and is under arrest for driving under the influence of alcohol. The driver doesn't want to go to the police station with you.

Casos

With you and a partner playing the roles, work through the following scenarios.

1. You are a police officer talking to someone who shows signs of being under the influence of alcohol and/or drugs.
2. You arrest some minors for committing vandalism.

Un paso más

Review the **Vocabulario adicional** in this lesson and complete the following sentences.

1. ¡Es mentira! Él nunca dice ____________.
2. Tengo las preguntas, pero no tengo ____________.
3. En la pared hay mucho ____________, pero mi ____________ y yo no escribimos nada. ¡No somos ____________!
4. Ella jura que no está endrogada, pero ésa es una ____________.
5. Antes de contestar, debe recordar que Ud. está ____________.

© 2017 Cengage Learning

LECCIÓN 7

PROBLEMAS DE LA CIUDAD

OBJECTIVES

Structures

- Stem-changing verbs (**e:i**)
- Irregular first-person forms
- Indirect object pronouns

Communication

- Investigating a crime: talking to victims, suspects, and witnesses; handling a medical emergency
- Giving physical descriptions

iLrn™

PROBLEMAS DE LA CIUDAD

Por la mañana: El agente Flores habla con el dueño de una licorería después de un robo, y le pide información sobre los ladrones.

Agente Flores	—¿Dice Ud. que los ladrones son muy jóvenes? ¿Puede describirlos?
Dueño	—Sí. El hombre es rubio, de ojos azules, y la mujer es pelirroja, de ojos verdes.
Agente Flores	—¿Puede decirme qué más recuerda?
Dueño	—El hombre mide unos seis pies, y ella mide unos cinco pies, dos pulgadas. Él es delgado. Ella es más bien gorda.
Agente Flores	—¿Algunas marcas visibles?
Dueño	—Él tiene un tatuaje en el brazo izquierdo. Ella tiene pecas.
Agente Flores	—Ud. no los conoce, ¿verdad? No son clientes...
Dueño	—No, pero sé que los puedo reconocer si los veo otra vez.
Agente Flores	—¿Qué clase de carro manejan?
Dueño	—Un Chevrolet amarillo, de dos puertas. Es un carro viejo.
Agente Flores	—¿Algo más?
Dueño	—Sí, creo que sí. Él fuma cigarrillos negros... de México... ¡y es zurdo!
Agente Flores	—Si recuerda algo más, puede llamarme a este número. Si no estoy, puede dejarme un mensaje.
Dueño	—Cómo no, señor.

Nombre ______________________ **Sección** ____________ **Fecha** ____________

Por la tarde: El agente Flores ve a un hombre que está parado frente a una escuela. Sospecha que el hombre les vende drogas a los estudiantes, porque sabe que muchos de ellos toman drogas.

Agente Flores	—¿Qué hace Ud. aquí? ¿Espera a alguien?
Hombre	—No... no hago nada...
Agente Flores	—¿Tiene alguna identificación? ¿Su licencia de conducir, por ejemplo?
Hombre	—No, aquí no. La tengo en casa, pero puedo mostrarle mi tarjeta de Seguro Social.
Agente Flores	—¿Quiere acompañarme al carro, por favor? Quiero hablar con Ud.

Por la noche: El agente Flores sale de la comisaría para ir a su casa. En la zona de estacionamiento, ve a un hombre en el suelo. Corre hacia él.

Agente Flores	—¿Qué tiene? ¿Está lastimado?
Hombre	—No... creo que... un ataque al corazón...
Agente Flores	—¿Tiene alguna medicina para el corazón?
Hombre	—Sí... en la guantera del carro...
Agente Flores	—(*Trae la medicina.*) Aquí está. (*Le da la medicina al hombre.*) Ahora voy a llamar a los paramédicos.

¡Escuchemos!

While listening to the dialogue, circle **V (verdadero)** if the statement is true and **F (falso)** if it is false.

1. El dueño de la licorería da información sobre un robo. V F
2. Los ladrones son dos hombres y una mujer. V F
3. La mujer es rubia, de ojos azules. V F
4. El hombre tiene un tatuaje en el brazo izquierdo. V F
5. El dueño puede reconocer a los ladrones si los ve otra vez. V F
6. Ellos manejan un Ford verde, de cuatro puertas. V F
7. El agente Flores sospecha que el hombre que está parado frente a una escuela es un ladrón. V F
8. El hombre puede mostrarle al agente su licencia de conducir. V F
9. En la zona de estacionamiento hay un hombre en el suelo. V F
10. El hombre tiene una medicina para el corazón en la guantera del carro. V F

© 2017 Cengage Learning

Nombre ______________ Sección ______________ Fecha ______________

VOCABULARIO

Cognados

el (la) estudiante
la medicina

Nombres

el cigarrillo *cigarette*
la clase *kind, type, class*
el (la) cliente(a) *customer*
el corazón *heart*
la guantera *glove compartment*
la licorería *liquor store*
el mensaje *message*
la peca *freckle*
el pie *foot*
la pulgada *inch*
el Seguro Social *Social Security*
el suelo *floor*
el tatuaje *tattoo*
la zona de estacionamiento *parking lot*

Verbos

acompañar *to accompany, to go (come) with*
conocer[1] *to know*
correr *to run*
decir (e:i)[2] *to say, to tell*
describir *to describe*
esperar *to wait (for)*
fumar *to smoke*
medir (e:i) *to measure*
mostrar (o:ue), enseñar *to show*
pedir (e:i) *to ask for, to request*
reconocer[3] *to recognize*
sospechar *to suspect*
traer[4] *to bring*

Adjetivos

amarillo(a) *yellow*
delgado(a) *thin, slender*
diestro(a) *right-handed*
gordo(a) *fat*
izquierdo(a) *left*
lastimado(a) *hurt, injured*
parado(a) *standing*
pelirrojo(a) *red-haired*
rubio(a), güero(a)[5] (*Méx.*) *blond(e)*
viejo(a) *old*
zurdo(a) *left-handed*

Otras palabras y expresiones

¿Algo más? *Anything else?*
el ataque al corazón *heart attack*
¡Cómo no! *Certainly!, Gladly!, Sure!*
Creo que sí *I think so*
de ojos (azules) *with (blue) eyes*
después de *after*
hacia *toward*
más bien, medio *rather*
mide seis pies *he is (measures) six feet tall*
por la mañana *in the morning*
por la noche *in the evening*
por la tarde *in the afternoon*
¿Qué más? *What else?*
¿Qué tiene? *What's wrong?*

---

[1]Irregular first person present indicative: **yo conozco**
[2]Irregular first person present indicative: **yo digo**
[3]Irregular first person present indicative: **yo reconozco**
[4]Irregular first person present indicative: **yo traigo**
[5]Also applies to anyone with fair skin.

© 2017 Cengage Learning

Nombre ______________________ Sección ____________ Fecha ____________

VOCABULARIO ADICIONAL

El tamaño (*Size*)

flaco(a) *thin, skinny*
grueso(a) *portly*

La raza/el color de la piel (*Race/skin color*)

asiático(a) *Asian*
blanco(a) *white/Caucasian*
mestizo(a) *mixed (any of two or more races)*
mulato(a) *mixed (black and white)*
negro(a) *black*

El pelo (*Hair*)

calvo(a), pelón(ona) *bald*
canoso(a) *grey-haired*
castaño(a), café *brown*
claro(a) *light*
corto(a) *short*
lacio(a) *straight*
largo(a) *long*
morocho(a) *dark-haired*
rizado(a), rizo(a), crespo(a) *curly*

Los ojos (*Eyes*)

azules *blue*
castaños,[1] **café** (*Méx.*) *brown*
grises *gray*
verdes *green*

Otras características

ciego(a) *blind*
cojo(a) *lame*
inválido(a), paralítico(a) *disabled, crippled*
mudo(a) *mute*
sordo(a) *deaf*
tartamudo(a) *person who stutters*

Notas Culturales

The extensive use of drugs is more evident in large cities. Because the majority of Hispanic immigrants come from villages and small towns, there are few drug addicts among first-generation immigrants. Nonetheless, their numbers increase dramatically beginning with the second generation, owing possibly to culture shock and living conditions.

ACTIVIDADES

Dígame... Answer the following questions, basing your answers on the dialogues.

1. ¿Con quién habla el agente Flores después del robo?

____

2. ¿Puede el dueño describir a los ladrones?

____

[1]In Spanish, very dark brown eyes are called **ojos negros.**

© 2017 Cengage Learning

Nombre ______________________ Sección ____________ Fecha ____________

3. ¿Cómo es el hombre? ¿Y la mujer?

____

4. ¿Qué marcas visibles tiene el hombre? ¿Y la mujer?

____

5. ¿Conoce el dueño de la licorería a los ladrones?

____

6. ¿Cree el dueño que puede reconocer a los ladrones si los ve otra vez?

____

7. ¿Qué clase de carro manejan los ladrones?

____

8. ¿Qué ve el agente Flores por la tarde?

____

9. ¿Qué sospecha el agente Flores?

____

10. ¿Tiene el hombre alguna identificación?

____

11. ¿Qué ve el agente Flores en la zona de estacionamiento?

____

12. ¿Qué tiene el hombre?

____

13. ¿Qué hace el agente Flores para ayudar al hombre?

____

Hablemos Interview a classmate, using the following questions. When you have finished, switch roles.

1. ¿Cómo es Ud.? ¿Cuánto mide?
2. ¿Puede describir a alguien de su familia?
3. ¿Qué clase de coche maneja Ud.?
4. ¿Su coche está en la zona de estacionamiento?
5. ¿Puede Ud. llamarme por teléfono mañana?
6. ¿Sabe Ud. qué drogas les venden a los estudiantes en las escuelas?

© 2017 Cengage Learning

Nombre ______ Sección ______ Fecha ______

Quiz

Vamos a practicar

A Rewrite the following sentences, using the new subjects and making all necessary changes.

1. Nosotros medimos la puerta. (ellos)

______

2. Nosotros seguimos (*follow*) a los ladrones. (yo)

______

3. Nosotras pedimos (*ask for*) más información. (el policía)

______

4. Nosotros conseguimos (*get*) la medicina. (Ud.)

______

5. Nosotros decimos la verdad (*truth*). (tú)

______

B Imagine that you are Officer Flores. Form sentences to tell what you do in your investigation of the liquor store holdup.

Modelo ir / a la licorería
Voy a la licorería.

1. ver / al dueño de la licorería

______

2. pedir / información

______

3. hacer / la descripción de los ladrones

______

4. decir / lo que (*what*) el dueño debe hacer mañana

______

5. salir / de la licorería

______

6. conducir / a la estación de policía

______

© 2017 Cengage Learning

Nombre ______________________ **Sección** ____________ **Fecha** ____________

C Answer the following questions using the cues provided.

MODELO ¿Quién les vende las drogas a los estudiantes? (un hombre alto)
Un hombre alto les vende las drogas.

1. ¿Qué drogas les venden a los jóvenes? (marihuana y cocaína)

____

2. ¿Ud. puede darme información? (sí) (*Use the* **Ud.** *form.*)

____

3. ¿Tú puedes decirme dónde está José? (sí) (*Use the* **tú** *form.*)

____

4. ¿Sus padres les hablan a Uds. de las drogas? (no)

____

5. ¿Qué le va a dar Ud. al señor? (la medicina)

____

Conversaciones breves

Complete the following dialogue, using your imagination and the vocabulary from this lesson.

El Sr. Rivas describe a una ladrona.

Agente Alcalá —____

Sr. Rivas —Sí, es alta, rubia, de ojos verdes, más bien delgada y muy bonita.

Agente Alcalá —____

Sr. Rivas —No recuerdo mucho... Mide unos cinco pies y diez pulgadas.

Agente Alcalá —____

Sr. Rivas —No, no tiene ninguna (*any*) marca visible.

Agente Alcalá —____

Sr. Rivas —Sí, yo creo que puedo reconocerla.

Agente Alcalá —____

Sr. Rivas —Un Mazda amarillo de cuatro puertas.

Agente Alcalá —____

Sr. Rivas —¡Ah, sí! ¡Ahora recuerdo! ¡Es zurda!

Agente Alcalá —____

© 2017 Cengage Learning

Nombre ______________________ Sección ____________ Fecha ____________

En estas situaciones

With a partner, act out the following situations in Spanish.

1. You are investigating a burglary. Ask if the witness can recognize the burglar if he/she sees him/her again. Ask how tall the burglar is, and if he/she has any visible marks. Ask also what kind of car the burglar drives.
2. You see a suspect standing near a school. Ask what he/she is doing there. Ask if he/she is waiting for a student, and if he/she has any identification.
3. You see someone who seems to be sick. Ask what's wrong. You get the person's heart medicine from his/her pocket and then say that you're going to call the paramedics.
4. Your partner is hurt. Ask a passerby to please call the police because there is a police officer who needs help.

Casos

With you and a partner playing the roles, work through the following scenarios.

1. You are a police officer. Interview a witness of a burglary.
2. You are a police officer and you see a suspicious-looking person standing near a playground. Approach the person and question him/her.
3. You are a police officer and notice a person lying on the sidewalk. Find out what the person's problem is and try to help him/her.

Un paso más

Review the **Vocabulario adicional** in this lesson and describe several people you know using as many words as possible from the list.

1. ____

____

2. ____

____

3. ____

____

4. ____

____

5. ____

____

© 2017 Cengage Learning

Casos de maltrato de miembros de la familia

Objectives

Structures

- Demonstrative adjectives and pronouns
- Special construction with **gustar, doler,** and **hacer falta**
- Direct and indirect object pronouns used together

Communication

- Investigating domestic abuse
- Reporting domestic violence

iLrn™

Casos de maltrato de miembros de la familia

Julia, una niña, llama a la policía porque su padrastro le está pegando a su mamá. El agente Vera va a la casa de la familia Aguirre para investigar la denuncia.

Agente Vera —Buenas tardes. ¿Es ésta la casa de la familia Aguirre?
Julia —Sí. Pase, por favor. Mi mamá y mi padrastro están encerrados en su recámara.
Agente Vera —¿Cuál es el problema?
Julia —Mi padrastro no tiene trabajo ahora y, en lugar de buscar otro trabajo, todos los días va a la cantina y vuelve borracho.
Agente Vera —¿Cómo consigue el dinero para la bebida?
Julia —Se lo pide a mi mamá, y si ella no se lo da, le pega, y se lo quita a la fuerza.
Agente Vera —¿Le pega con la mano?
Julia —Con la mano y con el cinto. A veces le dice que la va a matar.
Agente Vera —¿Tiene algún arma él?
Julia —Sí, tiene una navaja y una pistola.
Agente Vera —(*Toca a la puerta de la recámara.*) Sr. Aguirre, soy agente de policía, y necesito hablar con Ud. ¿Quiere salir un momento, por favor?

Nombre ______________________ Sección ____________ Fecha ____________

Sr. Aguirre —(*Desde adentro*) Ésta es mi casa. ¿Ud. tiene una orden del juez para entrar? Yo no tengo nada que hablar con Ud.

Agente Vera —No me hace falta una orden del juez para hablar con Ud.

Sra. Aguirre —(*Saliendo de la recámara*) Está enojado conmigo porque quiere dinero para comprar bebidas. Lo único que a él le gusta es beber.

Sr. Aguirre —(*Saliendo también*) Ése es un problema entre mi mujer y yo.

Agente Vera —Sra. Aguirre, Ud. está bastante lesionada.

Sra. Aguirre —Sí, me duele todo el cuerpo.

Agente Vera —Debe ver a un médico inmediatamente. ¿Está dispuesta a acusar a su marido de maltrato?

Sr. Aguirre —No. Ella hace lo que yo le digo. Y si Ud. quiere saber algo, me lo pregunta a mí.

Sra. Aguirre —(*No le hace caso a su marido, y le contesta al policía.*) Sí, señor agente.

Sr. Aguirre —(*A su esposa*) Tú no me debes hacer eso. Tú sabes que yo te trato bien cuando no estoy borracho. Te pido perdón.

Sra. Aguirre —No. Esta vez no te perdono. Ya estoy cansada de tus maltratos.

El Dr. Andrade notifica a la policía sus sospechas de que el niño Carlos Jiménez está siendo maltratado. La agente Rodríguez, a cargo del caso, habla con sus padres.

Agente Rodríguez —Buenos días. ¿Es Ud. el padre del niño Carlos Jiménez?

Sr. Jiménez —Sí, soy yo. ¿Qué se le ofrece?

Agente Rodríguez —Soy la agente Rodríguez, de la policía local. Ésta es mi identificación.

Sr. Jiménez —Pase y siéntese. ¿En qué puedo servirle?

Agente Rodríguez —Su hijo está ingresado en el hospital desde ayer. Ésta es la tercera vez que el niño ingresa en el hospital con lesiones más o menos graves y el médico sospecha que alguien lo está maltratando frecuentemente.

Sr. Jiménez —¿Qué? ¿Quién dice eso? Eso es mentira. Además, nadie tiene autoridad para decirnos cómo debemos castigar a nuestros hijos.

Agente Rodríguez —Está equivocado, Sr. Jiménez. En este país no se aceptan ciertas formas de disciplinar a los niños.

¡Escuchemos!

While listening to the dialogue, circle **V (verdadero)** if the statement is true and **F (falso)** if it is false.

1. El padrastro de Julia le está pegando a su mamá. V F
2. El señor y la señora Aguirre están en el portal de la casa. V F
3. El Sr. Aguirre trabaja en una cantina. V F
4. El Sr. Aguirre le pega a su esposa si ella no le da dinero. V F
5. Él siempre le pega a la esposa con la mano. V F
6. El Sr. Aguirre tiene una navaja y una pistola. V F
7. El policía necesita una orden del juez para hablar con el Sr. Aguirre. V F

© 2017 Cengage Learning

Nombre ______________________ Sección ____________ Fecha ____________

8. La Sra. Aguirre dice que lo único que le gusta a su esposo es beber. V F

9. Esta vez la Sra. Aguirre está dispuesta a acusar a su marido. V F

10. Ella va a perdonar a su esposo otra vez. V F

VOCABULARIO

Cognados

la autoridad
la familia
frecuentemente
local
violento(a)

Nombres

el arma (*f.*) *weapon*
la bebida *drinking, drink*
la cantina, la barra, el bar *bar*
el cinto, el cinturón, la correa *belt*
el cuerpo *body*[1]
el dinero *money*
la forma *way*
el (la) juez(a) *judge*
la lesión *injury*
el maltrato *abuse*
el (la) médico(a), el (la) doctor(a) *doctor*
la mentira *lie*
la navaja *switchblade, razor*
la orden *warrant, order*
el padrastro *stepfather*
el país *country*
el perdón *pardon, forgiveness*
el porqué *reason*
la recámara (*Méx.*), **el dormitorio, la pieza** *bedroom*
la sospecha *suspicion*
el trabajo *work, job*
la vez *time*

Verbos

aceptar *to accept*
acusar *to accuse*
beber, tomar *to drink*
castigar *to punish*
conseguir (e:i) *to get, to obtain*
disciplinar *to discipline*
doler (o:ue) *to hurt, to ache*
gustar *to be pleasing, to like*
hacer falta *to need, to lack*
ingresar *to be admitted (to), to enter*
investigar *to investigate*
maltratar, abusar (de) *to abuse*
matar *to kill*
pegar *to beat*
perdonar *to forgive*
preguntar *to ask (a question)*
quitar *to take away*
tratar *to treat*

Adjetivos

cansado(a) *tired*
cierto(a) *certain*
dispuesto(a) *willing*
encerrado(a) *locked up, closeted*
enojado(a) *angry*
ingresado(a) *admitted (to)*
lesionado(a) *injured*
tercero(a) *third*
todo(a)[2] *whole*

---

[1]In Spanish, a dead person is referred to as a **cadáver** not as a **cuerpo.**

[2]The adjective **todo(a)** precedes the article or the possessive: **todo el cuerpo; toda mi casa.**

© 2017 Cengage Learning

Nombre ______________________ Sección ______________ Fecha ______________

Otras palabras y expresiones

a cargo de *in charge of*
a la fuerza *by force*
adentro *inside*
ayer *yesterday*
bastante *quite, rather*
desde *from*
en lugar de *instead of*
ése, ésa *that one*
eso *that*
esta vez *this time*
estar equivocado(a) *to be wrong*
éste, ésta *this one*
hacerle caso a *to pay attention (to someone)*
lo que *what, that which*
lo único *the only thing*
más o menos *more or less*
nadie *nobody*
Siéntese. *Sit down.*
tocar a la puerta *to knock at the door*
todos los días *every day*
ya *at last, finally*

VOCABULARIO ADICIONAL

Armas de fuego

la ametralladora *machine gun*
la escopeta *shotgun*
el rifle *rifle*

Armas blancas (*Blades*)

el cuchillo *knife*
el puñal, la daga *dagger*

Explosivos (*Explosives*)

la bomba (de tiempo) *(time) bomb*
la dinamita *dynamite*
la granada de mano *hand grenade*

Algunos castigos corporales (*Some corporal punishments*)

ahorcar *to suffocate*
la bofetada, la galleta (*Cuba, Puerto Rico*) *slap*
la mordida *bite*
la nalgada *spanking, slap on the buttocks*
la paliza *beating*
la patada *kick*
la trompada, el puñetazo *punch*

Notas Culturales

- In Spanish-speaking cultures, the concept of **machismo,** in which males are seen as aggressive and authoritative, plays a part in traditional views of gender roles and family. Degrees of male authoritarianism vary widely, and in general, women are important contributors to decision making and share authority in the family. Many Latina women are also part of the work force, and more and more Latino men help with household chores and care of the children.

© 2017 Cengage Learning

Nombre ______________ Sección ______________ Fecha ______________

- In some Spanish-speaking countries, parents are still accustomed to disciplining their children through corporal punishment. This type of discipline is either not prohibited by law or is tolerated by the authorities. Generally speaking, mothers do the spanking, but if the misbehavior is serious, the father administers more serious punishment. He may hit the children with a belt or a leather strap. It is important, however, not to overgeneralize this disciplinary practice and to keep in mind that, in general, Latino families tend to be close-knit units in which all family members spend time together and help and support each other. Usually, unless questions of study or work arise, children continue to live with their parents until they get married, even beyond the time when they are no longer minors.

Actividades

Dígame... Answer the following questions, basing your answers on the dialogues.

1. ¿Quién es la persona violenta en la casa de Julia?

____

2. ¿Por qué le pega el padrastro de Julia a su mamá? ¿Con qué le pega?

____

3. ¿Cómo está el Sr. Aguirre en este momento? ¿Y la señora? ¿A quién debe ver ella inmediatamente?

____

4. ¿El Sr. Aguirre quiere hablar con el agente Vera?

____

5. ¿Qué piensa el Sr. Aguirre de la situación?

____

6. ¿Qué le duele a la Sra. Aguirre?

____

7. ¿Qué decide hacer la Sra. Aguirre?

____

8. ¿Es un hombre peligroso el Sr. Aguirre?

____

9. ¿Por qué está en el hospital el niño Carlos Jiménez?

____

© 2017 Cengage Learning

Nombre ______________________ **Sección** ____________ **Fecha** ____________

10. ¿Es la primera vez que el niño está allí?

____

11. ¿Qué sospecha el médico?

____

12. ¿Qué es lo que no se acepta en este país, según (*according to*) la agente Rodríguez?

____

Hablemos

Interview a classmate, using the following questions. When you have finished, switch roles. Answer the questions with details.

1. ¿Investiga Ud. a menudo casos de maltrato de miembros de la familia?
2. Si Ud. va a una casa para investigar una denuncia, ¿qué le dice primero a la familia?
3. Si Ud. sospecha que una persona le está pegando a un miembro de la familia, ¿qué hace?
4. ¿Está Ud. enojado(a) con alguien hoy? ¿Por qué?
5. ¿Qué toma Ud. cuando le duele la cabeza?
6. ¿Qué cosas importantes tiene en su recámara?
7. ¿Qué armas cree que son más efectivas para un policía? ¿Por qué?

Quiz

Vamos a practicar

A Change the demonstrative adjectives so that they agree with the new nouns.

1. este dinero, ____________ mentira, ____________ maltratos, ____________ cantinas
2. esas recámaras, ____________ forma, ____________ miembros de su familia, ____________ caso
3. aquel (*that over there*) país, ____________ armas, ____________ jueces, ____________ familia

B Complete the following sentences, using **doler, gustar,** or **hacer falta.**

Modelo A Luis ____________ este restaurante.
A Luis **le gusta** este restaurante.

1. A mí ____________ dinero porque necesito comprar ropa.
2. A Teresa ____________ todo el cuerpo.
3. A Roberto y a mí no ____________ el coche de Sergio porque es amarillo.

© 2017 Cengage Learning

4. ¿Cuánto ______ para comprar la casa que tú quieres?

5. Voy a tomar Advil porque ______ las manos.

C You are needed as a translator. Write the following dialogues in Spanish. Use direct and/or indirect object pronouns.

1. "What are you going to do, Anita?"
   "I'm going to tell him that I'm going to call the police."

   ______

   ______

2. "Do you give them money, Mr. Soto?"
   "No, I never give them anything!"

   ______

   ______

3. "Does your husband hit you, Mrs. Varela?"
   "Yes, he hits me when he's drunk."

   ______

   ______

D Answer the following questions, using the cues provided. Substitute direct and indirect object pronouns for the italicized objects.

Modelo ¿Quién *le* quita *el dinero a esa mujer?* (su marido)
Su marido **se lo** quita.

1. ¿Quién *le* dice *la verdad a Ud.?* (mi amigo)

   ______

2. ¿Quién no *les* perdona *los delitos a los ladrones?* (mi padre)

   ______

3. ¿Quién *les* consigue *bebidas a los menores de edad?* (nadie)

   ______

4. ¿Quién *le* va a preguntar *eso al padrastro?* (el agente)

   ______

© 2017 Cengage Learning

Nombre ______________________ Sección ____________ Fecha ____________

Conversaciones breves

Complete the following dialogue, using your imagination and the vocabulary from this lesson.

Un caso de maltrato:

Agente Rocha —______________________________

Vecina —El marido de mi vecina le está pegando.

Agente Rocha —______________________________

Vecina —Sí, siempre le pega. Y cuando está borracho, le pega mucho.

Agente Rocha —______________________________

Vecina —¿El dinero para bebidas? Su mujer me dice que si ella no se lo da, él se lo quita.

Agente Rocha —______________________________

Vecina —No sé si tiene armas.

Agente Rocha —______________________________

Vecina —No sé si va a estar dispuesta a acusar a su marido esta vez.

Agente Rocha —______________________________

En estas situaciones

With a partner, act out the following situations in Spanish.

1. You arrive at a house where there is a domestic squabble. Ask if you're at the right house, what is going on, if the stepfather is employed, and whether he is armed.
2. You are talking to a battered wife. See if she's hurt and if she needs to go to the hospital. Ask her if she wants to accuse her husband of abuse, and find out if she has a place to spend the night.
3. You go to a house where the parents are suspected of abusing their children. Introduce yourself. Explain that the local doctor suspects abuse because both children are in the hospital again with rather serious injuries. The parents deny everything.

Casos

With you and a partner playing the roles, work through the following scenarios.

1. You are a police officer questioning a child about the father's abuse of the mother.
2. Discuss child abuse and counseling with a parent who has been abusing his/her child.

© 2017 Cengage Learning

Nombre ______________________ Sección ____________ Fecha ____________

Un paso más Review the **Vocabulario adicional** in this lesson and match the questions or statements in column **A** with the answers in column **B.**

A		
1. ________	¿Es un rifle?	a. Porque hay una bomba.
2. ________	¿Cómo dice que lo va a matar?	b. Tiene que quitársela.
3. ________	¿Cómo castigan al niño?	c. Lo va a ahorcar.
4. ________	¿Por qué tenemos que salir del hotel?	d. Sí, revólveres y ametralladoras.
5. ________	¿Qué explosivos tiene?	e. Generalmente le dan una nalgada.
6. ________	El niño tiene una navaja.	f. Dinamita y granadas de mano.
7. ________	¿Le vas a dar una bofetada?	g. No, es una escopeta.
8. ________	¿La pandilla tiene armas de fuego?	h. No, una patada.

© 2017 Cengage Learning

Lección 9 La prueba del alcohol

Objectives

Structures

- Possessive pronouns
- Command forms: **Ud.** and **Uds.**
- Reflexive constructions
- Uses of object pronouns with command forms

Communication

- Traffic police: stopping and interviewing drivers; administering a sobriety test; giving detailed directions
- Identifying parts of a car

iLrn™

La prueba del alcohol

Son las tres de la madrugada. El agente López detiene a un hombre por conducir a cincuenta millas por hora, con las luces apagadas, en una zona residencial. El límite de velocidad es de treinta y cinco millas por hora. El hombre parece estar borracho.

Agente López —Arrime el carro a la acera y apague el motor, por favor.
Hombre —¿Qué pasa, agente?
Agente López —El límite de velocidad en este lugar es de treinta y cinco millas por hora, no de cincuenta.
Hombre —Es que estoy muy apurado.
Agente López —Déjeme ver su licencia de conducir, por favor.
Hombre —Está en mi casa...
Agente López —Muéstreme el registro del coche.
Hombre —No lo tengo. El coche no es mío. Es de mi tío.
Agente López —¿Cómo se llama Ud.?
Hombre —Me llamo Juan Lara.
Agente López —Su dirección y su edad, por favor.

Sr. Lara —Vivo en la calle Quinta, número quinientos veinte. Tengo veinte años.
Agente López —Bájese del carro, por favor. Párese con los talones juntos y ponga los brazos a los costados.
Sr. Lara —¡Le digo que estoy apurado!
Agente López —Usando la mano izquierda, tóquese la punta de la nariz con el dedo índice.
Sr. Lara —No puedo... pero no estoy borracho...
Agente López —Ahora cierre los ojos y eche la cabeza hacia atrás.
Sr. Lara —Me voy a caer...
Agente López —Bueno. Camine por esta línea hasta el final y vuelva por la misma línea. Dé nueve pasos.
Sr. Lara —No entiendo... ¿Cuántos pasos? No veo bien la línea.

El Sr. Lara no puede hacer lo que el agente le dice.

Agente López —Cuente con los dedos, así: uno, dos, tres, cuatro... cuatro, tres, dos, uno...
Sr. Lara —Uno, dos, tres, cuatro, tres... Voy a empezar de nuevo...
Agente López —Recite el abecedario, por favor.
Sr. Lara —A, be, ce, de... efe, jota... ene...
Agente López —Voy a leerle algo, Sr. Lara. Preste atención.

"Por la ley estatal Ud. tiene que someterse a una prueba química para determinar el contenido alcohólico de su sangre. Ud. puede elegir si la prueba va a ser de su sangre, orina o aliento. Si Ud. se niega a someterse a una prueba o si no completa una prueba, le vamos a suspender el derecho a manejar por seis meses. Ud. no tiene derecho a hablar con un abogado ni a tener un abogado presente antes de decir si va a someterse a una prueba, antes de decidir cuál de las pruebas va a elegir, ni durante la prueba elegida por Ud. Si Ud. no puede, o dice que no puede, completar la prueba elegida por Ud., debe someterse a cualquiera de las otras pruebas y completarla."

¡Escuchemos!

While listening to the dialogue, circle **V (verdadero)** if the statement is true and **F (falso)** if it is false.

1. El agente López detiene a un hombre a las tres de la madrugada. V F
2. El límite de velocidad en una zona residencial es de cincuenta millas por hora. V F
3. El hombre saca la licencia de conducir del bolsillo. V F
4. Él es el dueño del coche. V F
5. Juan Lara vive en la calle Quinta. V F
6. Juan no puede tocarse la nariz con el dedo índice. V F
7. Él no ve bien la línea. V F
8. Si Juan se niega a someterse a una prueba química no le pueden suspender el derecho a manejar. V F

© 2017 Cengage Learning

Nombre ______________________ Sección ____________ Fecha ____________

9. Juan puede elegir si la prueba va a ser de sangre, de orina o de aliento. V F

10. Si Juan elige una prueba y no puede completarla, no tiene derecho a someterse a otra de las pruebas. V F

VOCABULARIO

Cognados

el alcohol
alcohólico(a)
el límite
la línea
el motor
la orina
residencial
la velocidad
la zona

Nombres

el abecedario, el alfabeto *alphabet*
la acera, la banqueta (*Méx.*) *sidewalk*
la alcoholemia *blood alcohol level*
el aliento *breath*
la cabeza *head*
el contenido *content*
el dedo *finger*
el final *end*
el índice *index*
el límite de velocidad, la velocidad máxima *speed limit*
la madrugada *early morning*
la milla *mile*
la nariz *nose*
el paso *step*
la prueba *test*
la prueba del alcohol *sobriety test*
la punta *end, tip*
la sangre *blood*
el talón *heel*
el (la) tío (tía) *uncle (aunt)*

Verbos

apagar *to turn off*
arrimar *to pull over, to place nearby*
bajarse *to get out (off)*
caer(se)[1] *to fall*
completar *to complete*
contar (o:ue) *to count*
dejar *to allow, to let*
determinar *to determine*
elegir (e:i)[2] *to choose*
extender (e:ie) *to stretch out, to spread*
llamarse *to be named, to be called*
mostrar (o:ue), enseñar *to show*
pararse *to stand (up)*
poner[3] *to put*
recitar *to recite*
someterse a *to submit (oneself) to*
tocar *to touch*

Adjetivos

apagado(a) *out, turned off (light)*
elegido(a) *chosen*
estatal *of or pertaining to the state*
juntos(as) *together*
mismo(a) *same*
químico(a) *chemical*

---

[1]Irregular first person present indicative: **yo (me) caigo**
[2]First person present indicative: **yo elijo**
[3]Irregular first person present indicative: **yo pongo**

© 2017 Cengage Learning

Nombre ______________________ Sección ____________ Fecha ____________

Otras palabras y expresiones

a los costados *on the sides, at your sides*
así *like this*
conducir a cincuenta millas por hora *to drive fifty miles per hour*
dar un paso *to take a step*
de nuevo *over, again*
echar la cabeza hacia atrás *to tilt one's head back*
Es que... *It's just that . . .*
estar apurado(a), tener prisa *to be in a hurry*
prestar atención *to pay attention*

VOCABULARIO ADICIONAL

Vocabulario automovilístico

el aceite *oil*
el acelerador *accelerator, gas pedal*
el acumulador, la batería *battery*
el amortiguador (de choque) *shock absorber*
el arranque, el motor de arranque *starter*
el asiento *seat*
el asiento para el niño *child's car seat*
la baliza *hazard light*
la bomba de agua *water pump*
la bujía *spark plug*
el cambio de velocidad *gearshift*
el capó, la cubierta *hood*
el carburador *carburetor*
el cinturón de seguridad *safety belt*
el embrague *clutch*
el filtro *filter*
el foco *light*
el freno *brake*
el gasoil *Diesel*
la gasolina *gasoline*
la goma, el neumático, la llanta *tire*
el guardafangos *fender*
el limpiaparabrisas *windshield wiper*
la llanta pinchada (ponchada) *flat tire*
la luz de giro *turn signal*
el maletero, el portaequipajes, la cajuela (*Méx.*), **el baúl** (*Puerto Rico*) *trunk*
la palanca de cambio de velocidades *gearshift lever*
el portaguantes, la guantera *glove compartment*
la rueda *wheel*
el seguro *lock*
el silenciador *muffler*
el tablero *instrument panel*
el tanque *tank*
la tapicería *upholstery*
la ventanilla *window*
el volante, el timón (*Cuba*) *steering wheel*

Para dar direcciones

la cuadra (*América*) *block (one side of a city square)*
la manzana *block (city square)*
a (dos, cuatro,...) cuadras de aquí *(two, four, . . .) blocks from here*
Doble..., Voltee... *Turn . . .*
la esquina *corner*
hasta la... *up to . . .*
Siga derecho. *Go straight ahead.*

© 2017 Cengage Learning

Nombre ______________________ Sección __________ Fecha __________

Notas Culturales

- Alcoholism is stigmatized as a vice in most Spanish-speaking countries, but having several drinks or drinking excessively at social functions is acceptable on occasion. Latinos generally don't drink alone, but rather in groups, and rarely with the deliberate intention of getting drunk. In some countries, women drink as much as men; in other countries, women hardly drink at all. The frequency of drunkenness among women in Spanish-speaking countries is, overall, much lower than among women in the United States.
- In the majority of Hispanic countries, there is no age limit for the sale and consumption of alcoholic beverages, and, generally, where age limits exist, they are not enforced. Young people generally participate fully in social gatherings and parties, and it is not unusual for them to drink alcoholic beverages.
- The alcoholic beverages most consumed in Hispanic countries are beer, wine, tequila, rum, cognac, and whiskey. Cider, an alcoholic beverage, is the preferred beverage for toasts. Upon toasting, Spanish-speaking people generally say **¡Salud!** ("To your health!"). In Spain, one frequently says **¡Salud, amor y pesetas,**[1] **y tiempo para gastarlas!** ("Health, love, and *pesetas,* and the time to spend them!").

Actividades

Dígame... Answer the following questions, basing your answers on the dialogue.

1. ¿Por qué detiene al hombre el agente López?

____

2. ¿Cuál es el límite de velocidad en la zona residencial?

____

3. ¿Parece estar borracho el hombre?

____

4. ¿Por qué dice el hombre que está manejando a cincuenta millas por hora?

____

5. ¿Qué le pide el agente López?

____

6. ¿Tiene el hombre el registro del carro?

____

[1]The Spanish currency is now the **euro.**

© 2017 Cengage Learning

Nombre ______________________ Sección ____________ Fecha ____________

7. ¿Cómo se llama el hombre y cuántos años tiene?

____

8. ¿Cómo debe pararse?

____

9. ¿Qué debe hacer usando la mano izquierda?

____

10. ¿Qué debe hacer después de cerrar los ojos?

____

11. ¿Cuántos pasos debe dar el hombre?

____

12. ¿Para qué tiene que someterse el Sr. Lara a una prueba química?

____

Hablemos Interview a classmate, using the following questions. When you have finished, switch roles.

1. ¿Para qué es la prueba del alcohol?
2. ¿Cuáles son las tres clases de pruebas?
3. ¿Qué pasa si yo me niego a someterme a la prueba del alcohol?
4. Si yo me someto a la prueba del alcohol, ¿puede estar presente mi abogado(a)?
5. ¿Qué pasa si yo no puedo completar la prueba?
6. ¿Cómo se llama Ud.?
7. ¿Puede Ud. decirme su dirección y su edad?
8. ¿Puede Ud. cerrar los ojos y tocarse la punta de la nariz?

Quiz

Vamos a practicar

A Complete the following sentences with the Spanish equivalent of the words in parentheses.

1. Mi sangre es "O" positiva y ____________ es "A" negativa. (*his*)
2. Sus hijos viven en California y ____________ viven en México. (*mine*)

© 2017 Cengage Learning

Nombre ______________________ Sección ____________ Fecha ____________

3. Mi apartamento queda en la calle Azalea. ¿Dónde queda ____________, Sra. Vega? (*yours*)

4. Yo ______________________ a las seis y ellos ______________________ a las ocho. (*get up / get up*)

5. ¿A qué hora ______________________ Uds.? (*go to bed*)

6. Nosotros ______________________ ahora. (*go away*)

7. ¿Ud. ______________________ de la Sra. Peña? (*remember*)

B You have just stopped a woman for erratic driving. Use commands to tell her to do the following.

1. poner las manos en el volante

____

2. apagar el motor y bajarse del carro

____

3. prestar atención y no hablar

____

4. pararse con los brazos a los costados

____

5. extender los brazos, cerrar los ojos y echar la cabeza hacia atrás

____

C You suspect that two men who are creating a disturbance in the street are drunk. Use commands to tell them to do the following.

1. tocarse la nariz

____

2. caminar

____

3. recitar el alfabeto

____

4. contar con los dedos

____

© 2017 Cengage Learning

Nombre ______________________ Sección ____________ Fecha ____________

D Answer the following questions first affirmatively, then negatively.

Modelo ¿Se lo digo a ella?
Sí, **dígaselo.**
No, **no se lo diga.**

1. ¿Se las doy a Ud.?

   Sí, ______________________________.

   No, ______________________________.

2. ¿Lo completo ahora?

   Sí, ______________________________.

   No, ______________________________.

3. ¿Le suspendo el derecho a manejar?

   Sí, ______________________________.

   No, ______________________________.

4. ¿Me someto a la prueba de alcoholemia?

   Sí, ______________________________.

   No, ______________________________.

5. ¿Me bajo del carro?

   Sí, ______________________________.

   No, ______________________________.

6. ¿Pongo el seguro?

   Sí, ______________________________.

   No, ______________________________.

© 2017 Cengage Learning

Nombre ______________________ **Sección** ____________ **Fecha** ____________

Conversaciones breves

Complete the following dialogue, using your imagination and the vocabulary from this lesson.

Otra prueba del alcohol:

Hombre —______________________________

Agente —Lo detengo porque está manejando sin luz.

Hombre —______________________________

Agente —No, no puede irse (*leave*). ¿No sabe Ud. que el límite de velocidad en esta zona es de veinticinco millas por hora?

Hombre —______________________________

Agente —Deme su licencia, por favor.

Hombre —______________________________

Agente —Para manejar debe tener su licencia con Ud. Déjeme ver su registro.

Hombre —______________________________

Agente —¿El carro no es suyo (*yours*)? ¿De quién es?

Hombre —______________________________

Agente —Bájese del carro, por favor.

Hombre —______________________________

Agente —Lo siento, pero voy a tener que hacerle la prueba del alcohol.

Hombre —______________________________

Agente —Si no se somete a la prueba, le vamos a suspender el derecho a manejar por seis meses.

Hombre —______________________________

En estas situaciones

With two or more classmates, act out the following situations in Spanish.

1. You stop a woman for driving sixty miles per hour in a thirty-five-mile-per-hour zone. Order her to pull over to the curb, turn off the engine, and show you her driver's license and car registration.
2. You are giving a sobriety test to two teenagers caught racing their cars down Main Street. Order them to stretch their arms and touch their noses, to walk a straight line, and to count on their fingers. You find they are not drunk. You decide not to give them a ticket, but remind them about the speed limit.

Casos

With you and a partner playing the roles, work through the following scenarios.

1. While on patrol, you spot a reckless driver, whom you pull over. Explain why you have stopped the car and collect the appropriate personal data.
2. You have just pulled over a person suspected of DUI. Administer a field sobriety test.

© 2017 Cengage Learning

Nombre ______________________ Sección ______________ Fecha ______________

Un paso más

A Review the **Vocabulario adicional** in this lesson and match the items in column **A** with the Spanish equivalent in column **B.**

A	B
1. ________ turn signal	a. tapicería
2. ________ starter	b. guardafangos
3. ________ water pump	c. parabrisas
4. ________ carburetor	d. maletero
5. ________ oil	e. rueda
6. ________ tire	f. silenciador
7. ________ battery	g. limpiaparabrisas
8. ________ windshield wiper	h. portaguantes
9. ________ gas pedal	i. tanque
10. ________ spark plug	j. ventanilla
11. ________ steering wheel	k. aceite
12. ________ upholstery	l. bujía
13. ________ windshield	m. cambio de velocidades
14. ________ window	n. carburador
15. ________ glove compartment	ñ. baliza
16. ________ gearshift	o. acelerador
17. ________ wheel	p. capó
18. ________ hood	q. volante
19. ________ tank	r. luz de giro
20. ________ filter	s. asiento
21. ________ flat tire	t. llanta pinchada
22. ________ muffler	u. arranque
23. ________ trunk	v. filtro
24. ________ brake	w. bomba de agua
25. ________ fender	x. acumulador
26. ________ seat	y. freno
27. ________ hazard light	z. goma

© 2017 Cengage Learning

Nombre ______________________ **Sección** ____________ **Fecha** ____________

B You are a traffic policeman standing at the intersection of Novena Avenida and Calle 10, as indicated on the city map below. Give six people directions to the following places.

1. estación de policía:
2. hospital:
3. escuela secundaria:
4. hotel:
5. consulado de México:
6. mercado:

Sección del plano de una ciudad

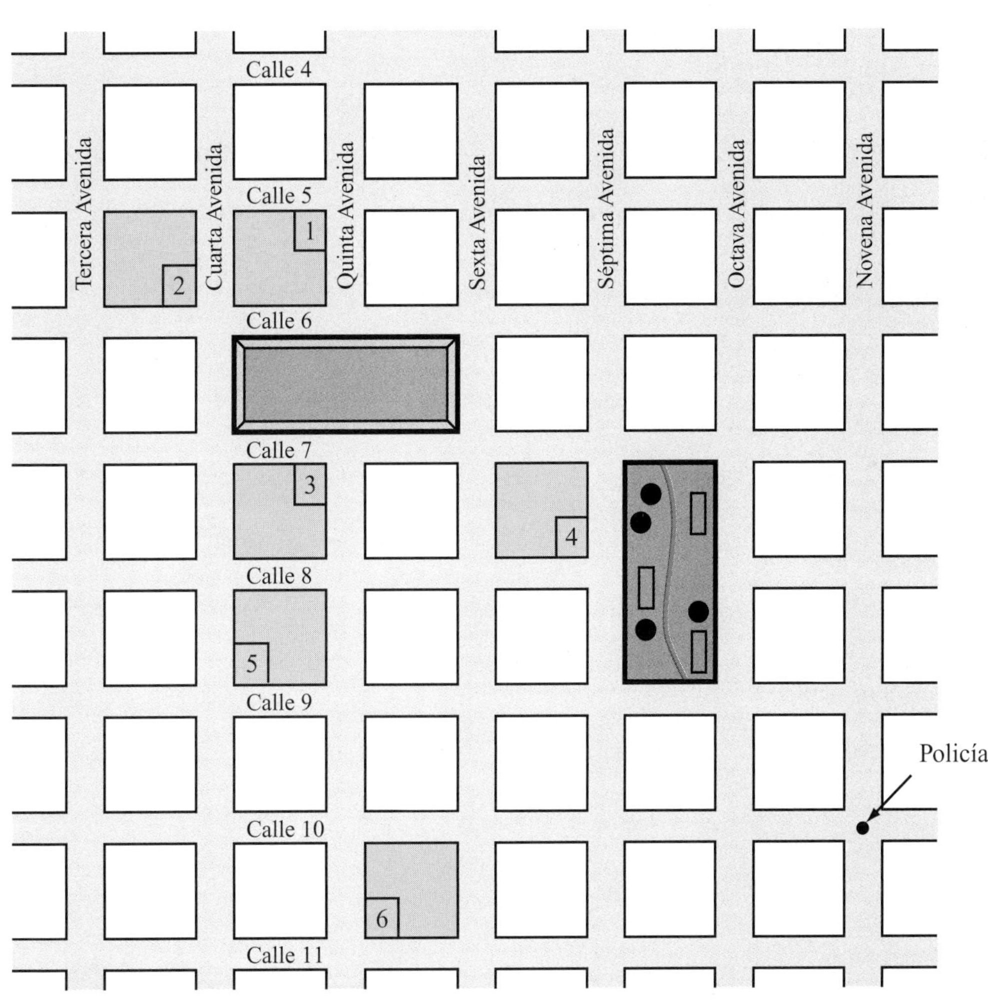

© 2017 Cengage Learning

La policía investiga un robo

Objectives

Structures

- The preterit of regular verbs
- The preterit of **ser, ir,** and **dar**
- Uses of **por** and **para**

Communication

- Investigating a burglary: interviewing victims and witnesses on location
- Describing the weather

iLrn™

La policía investiga un robo

Esta mañana la Sra. Ramos llamó por teléfono a la policía para denunciar un robo. Una hora después llegó a su casa el sargento Nieto, de la Sección de Robos.

El sargento Nieto habla con la Sra. Ramos:

Sargento Nieto —Buenos días, señora. Soy el sargento Nieto, de la Sección de Robos. Aquí está mi identificación.

Sra. Ramos —Buenos días, sargento. Llamé porque anoche entraron ladrones en la casa.

Sargento Nieto —¿Qué les robaron, señora?

Sra. Ramos —Muchas cosas: dos televisores, una cámara de vídeo, la computadora, el tocadiscos de discos compactos, varias joyas y unos ochenta dólares en efectivo.

Sargento Nieto —¿De qué marca son todos esos equipos?

Sra. Ramos —La computadora es de la IBM, los televisores son un JVC de diecinueve pulgadas y un RCA de veinticuatro pulgadas. Los demás equipos son también de la RCA.

Sargento Nieto —¿Tiene el número de serie de todos los equipos robados?

Sra. Ramos —Creo que sí. Nosotros los compramos a plazos y yo tengo guardados los contratos. Un momento.

Nombre ______________________ Sección ____________ Fecha ____________

La señora se va y vuelve con los contratos. El sargento Nieto los revisa.

Sargento Nieto —Aquí falta el contrato de uno de los televisores.
Sra. Ramos —Es verdad. Ahora me acuerdo de que lo tiré a la basura cuando terminé de pagarlo.
Sargento Nieto —Y... ¿no anotó el número de serie?
Sra. Ramos —No, no lo anoté. Ya sé que fue una tontería.
Sargento Nieto —¿Por dónde entraron los ladrones?
Sra. Ramos —Por la ventana del cuarto de mi hijo mayor. Forzaron la cerradura. Mire, como anoche llovió, dejaron algunas huellas de barro en la alfombra.
Sargento Nieto —¿Limpiaron Uds. la casa después del robo?
Sra. Ramos —No, no tocamos nada.
Sargento Nieto —Bien. Luego van a venir los técnicos para ver si dejaron algunas huellas digitales. Ud. no tiene idea de a qué hora fue el robo, ¿verdad?
Sra. Ramos —No. Mi hijo menor tiene el descanso de primavera. Lo llevamos a la playa y nos quedamos allá hasta hoy.
Sargento Nieto —¿Su hijo mayor también fue a la playa?
Sra. Ramos —Sí, todos fuimos y volvimos juntos.
Sargento Nieto —Bueno, eso es todo, Sra. Ramos. Ahora voy a hablar con los vecinos para continuar las averiguaciones.
Sra. Ramos —Yo hablé con los vecinos de al lado y ellos no vieron a nadie sospechoso rondando la casa.
Sargento Nieto —Y yo le di mi tarjeta, ¿verdad? Llámeme si tiene algo nuevo que decirme.
Sra. Ramos —Gracias por su ayuda, sargento. Y, por favor, si Ud. averigua algo, llámeme.
Sargento Nieto —Claro que sí, señora.

¡Escuchemos!

While listening to the dialogue, circle **V (verdadero)** if the statement is true and **F (falso)** if it is false.

1. El sargento Nieto llama a la Sra. Ramos para denunciar un robo. V F
2. Los ladrones entraron anoche en la casa de la familia Ramos. V F
3. La cámara de vídeo era de la marca IBM. V F
4. La Sra. Ramos tiene el número de serie de la computadora. V F
5. Los Ramos compraron los equipos a plazos. V F
6. Falta el contrato del tocadiscos. V F
7. Los ladrones entraron por la puerta de la calle. V F
8. Es una tontería no anotar el número de serie de los equipos. V F
9. Los técnicos van a venir para ver si los ladrones dejaron sus huellas digitales. V F
10. Los vecinos vieron a un hombre sospechoso rondando la casa. V F

© 2017 Cengage Learning

Nombre ______________________ Sección ____________ Fecha ____________

VOCABULARIO

Cognados

la cámara de vídeo[1]**, la videocámara**
el contrato
el disco compacto
el dólar
la serie
el (la) técnico(a)

Nombres

la alfombra *carpet*
la averiguación *investigation*
la basura *trash, garbage*
el barro, el fango *mud*
la cerradura *lock*
la computadora, el ordenador (*España*) *computer*
el cuarto, la habitación *room*
el descanso (las vacaciones) de primavera *spring break*
el equipo *equipment*
la huella *footprint*
la huella digital *fingerprint*
la joya *jewelry*
la mañana *morning*
la marca *brand*
el número de serie *serial number*
la playa *beach*
la primavera *spring*
el pueblo *town*
el televisor *television set*
la tontería *foolishness, nonsense*
las vacaciones *vacation*

Verbos

acordarse (o:ue) (de) *to remember*
anotar *to write down, to take note of*
averiguar *to find out*
comprar *to buy*
continuar *to continue*
faltar *to be missing, to lack*
forzar (o:ue) *to force*
irse *to go away, to leave*
limpiar *to clean*
quedarse *to stay*
revisar, chequear *to review, to check*
robar *to rob, to steal from*
rondar *to prowl*
terminar *to finish*
tirar, botar *to throw away*

Adjetivos

cercano(a) *near, nearby*
guardado(a) *put away, saved*
robado(a) *stolen, robbed*

Otras palabras y expresiones

a plazos *in installments, on time* (*payments*)
anoche *last night*
Claro que sí *Of course*
como *since, being that*
de al lado *next-door* (*neighbor, house*)
en efectivo *in cash*
los demás *the remaining* (*ones*)
luego *later, afterwards*
terminar de (+ *inf.*) *to finish* (*doing something*)

---

[1]"vídeo" is mostly used in Spain; in Latin America the word "video" is more common

© 2017 Cengage Learning

Nombre ______________________ Sección ______________ Fecha ______________

VOCABULARIO ADICIONAL

Algunos artículos usados para cometer delitos (*Some crime paraphernalia*)

el cortavidrios *glass cutter*
el documento falso *forged document*
la escala de soga *rope ladder*
la escalera de mano *hand ladder*
la identificación falsa *fake identification, forged ID*
la jeringuilla *hypodermic syringe*
la llave falsa, la ganzúa *skeleton key, picklock*
la máscara *mask*
la mordaza *gag*
la pata de cabra *crowbar*
la piedra *stone, rock*
la sierra de mano, el serrucho de mano *handsaw*
la soga *rope*

Para hablar del tiempo (*To talk about the weather*)

hacer buen tiempo *to have good weather*
hacer (mucho) calor *to be (very) hot*
hacer fresco *to be cool*
hacer (mucho) frío *to be (very) cold*
hacer mal tiempo *to have bad weather*
hacer (mucho) sol *to be (very) sunny*
hacer (mucho) viento *to be (very) windy*
la humedad *humidity*
la lluvia *rain*
llover (o:ue) *to rain*
la neblina, la niebla *fog*
nevar (e:ie) *to snow*
la nieve *snow*

Las estaciones (*Seasons*)

el invierno *winter*
el otoño *autumn*
el verano *summer*
la primavera *spring*

Notas Culturales

- Note that Latinos use a polite handshake when meeting someone for the first time. A handshake is also used for leave-taking.
- When saying hello or good-bye and when being introduced, Hispanic men and women almost always shake hands. When greeting each other, girls and women often place their cheeks together, kissing not each other's cheek but the air. In Spain, this kissing is done on both cheeks. Men who are close friends normally embrace and pat each other on the back.
- Remember that in the Southern hemisphere the seasons are reversed. For example, when it is winter in the United States, it is summer in Argentina.

© 2017 Cengage Learning

Nombre ______________________ Sección ____________ Fecha ____________

Actividades

Dígame... Answer the following questions, basing your answers on the dialogue.

1. ¿Para qué llamó la Sra. Ramos a la policía?

____

2. ¿Para qué fue el agente Nieto a su casa?

____

3. ¿Qué les robaron?

____

4. ¿De qué marca son los televisores? ¿Y la computadora?

____

5. ¿Sabe la Sra. Ramos todos los números de serie? ¿Por qué?

____

6. ¿Cómo entraron los ladrones en la casa?

____

7. ¿Para qué van a venir los técnicos?

____

8. ¿Adónde fueron la Sra. Ramos y su familia ayer?

____

9. ¿Qué más va a pasar?

____

10. ¿Qué le dio el sargento Nieto a la Sra. Ramos?

____

© 2017 Cengage Learning

Nombre ______________________ Sección ____________ Fecha ____________

Hablemos

Interview a classmate, using the following questions. When you have finished, switch roles.

1. ¿Adónde fue Ud. ayer?
2. ¿Le dio su identificación a alguien?
3. ¿Se quedó en casa anoche?
4. ¿Tiene Ud. una computadora en su casa? ¿De qué marca es? Cuando la compró, ¿anotó el número de serie?
5. ¿Se acuerda Ud. dónde compró su televisor? ¿Lo compró a plazos?
6. ¿Alguien lo (la) llamó a Ud. esta mañana? ¿Quién fue?
7. Si Ud. ve a alguien sospechoso rondando una casa, ¿qué hace?
8. ¿Llovió anoche? ¿Qué tiempo hizo?

Quiz

Vamos a practicar

A Change the following paragraph to indicate that the actions took place in the past. Pay special attention to the verbs in italics.

Cuando la familia García *sale* de su casa, los ladrones *entran* y le *roban* la computadora. Cuando la familia *regresa,* la Sra. García *llama* a la policía. *Habla* con el sargento Smith y le *da* el número de serie del equipo. El sargento le *dice* que va a investigar el caso. Por la tarde, el sargento *va* a la casa de los García.

____

____

____

____

____

B Fill in the blanks with **por** or **para** as needed.

1. Los ladrones entraron ____________ una ventana.
2. El sargento viene ____________ investigar el robo.
3. Me llamó ____________ teléfono ____________ decirme tonterías.
4. Ella guarda dinero ____________ su fiesta.
5. Compré una computadora ____________ mi hija ____________ muy poco dinero.

© 2017 Cengage Learning

Nombre ______________________ Sección ____________ Fecha ____________

6. No puede identificar la cámara de vídeo __________ no tener el número de serie.

7. __________ entrar en la casa, los ladrones forzaron la ventana.

8. Salimos __________ la mañana, pero la fiesta fue __________ la noche.

9. Nos fuimos de vacaciones __________ dos semanas.

10. Hay muchas nubes. Creo que está __________ llover.

C Write questions that elicit the following answers.

1. ____

   Anoche entramos por la ventana.

2. ____

   Fuimos a la casa de la Sra. Araújo.

3. ____

   Les di cien dólares.

4. ____

   No, no entendimos la conversación.

5. ____

   Volví a mi casa a las nueve y media.

6. ____

   Sí, yo fui el agente que investigó el robo.

Conversaciones breves

Complete the following dialogue, using your imagination and the vocabulary from this lesson.

Investigando un robo:

Agente —____

Mujer —Me robaron un televisor y una cámara de vídeo.

Agente —____

Mujer —El televisor es un RCA portátil, de diecinueve pulgadas y la cámara de vídeo, una Sony.

Agente —____

© 2017 Cengage Learning

Mujer —Hacía mucho calor y estábamos en la playa.

Agente —______

Mujer —Entraron por la ventana.

Agente —______

Mujer —¡Bah! Mis vecinos nunca ven nada. Siempre están mirando televisión.

Agente —______

En estas situaciones

With two or more classmates, act out the following situations in Spanish.

1. You are investigating a burglary. Ask the victim if he/she called the police, when the burglary took place, what the burglars took, and whether he/she knows how they got in.
2. You are talking to a burglary victim. Say that you are going to talk with the neighbors to try to find out if anybody saw anything. Explain that the technicians are going to come this afternoon to look for fingerprints. The victim asks you to call if you find out anything new.
3. You are talking to the neighbors of a person whose house was robbed. Introduce yourself and explain the reason for your visit. Ask if they saw anyone prowling around last night. They say they saw two suspicious young men in a strange car in front of the house, but they never got out. Tell them to call you if they remember anything new.

Casos

With you and a partner playing the roles, work through the following scenarios.

1. You are a police officer talking to a victim of a burglary.
2. You describe to your partner, who was not on duty last night, all you know about the break-in on Cisne Street.

Un paso más

A Review the **Vocabulario adicional** in this lesson and then list the paraphernalia that you associate with the following crimes.

1. el vandalismo ______

   ______
2. el homicidio ______

   ______
3. el uso de drogas ______

   ______

© 2017 Cengage Learning

4. el robo ______

______

5. el contrabando ______

______

6. la estafa (*swindle*) ______

______

B Review the expressions in the **Vocabulario adicional** for describing weather conditions. Describe what the weather is like in each of the following cities during the season that is indicated.

1. Phoenix, Arizona, en el verano: ______
2. Chicago, Illinois, en el otoño: ______
3. Portland, Oregón, en el invierno: ______
4. San Diego, California, en la primavera: ______
5. San Francisco, California, en el invierno: ______

© 2017 Cengage Learning

RECOMENDACIONES PARA PREVENIR EL ROBO EN LAS TIENDAS

RECOMENDACIONES PARA PREVENIR EL ROBO EN LAS TIENDAS

Read the information about shoplifting in the following pamphlet for shop owners. Try to guess the meaning of all cognates.

RECOMENDACIONES PARA PREVENIR EL ROBO EN LAS TIENDAS

1. Los empleados tienen que estar alertas. Ud. debe formular un método sistemático que todos los empleados puedan seguir[1] si ven a una persona robando.
2. Los empleados tienen que poder ver todo lo que[2] pasa en la tienda. Los mostradores[3] no deben ser más altos que el nivel de la cintura.[4] Se recomienda poner espejos[5] en los rincones[6] de la tienda.
3. Deben colocar[7] los mostradores cerca de la puerta de salida.[8] De este modo,[9] los clientes pasan frente a los cajeros.[10]
4. No recomendamos poner la mercancía más cara[11] cerca de la puerta.
5. Deben instalar cámaras de seguridad en varios puntos[12] de la tienda?

Debe haber una advertencia contra[13] el robo a la vista.

© Cengage Learning

[1]**puedan...** *can follow*
[2]**lo...** *what*
[3]*counters*
[4]*waist*
[5]**poner...** *to put mirrors*
[6]*corners*
[7]*place*
[8]*exit*
[9]**De...** *This way*
[10]*cashiers*
[11]*expensive*
[12]*locations*
[13]*against*

© 2017 Cengage Learning

Nombre ______________________ Sección __________ Fecha __________

Dígame...

1. Which of the following suggestions does the brochure make to prevent shoplifting?
   ___ **a.** Recomiendan tener una puerta en el fondo (*in the back*) de la tienda.
   ___ **b.** Cada empleado(a) debe decidir por sí mismo(a) (*by him/herself*) qué hacer si ve a una persona robando.
   ___ **c.** Es una buena idea poner en un lugar (*place*) muy visible una advertencia contra el robo en las tiendas.
   ___ **d.** Los mostradores deben ser muy bajos (*low*).
   ___ **e.** No deben poner los productos más caros cerca de la puerta.
   ___ **f.** Debe haber grabadoras ocultas (*hidden*).
2. If you were advising the owner of a store in a high-crime area, which of the anti-shoplifting measures in the Spanish brochure would you present as the most effective?

© 2017 Cengage Learning

Nombre ______________________ Sección ____________ Fecha ____________

REPASO

Práctica de vocabulario

A Circle the word or phrase that does not belong in each group.

1. automóvil carro dedo
2. aguja juicio abogada
3. mano derecho brazo
4. infracción de tránsito multa equipo
5. tragos corazón borracho
6. antes a plazos después
7. peca tío hijo
8. mentira cigarrillo fumar
9. rubio lastimado pelirrojo
10. hablar correr decir
11. aceptar abusar maltratar
12. volver pegar matar
13. enojada en este lugar adentro
14. agarra coge apaga
15. botan tiran averiguan
16. ordenador computadora cerradura
17. anoche cercano de al lado
18. cámara de vídeo guantera televisor

© 2017 Cengage Learning

Nombre ______________________ **Sección** ____________ **Fecha** ____________

B Circle the word or phrase that best completes each sentence.

1. No sé quién cometió (el delito / el derecho / la escuela).
2. ¿Dónde está el dinero? ¿En tu (joven / bolsillo / aguja)?
3. (El edificio / La pared / El chofer) está en el carro.
4. El reproductor MP3 es de ella; ella es (la clienta / la dueña / la estudiante).
5. No (recuerdo / detengo / empiezo) el nombre de este señor.
6. Maneja (dentro del / bajo los efectos del / a cargo del) alcohol.
7. ¿Es gordo o (delgado / amarillo / endrogado)?
8. El coche está (en la licorería / en la navaja / en la zona de estacionamiento).
9. Mide seis pies, cuatro (tatuajes / suelos / pulgadas).
10. Le va a pegar con un (miembro / cinto / aliento).
11. Vienen a las cuatro de la mañana. (¡De madrugada! / ¡Cualquiera! / ¡Durante!)
12. (Las huellas / Las monedas / Los números) digitales están en la ventana.
13. Yo voy con Roberto. Nosotros siempre vamos (cansados / callados / juntos).
14. Con el dinero que robó, el ladrón quiere (vender / limpiar / comprar) drogas.
15. Tenemos (más o menos / a la fuerza / en contra de) cien dólares.
16. Tiene que (echar / mostrar / dar) nueve pasos.
17. Eche la cabeza (hacia / juntos / luego) atrás.
18. Dejaron huellas de barro en la alfombra porque anoche (llovió / apagó / dejó).
19. Párese con los talones (a menudo / juntos / después).
20. Ponga los brazos (a los costados / a diez millas / de nuevo) del cuerpo.

© 2017 Cengage Learning

Nombre ____________________ Sección ____________ Fecha ____________

C Match the items in column **A** with the appropriate word or phrase in column **B**.

A

1. ____________ Muéstreme el registro, por favor.
2. ____________ ¿Ellas están muy enojadas con la vecina?
3. ____________ ¿De qué país son?
4. ____________ ¿Dices que él está muy enfermo?
5. ____________ ¿Qué puedo hacer?
6. ____________ ¿Cuándo lo viste?
7. ____________ ¿Con quién va Teresa?
8. ____________ ¿No va a conducir Juan?
9. ____________ ¿Cómo está tu tío?
10. ____________ ¿Qué tienes en el cuarto?
11. ____________ ¿Qué le van a hacer?
12. ____________ ¿Dónde está el hospital?
13. ____________ ¿Tú hablaste con él?
14. ____________ ¿Por qué no van a esa calle?
15. ____________ ¿Se van hoy?

B

a. Sí, está ingresado en el hospital.
b. Ayer.
c. Lo siento, pero no lo tengo conmigo.
d. No, porque está borracho.
e. A dos millas de aquí.
f. Porque el tránsito está prohibido.
g. De Colombia.
h. No sé. Tú tienes que decidir.
i. Sí, y vuelven la semana próxima.
j. Conmigo.
k. Sí, porque ella siempre dice tonterías.
l. La prueba del alcohol.
m. Un disco compacto.
n. Mejor.
o. No, porque él se niega a verme.

© 2017 Cengage Learning

Nombre ____________________ Sección ____________ Fecha ____________

D Crucigrama

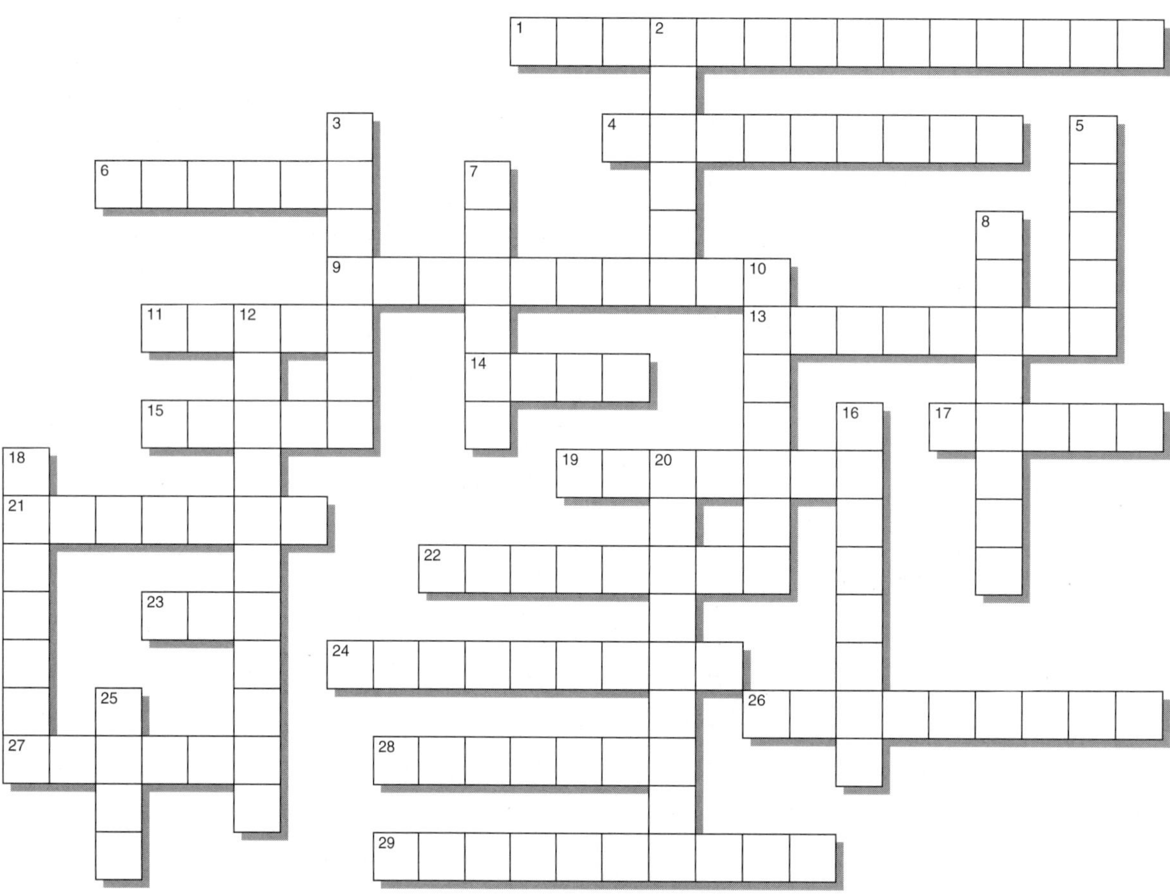

HORIZONTALES

1. con frecuencia
4. ¿Cuál es la ____________ máxima?
6. ¿Es por la ____________ o por la tarde?
9. María dice que son de Lima, pero ella está ____________; son de Santiago.
11. Tóquese la punta de la ____________.
13. *to forgive,* en español
14. un revólver, por ejemplo
15. No es diferente; es el ____________.
17. Escribe con la mano izquierda porque es ____________.
19. opuesto de "gorda"
21. persona de uniforme que anda en patrullero
22. El Empire State, por ejemplo
23. opuesto de "con"
24. Es el esposo de mi mamá, pero no es mi papá; es mi ____________.
26. carro
27. toma
28. mostrar
29. alfabeto

© 2017 Cengage Learning

Nombre ______________________ Sección ____________ Fecha ____________

VERTICALES

2. Ella ___________ de uno a diez en español.
3. parecer: yo ___________
5. Quiero ése en ___________ de éste.
7. opuesto de "dar"
8. cinto
10. Luis tiene prisa: está ___________.
12. Tienes que manejar a 25 millas por hora en un distrito ___________.
16. Es muy tarde y no hay ___________ tiempo para terminar el informe hoy.
18. bar
20. Se puede comprar bebidas alcohólicas en una ___________.
25. No me hace ___________.

Práctica oral

Listen to the following exercise on the audio program. The speaker will ask you some questions. Answer the questions, using the cues provided. The speaker will confirm the correct answer. Repeat the correct answer.

1. ¿Cuánto mide Ud.? (cinco pies, diez pulgadas)
2. ¿Qué marcas visibles tiene Ud.? (un tatuaje en el brazo izquierdo)
3. ¿Adónde fue Ud. ayer? (a la comisaría)
4. ¿Con quién habló Ud. ayer? (con el técnico)
5. ¿A quién vio Ud. anoche? (a mi familia)
6. ¿A qué hora volvió a su casa anoche? (a las ocho)
7. ¿Hay alguien en su casa en este momento? (no)
8. Cuando Ud. necesita dinero, ¿a quién se lo pide? (a nadie)
9. ¿Le robaron a Ud. algo esta mañana? (sí, mis joyas)
10. ¿De qué marca es su televisor? (Sony)
11. ¿Cuándo compró Ud. su televisor? (en abril)
12. ¿Sabe Ud. el número de serie de su videocámara? (no)
13. ¿A quiénes llama Ud. si alguien está lastimado? (a los paramédicos)
14. ¿Cómo se llama la doctora? (Luisa Morales)
15. ¿Quién pagó una multa esta tarde? (la señora de al lado)
16. Cuando Ud. sospecha que alguien maneja bajo la influencia del alcohol, ¿qué hace? (la prueba del alcohol)
17. ¿Alguien se negó a someterse a la prueba del alcohol? (sí, la Srta. Silva)
18. Si alguien maneja muy rápido, ¿lo detiene Ud.? (sí)
19. ¿Recuerda Ud. la advertencia Miranda? (claro que sí)

© 2017 Cengage Learning

Nombre ______________________ Sección ____________ Fecha ____________

20. ¿Puede leerle la advertencia Miranda a alguien en español? (sí)

21. ¿Puede Ud. interrogar a un detenido en español? (sí)

22. ¿Siempre entiende bien cuando alguien le habla en español? (a veces)

23. ¿A quién interrogó Ud. hoy? (al esposo de una mujer maltratada)

24. ¿Ya terminó la averiguación? (sí)

25. ¿Investiga Ud. casos de maltrato a menudo? (sí, frecuentemente)

© 2017 Cengage Learning

Lección 11 ¡Más robos!

Objectives

Structures

- Time expressions with **hacer**
- Irregular preterits
- The preterit of stem-changing verbs (**e:i** and **o:u**)
- Command forms: **tú**

Communication

- Investigating a burglary: reporting a robbery; interviewing victims at the police station
- Indicating times of the day

iLrn™

¡Más robos!

El Sr. Gómez vino a la comisaría a denunciar el robo de su carro. Ahora está hablando con el sargento Alcalá, de la Sección de Robos.

Sargento Alcalá —¿Cuándo le robaron su carro?
Sr. Gómez —Anoche. Mi hijo lo dejó estacionado frente a la casa y yo creo que no lo cerró con llave.
Sargento Alcalá —¿El carro es suyo o de su hijo?
Sr. Gómez —Es mío, pero anoche mi hijo me lo pidió prestado para ir a una fiesta. Él fue el último que lo manejó.
Sargento Alcalá —¿A qué hora regresó su hijo?
Sr. Gómez —Como a las once.
Sargento Alcalá —¿Vio el carro Ud. a esa hora?
Sr. Gómez —Sí, señor. Y él me dio la llave cuando llegó.
Sargento Alcalá —Por favor, dígame la marca, el modelo y el año de su carro.
Sr. Gómez —Es un Ford Taurus, azul claro, del año dos mil cinco.
Sargento Alcalá —¿Cuál es el número de la placa de su carro?

Sr. Gómez —PED 530.
Sargento Alcalá —¿Está asegurado su carro?
Sr. Gómez —Sí, señor, contra todo riesgo.
Sargento Alcalá —¿Ya está totalmente pagado el carro, Sr. Gómez?
Sr. Gómez —No, todavía debo muchos plazos.
Sargento Alcalá —¿Está atrasado en los pagos?
Sr. Gómez —La verdad es que no estoy al día. Debo como dos meses. Es que tuvimos que pagar muchas cuentas, pero ahora mi esposa consiguió un buen trabajo.
Sargento Alcalá —Muy bien. Voy a entregarles las copias del informe a los patrulleros.
Sr. Gómez —A ver si lo encuentran pronto. Muchas gracias, sargento.
Sargento Alcalá —No hay de qué, Sr. Gómez.

La Sra. Vega también vino a la comisaría a denunciar un robo. Ahora está hablando con el sargento Rivas.

Sra. Vega —¡No puedo creerlo! Hace veinte años que vivo aquí y nunca antes hubo un robo en el vecindario.
Sargento Rivas —¿Revisó bien la casa para ver todo lo que le falta?
Sra. Vega —Sí. Hice una lista de lo que falta: cubiertos de plata, la videocasetera, una grabadora, una cámara de vídeo y una computadora.
Sargento Rivas —¿Se llevaron algún arma?
Sra. Vega —¡Ah, sí...! Una pistola de mi esposo.
Sargento Rivas —Esa pistola, ¿está registrada?
Sra. Vega —Creo que sí, pero no estoy segura. Mi esposo murió el año pasado.
Sargento Rivas —Anóteme la marca, descripción y valor aproximado de todos los objetos robados, por favor.
Sra. Vega —Muy bien.
Sargento Rivas —¿Son todos los objetos robados propiedad de Ud.?
Sra. Vega —Sí, señor. Son míos.
Sargento Rivas —Bien, vamos a hacer todo lo posible por recobrarlos. (*Al agente Soto*) Lleva a la Sra. Vega a su casa, por favor. Después ven a mi oficina y tráeme los informes que te pidió el sargento Viñas.

¡Escuchemos!

While listening to the dialogue, circle **V (verdadero)** if the statement is true and **F (falso)** if it is false.

1. El Sr. Gómez le dice al sargento Alcalá que le robaron su computadora.
2. El hijo del Sr. Gómez dejó el carro estacionado frente a su casa.
3. El Sr. Gómez cree que su hijo no dejó el carro cerrado con llave.
4. El hijo del Sr. Gómez no manejó el carro anoche.
5. El carro del Sr. Gómez está asegurado contra todo riesgo.
6. El Sr. Gómez compró el carro a plazos.

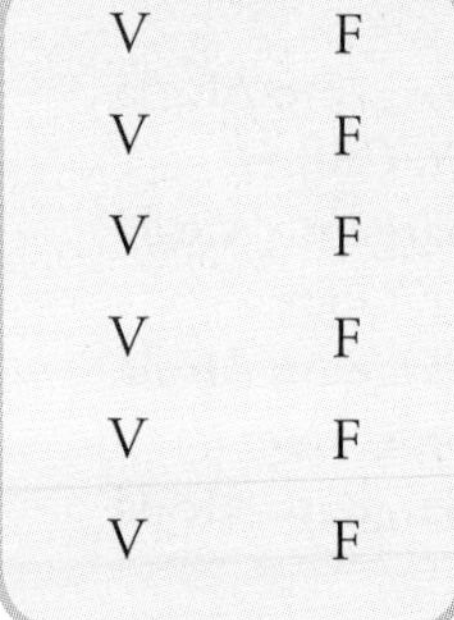

© 2017 Cengage Learning

7. El Sr. Gómez está al día en los pagos. V F
8. El sargento Alcalá va a entregarles las copias del informe a los patrulleros. V F
9. En el vecindario de la Sra. Vega hay muchos robos. V F
10. El esposo de la Sra. Vega estaba en la playa anoche. V F

VOCABULARIO

Cognados

aproximado(a)
la copia
la descripción
la lista
el modelo
el objeto
registrado(a)

Nombres

el año *year*
los cubiertos *silverware (forks, knives, etc.)*
la cuenta *bill*
el empleo, el trabajo *job*
la fiesta *party*
la grabadora *tape recorder*
el pago *payment*
la placa, la chapa *license plate*
la plata *silver*
el plazo *installment*
la propiedad *property*
el riesgo *risk*
el valor *value*
la verdad *truth*
la videocasetera, la videograbadora *videocassette recorder (VCR)*

Verbos

deber *to owe*
encontrar (o:ue) *to find*
entregar *to give, to turn over (i.e., something to someone)*
llevarse *to steal (literally, to carry away)*
morir (o:ue), fallecer *to die, to pass away*
recobrar *to recover*

Adjetivos

asegurado(a) *insured*
atrasado(a) *behind*
cerrado(a) *closed, locked*
claro(a) *light (in color)*
estacionado(a) *parked*
pagado(a) *paid (for)*
pasado(a) *last*
todo(a) *all*
último(a) *last (in a series)*

Otras palabras y expresiones

al día *up to date*
como *about, approximately*
contra *against*
hubo *there was (were)*
nunca antes *never before*
pedir prestado(a) *to borrow*
todo lo posible *everything possible*
totalmente *totally*

© 2017 Cengage Learning

Nombre ____________ Sección ________ Fecha ________

VOCABULARIO ADICIONAL

Pasado, presente y futuro (*Past, present, and future*)

a la mañana *in the morning*
a la noche *in the evening*
a la tarde *in the afternoon*
a mediados de mes *about the middle of the month*
a mediados de semana *about the middle of the week*
a medianoche *at midnight*
al amanecer, de madrugada *at dawn, at daybreak*
al anochecer *at dusk*
al mediodía *at noon*
anteanoche, antes de anoche *the night before last*
anteayer, antes de ayer *the day before yesterday*
el año que viene, el año próximo *next year*
durante el día *during the day*
durante la noche *during the night*
el mes pasado *last month*
el mes que viene, el mes próximo *next month*
pasado mañana *the day after tomorrow*
la semana pasada *last week*
la semana que viene, la semana próxima *next week*
temprano *early*

Otras palabras y expresiones

el reproductor de DVD *DVD player*
el reproductor MP3 *MP3 player*
el videojuego *videogame*

Notas Culturales

- Automobile insurance is not mandatory in many Spanish-speaking countries, and thus the habit of insuring cars is not as widespread in Latin America as it is in the United States. Many Latinos who immigrate to the United States leave their cars uninsured, either out of habit, because they are unaware that automobile insurance is mandatory, or because they cannot afford to pay high insurance premiums.
- In most Latino families children generally live with their parents until they get married or go away to college. They have a very close relationship not only with their parents, but also with their grandparents and other members of the extended family.

Actividades

Dígame... Answer the following questions, basing your answers on the dialogues.

1. ¿Para qué fueron el Sr. Gómez y la Sra. Vega a la comisaría? ¿Con quién está hablando el Sr. Gómez ahora?

____

2. ¿Quién fue el último que manejó el carro? ¿Dónde lo dejó estacionado?

____

3. ¿Puede Ud. describir el carro del Sr. Gómez?

____

© 2017 Cengage Learning

Nombre ________________________ Sección ____________ Fecha ____________

4. ¿Está totalmente pagado el carro del Sr. Gómez?

___

5. ¿Cuántos meses debe el Sr. Gómez? ¿Por qué está atrasado en los pagos?

___

6. ¿Cuántos años hace que la Sra. Vega vive en el barrio?

___

7. ¿Hubo antes algún robo en el vecindario?

___

8. ¿Qué hizo la Sra. Vega después del robo?

___

9. ¿Qué se llevaron los ladrones?

___

10. ¿Está registrada la pistola del Sr. Vega?

___

11. ¿De quién son los objetos robados?

___

12. ¿Qué va a hacer el agente Soto?

___

Hablemos Interview a classmate, using the following questions. When you have finished, switch roles.

1. ¿Cuánto tiempo hace que Ud. trabaja en el Departamento de Policía?
2. ¿Hacen Uds. todo lo posible por recobrar objetos robados?
3. ¿Cuándo fue la última vez que Ud. hizo un informe sobre (*about*) un robo de un carro?
4. ¿Cuál es el número de la chapa de su carro?
5. ¿Está Ud. atrasado(a) en los pagos de su carro?
6. ¿Está asegurado su carro?
7. ¿Cerró Ud. con llave su carro anoche?
8. ¿Hubo algún robo en su barrio recientemente (*recently*)?

© 2017 Cengage Learning

Nombre ______________________ Sección ____________ Fecha ____________

Quiz

Vamos a practicar

A Create sentences with the elements provided, using **hace** + ***time*** + **que** + ***verb.***

1. tres años / (yo) tener / carro

   ____

2. dos horas / sargento Alcalá / hablar / Sr. Gómez

   ____

3. ¿Cuántos años / (Ud.) vivir / en esa casa?

   ____

4. quince minutos / (yo) revisar / la casa

   ____

5. veinte años / mi esposo / tener / esas pistolas

   ____

6. media hora / la Sra. Vega / anotar / la marca / los objetos robados

   ____

7. dos meses / (nosotros) no estar / al día

   ____

B Rewrite the following sentences in the preterit tense according to the cues given.

Modelo Hoy la agente Rojas viene a entregar el informe.
Ayer **la agente Rojas *vino* a entregar el informe.**

1. Tengo que anotar todos los datos.
   Ayer ______________________.
2. Estamos en la fiesta de una vecina.
   Anoche ______________________.
3. No puedo comprar un seguro contra todo riesgo.
   Cuando compré el carro ______________________.
4. Ellos lo saben.
   Anoche ______________________.
5. La Sra. Ramos hace la denuncia en la estación de policía.
   Ayer ______________________.

© 2017 Cengage Learning

Nombre ______________________ Sección ____________ Fecha ____________

6. No quiere decir nada.
   Anoche ______________________________.
7. La señora dice la verdad.
   Ayer ______________________________.
8. Conduzco el coche de mi tío a toda velocidad.
   Anoche ______________________________.
9. Sirven tequila en la fiesta.
   El sábado pasado ______________________________.
10. Elsa duerme muy mal.
    Anoche ______________________________.
11. Uds. no le piden nada.
    Ayer ______________________________.
12. Muchas personas prefieren ir a México.
    El año pasado ______________________________.

C Doña Marta wants her son Roberto to help her out. She gives Roberto the following instructions. Use the Spanish equivalent of each command in parentheses.

Doña Marta —__________ (*Come*) aquí, Roberto. __________ (*Do me*) un favor: __________ (*bring me*) hoy los libros a la oficina, pero __________ (*don't give them*) a mi secretaria; __________ (*put them*) en mi escritorio (*desk*). __________ (*Call*) a tu papá y __________ (*tell him*) que necesito hablar con él. __________ (*Give him*) el número de teléfono de mi nuevo trabajo. Esta noche, __________ (*go*) a la casa de tu hermano Diego y __________ (*ask him*) si puede venir a casa mañana. Pero __________ (*come back*) a las ocho porque tienes que estudiar. ¡Ah!, si no puedes hablar con tu papá, __________ (*write him*) una nota.

Conversaciones breves

Complete the following dialogues, using your imagination and the vocabulary from this lesson.

El sargento Miño habla con la Sra. Paz del robo de su carro.

Sargento Miño —______________________________

Sra. Paz —No, no estoy al día. Debo como cuatro meses.

Sargento Miño —______________________________

Sra. Paz —No, no tengo seguro.

© 2017 Cengage Learning

Nombre ______________________ Sección ____________ Fecha ____________

Sargento Miño —______________________

Sra. Paz —Lo dejé en la calle. No lo puse en el garaje anoche.

Sargento Miño —______________________

Sra. Paz —No, no las tengo. Las dejé en el coche.

Sargento Miño —______________________

Sra. Paz —Sí, yo sospecho de mi vecino...

Sargento Miño —______________________

Sra. Paz —Es un Mazda 2002, de cuatro puertas.

Sargento Miño —______________________

El Sr. Ortega denuncia un robo.

Agente Barrios —¿Hizo Ud. una lista de lo que falta?

Sr. Ortega —______________________

Agente Barrios —¿Puede darme la marca, descripción y valor aproximado de los objetos robados?

Sr. Ortega —______________________

____

____

Agente Barrios —¿De quién son los objetos robados, señor?

Sr. Ortega —______________________

En estas situaciones

With two or more classmates, act out the following situations in Spanish.

1. You are speaking to someone who has just come to the police station to report that his/her car was stolen. Question the owner about where he/she left the car, when it was stolen, whether it was locked, and whether it was insured. Ask for a description of the vehicle.
2. You are investigating a burglary. Ask the victim if he/she checked the house carefully to see what is missing. Find out if the burglars took any weapons. Finally, request that he/she write down the description and the approximate value of the DVD player, the computer, the MP3 player, and the silverware. Say that you'll let him/her know right away if you find the stolen items.

© 2017 Cengage Learning

Nombre ______________________________ Sección ____________ Fecha ____________

Casos With you and a partner playing the roles, work through the following scenarios.

1. You are a desk sergeant speaking with a man/woman who is reporting the theft of his/her car.
2. You are an officer speaking with a person whose home has been burglarized.

Un paso más Review the **Vocabulario adicional** in this lesson and complete the following minidialogues.

1. —¿Cuándo viene Teresa?

   —El 16 de agosto, creo... A ____________.

   —¿Y Jorge?

   —El viernes al mediodía. Hoy es miércoles. Llega ____________.

2. —¿Van temprano?

   —¡Muy temprano! ¡De ____________!

3. —¡Va a llegar muy tarde! ¡Son las once y media de la noche!

   —¡Casi (*Almost*) ____________!

4. —¿Qué fecha es hoy?

   —El 12 de noviembre.

   —¿Cuándo regresó Rafael?

   —El 10... ¡____________!

   —¿Y Ana María?

   —Ella regresó el ____________. El 20 de octubre, creo.

5. —¿Cuándo prefieres hacer la tarea?

   —Generalmente la hago ____________.

6. —¿En qué momento del día usas el reproductor de DVD?

   —Lo uso ____________. Veo películas con mi hermano.

© 2017 Cengage Learning

Lección 12 Con un agente de la Sección de Tránsito

Objectives

Structures

- The imperfect tense
- The past progressive
- The preterit contrasted with the imperfect
- **En** and **a** as equivalents of ***at***

Communication

- Traffic police: giving a ticket; issuing a warning; talking to a woman who left her baby in a locked car
- Identifying road signs

iLrn™

Con un agente de la Sección de Tránsito

Con la conductora de un coche que se pasa un semáforo con la luz roja.

Agente Reyes —Buenas tardes, señora.
Mujer —Buenas tardes, señor. ¿Por qué me detuvo? Yo no iba muy rápido.
Agente Reyes —No, pero pasó un semáforo en rojo.
Mujer —¡Pero yo empecé a cruzar la calle cuando el semáforo tenía la luz amarilla!
Agente Reyes —Pero antes de terminar de cruzarla ya estaba la luz roja.
Mujer —Bueno, yo no tengo la culpa de eso. La luz cambió muy rápido.
Agente Reyes —Ud. sólo debe iniciar el cruce de la calle con luz amarilla si está tan cerca de la línea de parada que no tiene tiempo para parar.
Mujer —Pero el carro de atrás venía a demasiada velocidad.
Agente Reyes —Lo siento, señora, pero tengo que imponerle una multa. Firme aquí, por favor.

En la autopista, con un conductor que cambia de carriles imprudentemente.

Agente Reyes —Señor, está cambiando de carriles imprudentemente. En cualquier momento va a causar un accidente.

Conductor —Es que tengo mucha prisa. No quiero llegar tarde al trabajo. Debo llegar a las siete.
Agente Reyes —Ésa no es una excusa válida. Ud. está poniendo en peligro su vida y la de los demás.
Conductor —Es que mi jefe me dijo que si llegaba tarde otra vez me iba a despedir.
Agente Reyes —Bien. Esta vez solamente le voy a dar una advertencia. Aquí la tiene. Buenos días y maneje con cuidado.
Conductor —Muchísimas gracias, agente.

Con una señora que dejó a su bebé en un carro cerrado.

Señora —¿Qué sucede, agente?
Agente Reyes —Abra la puerta, por favor. ¿Es Ud. la madre de este bebé?
Señora —Sí, señor. Lo dejé solamente por un momento.
Agente Reyes —Eso es muy peligroso, señora. Alguien puede secuestrar al bebé. Además, la temperatura en el coche es muy alta. Es de unos 115 grados.

Eran las cuatro de la tarde cuando el agente regresó a la oficina.

¡Escuchemos!

While listening to the dialogue, circle **V (verdadero)** if the statement is true and **F (falso)** if it is false.

1.	El agente detuvo a la conductora porque iba muy rápido.	V	F
2.	Ella se detuvo en un semáforo en rojo.	V	F
3.	Antes de terminar de cruzar la luz estaba roja.	V	F
4.	La conductora dice que la luz cambió muy rápido.	V	F
5.	También dice que el carro de atrás venía a demasiada velocidad.	V	F
6.	El agente detuvo al conductor por cambiar de carriles imprudentemente.	V	F
7.	Tener mucha prisa es una excusa válida.	V	F
8.	El agente le impuso una multa al conductor imprudente.	V	F
9.	La señora dejó al bebé en el carro abierto.	V	F
10.	Eran las cuatro de la tarde cuando el agente regresó a su casa.	V	F

© 2017 Cengage Learning

Nombre ______________________ Sección ____________ Fecha ____________

VOCABULARIO

Cognados

la excusa
la temperatura
válido(a)

Nombres

la advertencia *warning*
la autopista *highway*
el bebé *baby*
el carril, la vía *lane*
el (la) conductor(a), el chofer *driver*
el cruce *crossing, intersection*
el grado *degree*
el (la) jefe(a) *boss*
la línea de parada *stop line*
la oficina *office*
el semáforo *traffic light*

Verbos

cambiar *to change*
causar *to cause*
cruzar *to cross*
despedir (e:i) *to fire (from a job)*
firmar *to sign*
girar, doblar *to turn*
iniciar *to begin*
parar *to stop*
secuestrar *to kidnap*

Adjetivos

alto(a) *high*
demasiado(a) *excessive, too much*

Otras palabras y expresiones

atrás *behind*
cerca (de) *close*
con cuidado *carefully*
es de unos... grados *it's about . . . degrees*
imponer (dar) una multa *to impose a fine, to give a ticket*
imprudentemente *imprudently, recklessly*
llegar tarde *to be late*
¡Maneje con cuidado! *Drive safely!*
mejor *better, best*
pasarse la luz roja *to go through a red light*
poner en peligro *to endanger*
rápido *fast*
tan *so*
tener la culpa (de), ser culpable (de) *to be at fault, to be guilty*
tener razón *to be right*

© 2017 Cengage Learning

Nombre ______________________ Sección ____________ Fecha ____________

VOCABULARIO ADICIONAL

Señales de tránsito (*Traffic signs*)

Narrow Bridge

Yield

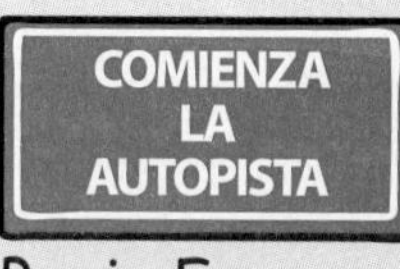

Begin Freeway

Stop

One Way

R.R. Crossing
(*ferrocarril*)

Dangerous Curve

Don't Litter

Detour

Danger

No Parking

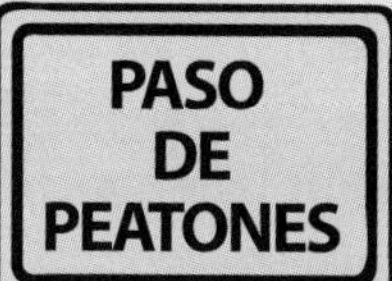

Pedestrian Crossing

Two-way
Traffic

Slow Traffic
Right Lane

Keep to the
Right

Private Property
(No Trespassing)

© 2017 Cengage Learning

Nombre ______________________ Sección ______________ Fecha ______________

Más señales de tránsito

Despacio *Slow*
Escuela, cruce de niños *School crossing*
Estacionamiento de emergencia solamente *Emergency parking only*
Estacionamiento para residentes *Resident parking*
Mantenga su derecha *Keep right*
No entre *Do not enter, Wrong way*
No pasar, No rebasar (*Méx.*) *Do not pass*
Prohibido el cruce de peatones *No pedestrian crossing*
Prohibido girar en rojo *No turn on red*
Prohibido pasar *No trespassing*
Termina la doble vía *End of divided road*
Velocidad máxima *Speed limit*
Zona de grúa *Tow zone*

Notas Culturales

- In most Latin American countries and Spain, gasoline and automobiles are much more expensive than they are in the United States. For this reason, motorcycles are very popular, especially among young people.
- The metric system is used in Spanish-speaking countries. One kilometer is equivalent to 0.6 miles; one gallon is equivalent to 3.8 liters. See *Appendix D: Weights and Measures* for more information about the metric system and conversions.

Actividades

Dígame... Answer the following questions, basing your answers on the dialogues.

1. ¿Por qué detuvo el agente Reyes a la mujer?

____

2. ¿Con qué luz empezó a cruzar la calle?

____

3. ¿Cuándo se puede iniciar el cruce de una calle con luz amarilla?

____

4. ¿Qué hacía el conductor que venía en el carro de atrás, según (*according to*) la mujer?

____

5. ¿Por qué estaba poniendo en peligro su vida y la de los demás el otro conductor?

____

6. ¿Por qué no quiere llegar tarde al trabajo?

____

© 2017 Cengage Learning

Nombre ______________ Sección ______ Fecha ______

7. ¿El agente Reyes le impone una multa a este conductor? ¿Qué le da?

____

8. ¿Qué encontró el agente en un coche cerrado?

____

9. ¿Por qué es peligroso dejar a un bebé solo en un coche?

____

10. ¿Qué hora era cuando el agente Reyes regresó a la oficina?

____

Hablemos Interview a classmate, using the following questions. When you have finished, switch roles.

1. ¿Cuál es la velocidad máxima en la autopista de tu estado?
2. Si manejo en la autopista a noventa millas por hora, ¿me van a imponer una multa por exceso de velocidad?
3. ¿Qué señal indica que debe dejar pasar a otro carro?
4. ¿Tiene Ud. que manejar muy rápido a veces? ¿Cuándo?
5. Generalmente, ¿cuántas multas impone Ud. en un día?
6. ¿Llega Ud. tarde al trabajo a veces?
7. ¿Qué hora era cuando Ud. regresó a su casa anoche?

Quiz

Vamos a practicar

A Complete the following sentences, using the preterit or the imperfect of the verbs given.

1. El coche que yo ______ (ver) ______ (ir) a más de noventa millas por hora.
2. Ayer yo le ______ (decir) a mi jefe que ______ (necesitar) otro carro.
3. La luz ______ (cambiar) cuando yo ______ (estar) cruzando la calle.
4. Él ______ (venir) a setenta millas por hora cuando el policía lo ______ (detener).
5. ______ (Ser) las tres de la tarde cuando ellas ______ (llegar).
6. El carro que yo ______ (tener) ______ (ser) rojo.

© 2017 Cengage Learning

Nombre ______________________ Sección ____________ Fecha ____________

B Complete the following sentences with the Spanish equivalent of the words in parentheses.

1. Mi esposa no está ____________ (*at home*) ahora.
2. Puedes irte, pero debes volver ____________ (*at eight*).
3. La hija del conductor está ____________ (*at school*).
4. Ella no está ____________ (*at the party*).

C Complete the following exchanges using the past progressive forms of the verbs given.

1. —¿Qué ____________ (hacer) él cuando tú llegaste?
   —____________ (Leer) el anuncio.
2. —¿Qué ____________ (decir) Uds.?
   —____________ (Decir) que tenías que parar.
3. —¿Qué ____________ (escribir) tú?
   —____________ (Escribir) el informe.

Conversaciones breves

Complete the following dialogue, using your imagination and the vocabulary from this lesson.

La agente Nieto, de la Policía de Patrulla, habla con el Sr. Soto.

Agente Nieto —Ud. iba manejando a ochenta millas por hora, señor.

Sr. Soto —____

Agente Nieto —Déjeme ver su licencia de conducir, por favor.

Sr. Soto —____

Agente Nieto —También se pasó Ud. una luz roja en la calle Magnolia y cambió de carriles imprudentemente.

Sr. Soto —____

Agente Nieto —Ésa no es una excusa válida.

Sr. Soto —____

Agente Nieto —Lo siento, pero voy a tener que darle una multa por exceso de velocidad y por pasarse una luz roja.

En estas situaciones

With a partner, act out the following situations in Spanish.

1. You pull over a car that has just run a red light. The driver says he/she didn't know that there was a light there and didn't see it. Tell the driver that you have to give him/her a ticket. Advise him/her to drive carefully.

© 2017 Cengage Learning

Nombre ______________________ Sección ____________ Fecha ____________

2. You stop someone who seems to be driving recklessly. He/She was going more than 60 miles per hour and was changing lanes too quickly when you stopped him/her. The driver explains he/she was going to see his/her mother in the hospital. Say that this time you're issuing a warning, but next time you're going to give him/her a ticket.

Casos With you and a partner playing the roles, work through the following scenarios.

1. Stop someone for running a red light.
2. Give someone a warning for reckless driving.

Un paso más Review the **Vocabulario adicional** in this lesson and indicate in Spanish which signs the following people are not obeying.

1. A cyclist is trying to enter a highway.

   ____

2. A driver is speeding.

   ____

3. A driver is trying to park in a zone designated for emergency vehicles.

   ____

4. Someone is driving above the speed limit in a school zone.

   ____

5. A passenger in a car just threw a paper bag out the window.

   ____

6. Someone is going over a fence to get his frisbee.

   ____

7. A driver is passing another car illegally.

   ____

8. Cars must stop, but this person drives through.

   ____

9. A driver just turned the wrong way onto a one-way street.

   ____

10. A car is going 40 miles per hour in the left lane of a highway, holding up the cars behind.

   ____

© 2017 Cengage Learning

LECCIÓN 13 UN ACCIDENTE

OBJECTIVES

Structures

- **Hace** meaning ***ago***
- Changes in meaning with the imperfect and preterit of **conocer, saber,** and **querer**

Communication

- Witnessing an accident: interviewing witnesses; talking to accident victims
- Recognizing parts of the body

iLrn™

UN ACCIDENTE

Hubo un accidente en la carretera. Un camión chocó con un carro y una motocicleta. El hombre que manejaba el carro y sus dos pasajeros murieron. El agente Peña, que acaba de llegar, está tratando de ayudar al muchacho que venía en la motocicleta.

Agente Peña —No trate de levantarse. Quédese quieto.
Muchacho —¿Qué pasó? Me siento mareado...
Agente Peña —Hubo un accidente. ¿Le duele algo?
Muchacho —Sí. La pierna derecha y la mano izquierda...
Agente Peña —A ver... Voy a ponerle una venda para parar la sangre.
Muchacho —¿Qué le pasó a la chica que venía conmigo?
Agente Peña —Se lastimó la cara y los brazos, pero no es serio... Nosotros queríamos llevarla al hospital, pero ella no quiso ir. Se fue a su casa.
Muchacho —Por suerte los dos llevábamos puestos los cascos de seguridad.
Agente Peña —¿Sabía Ud. que en este estado el uso del casco de seguridad es obligatorio?
Muchacho —No, no lo sabía. ¿Y... mi motocicleta? Hace solamente un mes que la compré.
Agente Peña —Lo siento. Está debajo del camión. Por suerte Uds. saltaron a tiempo.

Nombre ______________________ Sección ____________ Fecha ____________

El agente va hacia el camión y ve que hay un incendio en la cabina. Corre y apaga el incendio con un extinguidor de incendios. El hombre que manejaba el camión está a un lado del camino.

Agente Peña —¿Cómo se siente?

Hombre —Todavía estoy temblando. Hice todo lo posible para evitar el choque, pero no pude.

Agente Peña —¿Qué recuerda del accidente?

Hombre —El chofer del coche trató de rebasar sin darse cuenta de que una motocicleta venía en sentido contrario. Trató de desviarse, pero perdió el control del vehículo, y chocó con mi camión.

Agente Peña —Mire, ya vino la ambulancia. Van a llevarlo al hospital a Ud. también. ¿Quiere llamar a alguien?

Hombre —Sí, a mi esposa, pero la tienda donde ella trabaja no se abre hasta las diez. Además, yo no necesito ir al hospital.

Agente Peña —Es una precaución. Probablemente le van a tomar radiografías y el médico lo va a examinar. Necesito su nombre y su dirección.

Hombre —Rafael Soto, calle La Sierra, 517.

Agente Peña —¿Cuál es su número de teléfono?

Hombre —328-9961.

Escuchemos! While listening to the dialogue, circle **V (verdadero)** if the statement is true and **F (falso)** if it is false.

1. Un camión chocó con un carro y con una motocicleta. V F
2. Las tres personas que venían en el carro murieron en el accidente. V F
3. La chica que venía en la motocicleta también murió. V F
4. Al muchacho de la motocicleta no le duele nada. V F
5. El uso del casco de seguridad es obligatorio en ese estado. V F
6. El chofer del camión no hizo nada para evitar el accidente. V F
7. El chofer del coche trató de rebasar cuando la motocicleta venía en sentido contrario. V F
8. La tienda donde trabaja la esposa del camionero se abre a las nueve. V F
9. El camionero dice que no necesita ir al hospital. V F
10. Le van a tomar radiografías y el médico lo va a examinar. V F

© 2017 Cengage Learning

Nombre ________________ Sección ________ Fecha ________

VOCABULARIO

Cognados

la ambulancia
el control
la motocicleta
la precaución
serio(a)
el vehículo

Nombres

la cabina *cab (of a truck)*
el camino *road*
el camión *truck*
la cara *face*
la carretera *highway*
el (la) chico(a), el (la) chamaco(a) (*Méx.*) *young boy/girl*
el choque *collision, crash*
el extinguidor de incendios, el extintor de incendios (*Esp.*) *fire extinguisher*
el hueso *bone*
el lado *side*
el (la) pasajero(a) *passenger*
la pierna *leg*
la radiografía *X-ray*
la venda *bandage*

Verbos

apagar *to put out (a fire)*
chocar *to collide, to run into, to hit*
desviarse *to swerve*
examinar, chequear *to examine*
lastimarse *to get hurt*
levantarse *to get up*
rebasar (*Méx.*), **pasar** *to pass (a car)*
saltar *to jump*
sentirse (e:ie) *to feel*
temblar (e:ie) *to shake, to tremble, to shiver*

Adjetivos

derecho(a) *right*
desmayado(a) *unconscious*
mareado(a) *dizzy*
obligatorio(a) *compulsory*
quebrado(a) *broken*
quieto(a) *still, quiet, calm*

Otras palabras y expresiones

a tiempo *on time, just in time*
acabar de (+ *inf.*) *to have just (done something)*
darse cuenta de *to realize, to become aware of*
debajo de *under, underneath, below*
en sentido contrario *in the opposite direction*
hace un mes *a month ago*
por suerte *fortunately*

© 2017 Cengage Learning

Nombre ______________________ Sección ______________ Fecha ______________

VOCABULARIO ADICIONAL

Las partes del cuerpo (*Parts of the body*)

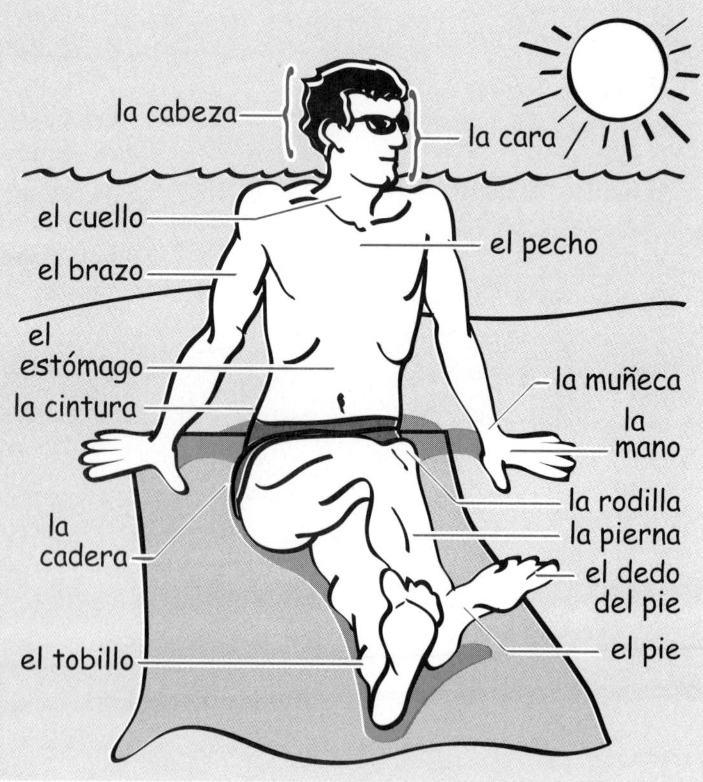

© 2017 Cengage Learning

Los dedos de la mano

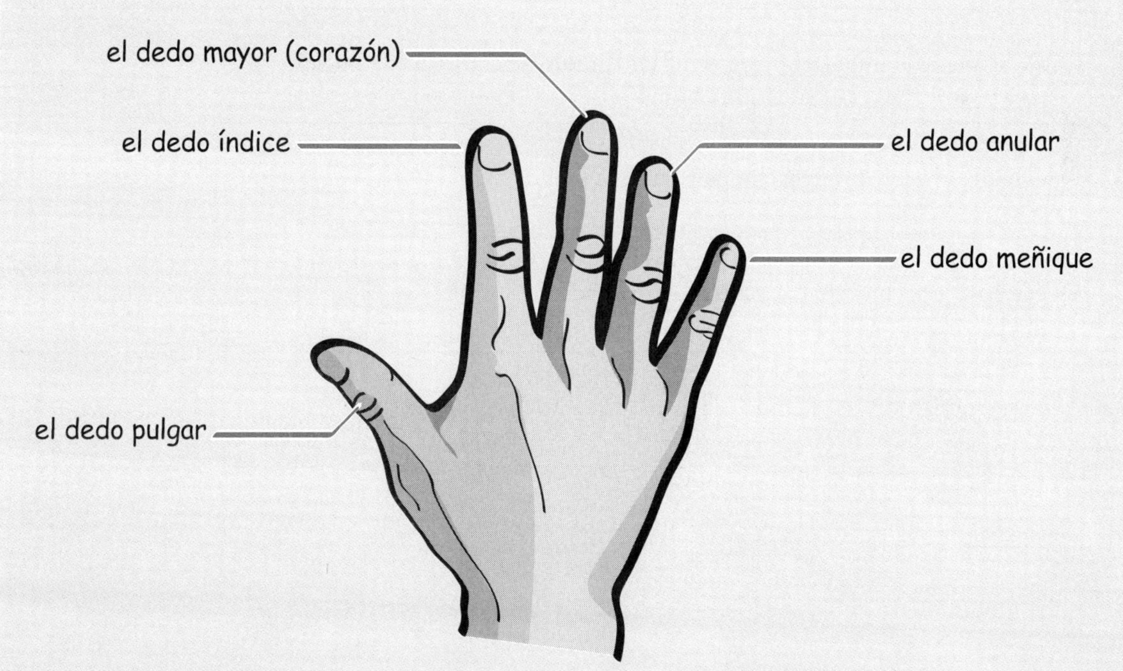

© 2017 Cengage Learning

Nombre ______________________ Sección ____________ Fecha ____________

Notas Culturales

- As a result of the North American Free Trade Agreement (NAFTA), every day more Mexican trucks are traveling U.S. highways, particularly in California, Arizona, New Mexico, and Texas. Standardized visual traffic signs are used throughout the world; however the U.S. highway system relies more extensively on written signs, which truckers who do not read English cannot understand. This poses some challenges and perhaps risks for all drivers.
- To avoid confusion among Mexican drivers accustomed to the metric system, highway signs near the Mexican border often post speed limits in both miles and kilometers. This can also be seen close to the Canadian border.

Actividades

Dígame... Answer the following questions, basing your answers on the dialogue.

1. ¿Con qué chocó el camión?

   ____

2. ¿Quiénes murieron?

   ____

3. ¿Qué está haciendo el agente Peña?

   ____

4. ¿Cómo se siente el muchacho que venía en la motocicleta? ¿Qué le duele?

   ____

5. ¿Qué le van a hacer al muchacho para parar la sangre?

   ____

6. ¿Qué le pasó a la chica que venía con el muchacho?

   ____

7. ¿Adónde querían llevar a la muchacha? ¿Por qué no la llevaron?

   ____

© 2017 Cengage Learning

Nombre ____________________ Sección ____________ Fecha ____________

8. ¿Adónde se fue?

____

9. ¿Qué ve el agente cuando va hacia el camión? ¿Qué hace él?

____

10. ¿Cómo se siente el hombre que manejaba el camión?

____

11. ¿Cómo ocurrió (*happened*) el accidente?

____

12. ¿A quién quiere llamar el hombre?

____

13. ¿Qué le van a hacer al hombre en el hospital?

____

Hablemos Interview a classmate, using the following questions. When you have finished, switch roles.

1. ¿Cómo se siente Ud.?
2. ¿Le duele algo ahora?
3. ¿Qué tipo de vehículo le gusta manejar?
4. Cuando un(a) policía llega a un accidente en la autopista, ¿qué debe hacer primero?
5. ¿Es obligatorio el uso del casco de seguridad en este estado?
6. ¿Sabe Ud. a qué hora se abren las tiendas en esta ciudad? ¿A qué hora se cierran?

© 2017 Cengage Learning

Nombre ______________________ **Sección** ____________ **Fecha** ____________

Quiz

Vamos a practicar

A Tell how long ago the following things happened.

Modelo Estamos en el año 2010.
Julio vino a este estado en el año 2008.
Hace dos años que Julio vino a este estado.

1. Estamos en septiembre.

   Nosotros llegamos en junio.

   ____

2. Son las diez de la mañana.

   Ella se levantó a las seis.

   ____

3. Son las diez y veinte.

   Las tiendas se abren a las diez.

   ____

4. Hoy es viernes.

   Hubo un accidente el miércoles.

   ____

B Complete the following sentences with the Spanish equivalent of the words in parentheses.

1. Yo ___________ (*didn't know*) a la mamá de Claudia. ___________ (*I met her*) anoche en el hospital.
2. Ellos ___________ (*knew*) que nosotros estábamos aquí; no vinieron porque ___________ (*they didn't want*) venir.
3. Yo ___________ (*didn't want*) comprar la motocicleta, pero decidí comprarla.
4. Yo no sé ___________ (*what*) es tu dirección.
5. ¿Dónde ___________ (*are sold*) esos cascos de seguridad?

© 2017 Cengage Learning

Nombre ______________________ Sección ____________ Fecha ____________

Conversaciones breves

Complete the following dialogue, using your imagination and the vocabulary from this lesson.

Hubo un accidente en la autopista.

Agente Smith —Quédese quieto. No trate de levantarse.

Hombre —____________________

Agente Smith —Un camión chocó con su carro. ¿Le duele algo?

Hombre —____________________

Agente Smith —Déjeme ponerle una venda para parar la sangre.

Hombre —____________________

Agente Smith —¿No recuerda el accidente?

Hombre —____________________

Agente Smith —Aquí viene la ambulancia para llevarlo al hospital.

Hombre —____________________

En estas situaciones

With a partner, act out the following situations in Spanish.

1. You are talking to an accident victim. Tell him/her to stay still and ask him/her what hurts. Tell the victim his/her son is hurt but not seriously. Say that an ambulance is coming, and it will take both of them to the hospital.
2. While on traffic duty, you see a motorcyclist collide with a car. When you question the motorcyclist, the person seems not to feel well and asks what happened. Explain that the motorcycle collided with a car coming in the opposite direction. The motorcyclist was driving too fast to avoid the collision. He/She was wearing a helmet but is injured nevertheless. Unfortunately, the person doesn't want to go to the hospital and says he/she doesn't like hospitals, ambulances, and doctors.

Casos

With you and a partner playing the roles, work through the following scenarios.

1. You are a police officer helping an accident victim who is badly hurt and very scared.
2. You are a police officer talking to someone who witnessed an accident on the highway.

© 2017 Cengage Learning

Nombre ______________________ Sección ______________ Fecha ______________

Un paso más

A Review the **Vocabulario adicional** in this lesson and name the part of the body that corresponds to each number.

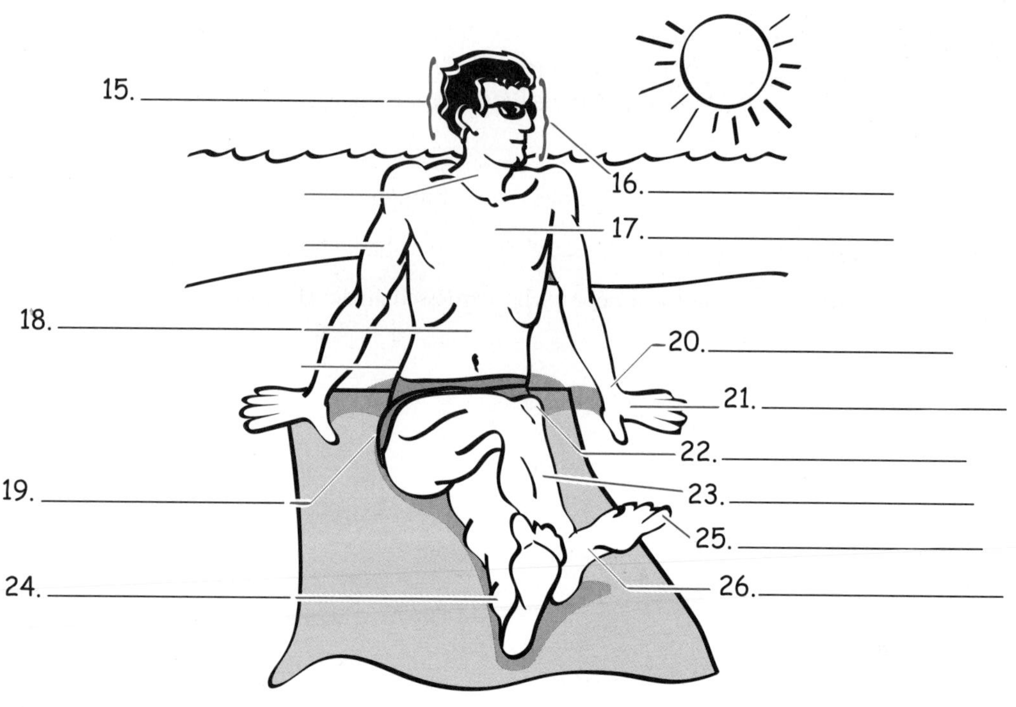

© 2017 Cengage Learning

Nombre ______________________ Sección ____________ Fecha ____________

B Review the **Vocabulario adicional** in this lesson once again, and name the finger that corresponds to each number.

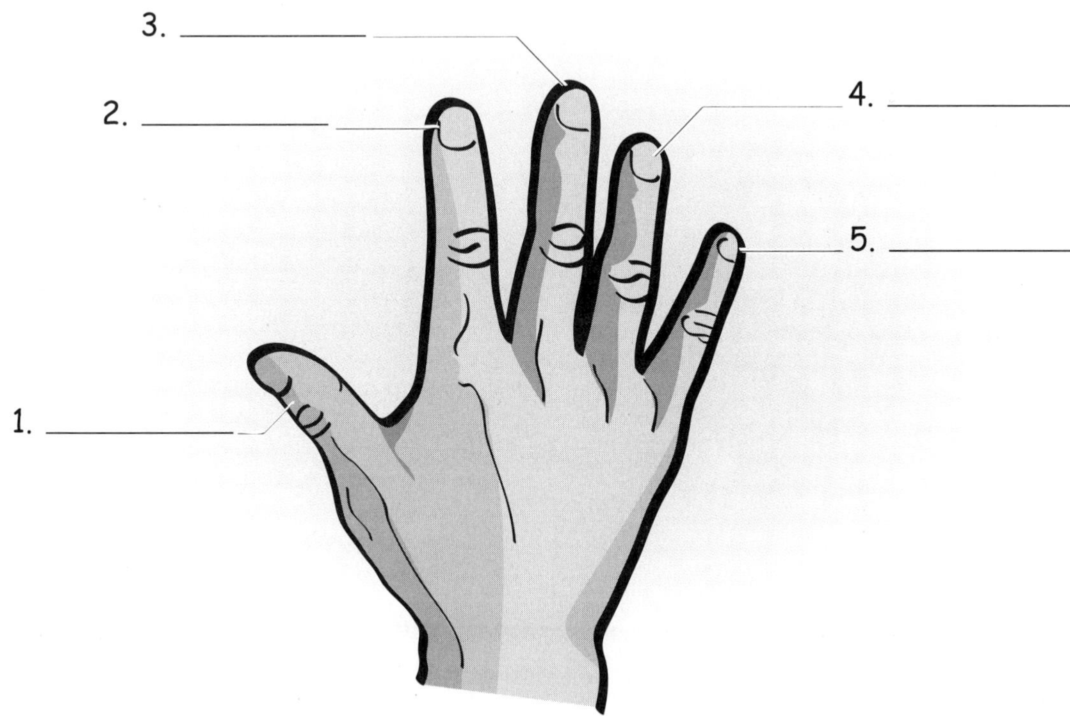

© 2017 Cengage Learning

Lección 14 Interrogatorios

Objectives

Structures

- The past participle
- The present perfect tense
- The past perfect (pluperfect) tense

Communication

- Interrogating a suspect
- Talking to a witness

iLrn™

Interrogatorios

El sargento Vega acaba de detener a Carlos Guzmán. Le ha leído la advertencia Miranda y ahora empieza a interrogarlo.

Sargento Vega —¿Entiende Ud. los derechos que le he leído?
Sr. Guzmán —Sí, señor, pero yo no necesito un abogado porque soy inocente.
Sargento Vega —¿Sabe Ud. de qué se le acusa? ¿Entiende Ud. la acusación?
Sr. Guzmán —Sí, señor. Se me acusa de un robo que yo no cometí.
Sargento Vega —Bien, la computadora que Ud. trató de empeñar era robada.
Sr. Guzmán —Sí, eso me han dicho, pero yo no lo sabía.
Sargento Vega —¿Cómo llegó a sus manos esa computadora?
Sr. Guzmán —Se la compré a un hombre que me ofreció una ganga.
Sargento Vega —¿No sospechó Ud. que era robada? Comprar artículos robados es un delito mayor.
Sr. Guzmán —Yo no sabía que él la había robado. Me dijo que tenía que venderla urgentemente porque se había quedado sin trabajo.
Sargento Vega —¿Dónde estaba Ud. la noche del sábado veinte de abril?
Sr. Guzmán —En un bar de la calle Franklin.

Sargento Vega —¿A qué hora salió de allí?
Sr. Guzmán —Después de las doce de la noche.
Sargento Vega —Sin embargo, yo he hablado con testigos que dicen que lo vieron a eso de las diez de la noche en el edificio donde ocurrió el robo.
Sr. Guzmán —No puede ser. El dueño del bar puede decirle que yo estoy allí todas las noches hasta muy tarde.
Sargento Vega —Sí, pero un empleado me dijo que esa noche Ud. había salido de allí antes de las diez.
Sr. Guzmán —Eso es mentira. Es alguien que me quiere perjudicar.

El sargento arresta al hombre.

El detective Rubio interroga al Sr. Darío, un hombre acusado de estafa.

Detective Rubio —Ud. le vendió un collar de perlas a la Sra. Carmen Hernández, ¿verdad?
Sr. Darío —Sí, señor. Hace una semana.
Detective Rubio —¿Ud. le dijo a la señora que las perlas eran de cultivo?
Sr. Darío —No, señor.
Detective Rubio —Pero Ud. le cobró las perlas como de primera calidad.
Sr. Darío —Bueno, también yo le había dicho que el collar tenía un gran valor sentimental para mí.
Detective Rubio —Ud. no le dijo la verdad. Sinceramente, yo creo que Ud. la engañó, pero el jurado va a decidir si la estafó o no. Yo no soy el que lo va a juzgar.

¡Escuchemos!

While listening to the dialogue, circle **V (verdadero)** if the statement is true and **F (falso)** if it is false.

1. El sargento Vega le ha leído la advertencia Miranda al Sr. Guzmán. V F
2. El Sr. Guzmán dice que él necesita un abogado. V F
3. Él dice que sabía que la computadora era robada. V F
4. Le compró la computadora a un hombre que le ofreció una ganga. V F
5. Comprar artículos robados es un delito mayor. V F
6. El sábado el Sr. Guzmán estaba en el bar de la calle Franklin. V F
7. El Sr. Guzmán dice que salió del bar a eso de las diez de la noche. V F
8. Ningún testigo vio al Sr. Guzmán en el edifício donde ocurrió el robo. V F
9. El Sr. Darío le vendió un collar de perlas a la Sra. Hernández. V F
10. Las perlas del collar eran de primera clase. V F

© 2017 Cengage Learning

Nombre ______________________ Sección ____________ Fecha ____________

VOCABULARIO

Cognados

la acusación
el artículo
el (la) detective
inocente
sentimental

Nombres

el collar *necklace*
el delito mayor, el delito grave *felony*
el (la) empleado(a) *employee, clerk*
la estafa *swindle, fraud*
la ganga *bargain*
el jurado *jury*
la perla *pearl*
el (la) testigo *witness*

Verbos

cobrar *to charge, to collect*
empeñar *to pawn*
engañar *to cheat, to deceive*
estafar *to swindle*
juzgar *to judge*
ocurrir, pasar *to occur*
ofrecer[1] *to offer*
perjudicar *to cause damage, to hurt*

Adjetivo

gran *great*

Otras palabras y expresiones

a eso de *at about (used with time)*
como de *as, like*
de cultivo *cultured (pearl)*
de primera calidad *first class, top quality*
para mí *for me*
quedarse sin trabajo *to lose one's job*
sin embargo *nevertheless, however*
sinceramente *sincerely*
urgentemente *urgently*

VOCABULARIO ADICIONAL

El juicio (*Trial*)

el (la) abogado(a) defensor(a) *counsel for the defense*
absuelto *acquitted*
el (la) acusado(a), el (la) reo *defendant*
la apelación *appeal*
apelar *to appeal*
la cárcel, la prisión *jail, prison*
el centro de reclusión de menores *juvenile hall*
comparecer ante un juez *to appear in court*
el (la) cómplice *accomplice*
confesar (e:ie) *to confess*
la confesión *confession*
la corte, el juzgado *court*
culpable *guilty*
declarar culpable *to convict*
la demanda *lawsuit*
demandar *to sue*
dictar sentencia, sentenciar *to sentence*
el fallo, el veredicto *decision, verdict*
el (la) fiscal *prosecutor, district attorney*
el (la) intérprete *interpreter*
los miembros del jurado *jury members*
el (la) perito *expert*

---

[1]Irregular first person present indicative: **yo ofrezco**

© 2017 Cengage Learning

Nombre ______________________ Sección ______________ Fecha ______________

presentar una apelación *to file an appeal*
procesado(a) *indicted*
la prueba *evidence*
la sentencia, la condena *sentence*
el (la) taquígrafo(a) *court reporter, stenographer*
el Tribunal Supremo *Supreme Court*

Notas Culturales

- The justice system in Spanish-speaking countries is very different from that of the United States. Juries do not exist, and the guilt or innocence of the accused is decided by either a judge or a tribunal. Punishments are determined in accordance with a code that establishes minimum and maximum sentences for various categories of offense.
- Many people from Spanish-speaking countries do not want to serve jury duty because they don't believe in the jury system. To them, people who are not trained to interpret the law should not decide legal matters.

Actividades

Dígame... Answer the following questions, basing your answers on the dialogues.

1. ¿Qué acaba de hacer el sargento Vega?

   ____

2. ¿Por qué dice el Sr. Guzmán que no necesita un abogado?

   ____

3. ¿De qué se le acusa?

   ____

4. ¿Qué dice el sargento Vega de la computadora que el Sr. Guzmán trató de empeñar?

   ____

5. Según (*According to*) el Sr. Guzmán, ¿cómo consiguió la computadora?

   ____

6. Según el Sr. Guzmán, ¿dónde estaba la noche del robo? ¿Hasta qué hora estuvo allí?

   ____

© 2017 Cengage Learning

Nombre ______________________ Sección ____________ Fecha ____________

7. ¿Qué han dicho los testigos?

____

8. ¿Qué hizo el Sr. Darío hace una semana?

____

9. ¿Por qué cree el detective Rubio que el Sr. Darío no le dijo la verdad a la Sra. Hernández?

____

10. ¿Qué va a tener que decidir el jurado?

____

Hablemos Interview a classmate, using the following questions. When you have finished, switch roles.

1. ¿Recuerda Ud. dónde estaba la noche del cuatro de julio?
2. ¿Ha empeñado Ud. algo?
3. ¿Cuánto tiempo hace que Ud. compró su carro?
4. ¿Cómo llegó a sus manos su televisor?
5. ¿Ha vendido Ud. alguna vez (*ever*) un artículo de gran valor?
6. ¿Ha sido estafado(a) alguna vez?
7. ¿Se ha quedado Ud. sin trabajo alguna vez?
8. ¿Ha sido Ud. testigo de algún delito grave?

Quiz

Vamos a practicar

A Complete the following sentences with the Spanish equivalent of the words in parentheses.

1. Todas las ventanas estaban ____________ (*closed*), pero la puerta estaba ____________ (*open*).
2. El hombre estaba ____________ (*dead*).
3. La ropa está ____________ (*made*) en la República Dominicana.
4. La información está ____________ (*written*) en español.
5. Los objetos eran ____________ (*stolen*).
6. Armando tenía un brazo ____________ (*broken*).

© 2017 Cengage Learning

Nombre ______________________ Sección ______________ Fecha ______________

B Rewrite the following sentences, first in the present perfect, then in the past perfect.

1. Me dice la verdad.

____

____

2. Lo interrogan.

____

____

3. Le decimos que no.

____

____

4. Esa mujer me ofrece una ganga.

____

____

5. ¿Uds. son testigos?

____

____

6. Yo no compro artículos robados.

____

____

7. Los testigos no pueden hablar con el detective.

____

____

8. Empeñan un collar de perlas y otras joyas.

____

____

© 2017 Cengage Learning

Nombre ______________________ **Sección** __________ **Fecha** __________

Conversaciones breves

Complete the following dialogue, using your imagination and the vocabulary from this lesson.

El teniente Casas interroga a Juan Luna.

Casas —______________________

Luna —No, yo no estuve en ese edificio anoche.

Casas —______________________

Luna —¿Dos testigos dijeron eso? ¡No puede ser!

Casas —______________________

Luna —¿La computadora? Me la dio un amigo...

Casas —______________________

Luna —Bueno, yo no sabía que era robada.

Casas —(*Le lee la advertencia Miranda.*)______________________

Luna —Sí, entiendo.

Casas —______________________

Luna —No. No quiero hablar con un abogado...

Casa —______________________

En estas situaciones

With a partner, act out the following situations in Spanish.

1. You are interrogating a suspect. Ask where he/she was yesterday at 3 P.M. Say that three witnesses saw him/her at the school talking to some children. The suspect claims to have been talking on the telephone with a friend. Find out the friend's name, address, and telephone number.
2. You are talking to a witness. Ask if he/she is sure about the identification of the person he/she saw in the building the night of the robbery. The man he/she described was not there.

Casos

With you and a partner playing the roles, work through the following scenarios.

1. You are an officer interrogating a robbery suspect.
2. You are an officer talking to a suspect about his/her legal rights.

© 2017 Cengage Learning

Nombre ______________________ Sección ____________ Fecha ____________

Un paso más

A Review the **Vocabulario adicional** in this lesson and complete the following sentences with an appropriate expression from the list.

1. Él fue __________ (*indicted*) por el gran jurado y ahora está esperando el juicio.
2. Si Ud. le dijo al __________ (*defendant*) dónde estaba el dinero, Ud. es __________ (*accomplice*) del delito.
3. El __________ (*prosecutor*) dice que el acusado es culpable y el __________ (*counsel for the defense*) dice que es inocente.
4. Los __________ (*experts*) examinan las pruebas.
5. Ella confesó su delito, pero la __________ (*confession*) no fue aceptada porque no le habían dicho que su abogado __________ (*could*) estar presente.
6. La testigo no pudo __________ (*identify*) al acusado.
7. Hoy vamos a saber el __________ (*verdict*) del jurado. Si es culpable, el juez la va a __________ (*sentence*) la semana que viene.
8. La __________ (*court reporter*) escribe todo lo que dicen los testigos.
9. La __________ (*sentence*) fue de dos años en un __________ (*juvenile hall*).

B Match the questions or statements in column **A** with the responses in column **B.**

A

1. __________ ¿Lo arrestaron?
2. __________ ¿El acusado fue declarado culpable?
3. __________ ¿El acusado no habla inglés?
4. __________ ¿Te estafaron?
5. __________ ¿Qué decidieron los miembros del jurado?
6. __________ ¿Presentaron una apelación?
7. __________ ¿Fue absuelto?
8. __________ ¿Qué prueba tienen contra él?

a. Lo encontraron culpable.
b. No. Necesita un intérprete.
c. No, culpable.
d. Sí, pero el Tribunal Supremo no la aceptó.
e. Sus huellas digitales.
f. Sí, va a comparecer ante un juez mañana.
g. Sí, les voy a poner una demanda.
h. Sí, pero va a apelar ante (*before*) el Tribunal Supremo.

© 2017 Cengage Learning

CON LA POLICÍA SECRETA

OBJECTIVES

Structures

- The future tense
- The conditional tense

Communication

- Working undercover: infiltrating a gang; arresting solicitors of prostitution
- Investigating drug use and distribution

iLrn™

CON LA POLICÍA SECRETA

Isabel Cabrera, agente de la policía secreta, ha sido asignada a la Sección de Servicios Especiales. Se ha matriculado en una escuela secundaria del barrio hispano para infiltrarse en una pandilla que distribuye drogas en la escuela. Ahora, la agente Cabrera habla con María, una estudiante cuyo novio podría ser miembro de una pandilla.

Agente Cabrera —Tú hablas español, ¿verdad?
María —Sí, lo aprendí en casa. Soy latina.
Agente Cabrera —Yo no hablo bien el inglés. ¿Podrías ayudarme con mis clases?
María —Sí, aunque yo soy muy mala estudiante. ¿De dónde vienes, Isabel?
Agente Cabrera —De Texas. Vinimos a Chicago hace una semana.
María —¿Te gusta Chicago?
Agente Cabrera —Sí, pero aquí no tengo amigos.
María —Tú verás que pronto encuentras amigos aquí.
Agente Cabrera —Espero que sí. ¿Qué se hace aquí para pasarlo bien?
María —No sé, vamos al cine, tenemos fiestas... Ya sabes, hay de todo, si tienes dinero: bebida, yerba, piedra...
Agente Cabrera —Aquí tengo cien dólares que me regaló mi tía.
María —Si quieres, mi novio nos conseguirá una botella de tequila, y te presento a algunos de nuestros amigos.

Nombre ______________________ **Sección** __________ **Fecha** __________

Agente Cabrera —Me gustaría conocerlos. ¿Cómo se llama tu novio?
María —Roberto Álvarez.

A las once de la noche, la agente Rosales, vestida como una prostituta, tiene a su cargo detener hombres que solicitan sexo en una calle de la ciudad. Un hombre que maneja un carro azul se acerca a ella y la saluda. Empiezan a hablar.

Hombre —Hola... ¿Quieres pasar un buen rato?
Agente Rosales —Tú lo pasarás mejor...
Hombre —Eso espero. Sube.
Agente Rosales —¿Adónde me llevas?
Hombre —Vamos a un motel. Quiero pasar toda la noche contigo.
Agente Rosales —Bueno, hace falta algo más que querer...
Hombre —Aquí tienes cien dólares y si haces todo lo que yo quiero, te daré más.
Agente Rosales —No hace falta. Esto es suficiente. Está Ud. detenido. (*Le empieza a leer la advertencia Miranda.*)
Hombre —Por favor, soy un hombre de negocios y esto me perjudicaría muchísimo. Mire, aquí tiene mil dólares.
Agente Rosales —Eso es un intento de soborno. Su situación se agrava, señor.

¡Escuchemos!

While listening to the dialogue, circle **V (verdadero)** if the statement is true and **F (falso)** if it is false.

1. María es una agente de la policía secreta. V F
2. El novio de María podría ser miembro de una pandilla. V F
3. María es muy buena estudiante. V F
4. Hay una pandilla que distribuye drogas en la escuela. V F
5. La agente dice que vinieron de Oregón hace una semana. V F
6. La agente Rosales se viste de prostituta para detener hombres que solicitan sexo. V F
7. Un hombre le dice que quiere pasar la noche con ella. V F
8. Si hace todo lo que él quiere, el hombre le dará cien dólares. V F
9. El hombre es un profesor de la escuela secundaria. V F
10. El hombre le ofrece mil dólares para que no lo arreste. V F

© 2017 Cengage Learning

Nombre ______________________ Sección ____________ Fecha ____________

VOCABULARIO

Cognados

el (la) latino(a), hispano(a)
el motel
el (la) prostituto(a)
el servicio
el sexo
suficiente
la tequila

Nombres

la botella *bottle*
el cine *movie theater, the movies*
la escuela secundaria[1] *junior high school, high school*
el hombre (la mujer) de negocios *businessman (woman)*
el intento *attempt*
la piedra (*coll.*), **el crac** *rock (crack cocaine)*
la policía secreta *undercover police*
el soborno *bribe*
la yerba (*coll.*) *marijuana*

Verbos

agravarse *to get worse, to worsen*
aprender *to learn*
costar (o:ue) *to cost*
distribuir[2] *to distribute*
encontrar (o:ue) *to find*
infiltrar(se) *to infiltrate*
matricularse *to register, to enroll (in a school)*
presentar *to introduce*
regalar *to give (a gift)*
responder *to respond*
saludar *to greet*
solicitar *to solicit*

Adjetivos

asignado(a) *assigned*
secreto(a) *secret*

Otras palabras y expresiones

aunque *although*
contigo *with you (informal)*
cuyo(a) *whose*
hay de todo *you can find everything*
muchísimo *very much*
pasarlo bien, pasar un buen rato *to have a good time*
tener a su cargo *to be in charge of*

VOCABULARIO ADICIONAL

Nombres comunes de algunas drogas

el ácido[3] *LSD*
la anfetamina *amphetamine*
la cocaína, la coca *cocaine*
el hachich, el hachís[4] *hashish*
la heroína *heroin*

---

[1]**Escuela primaria (elemental)** *grade school*
[2]Present tense: **distribuyo, distribuyes, distribuye, distribuimos, distribuyen**
[3]Colloquialisms: **el pegao, el sello, la pastilla**
[4]Colloquialisms: **el chocolate, el kif, la grifa**

© 2017 Cengage Learning

Nombre ______________________ Sección ______________ Fecha ______________

el leño, la cucaracha, el porro *joint*
la marihuana, la mariguana *marijuana*
la metadona *methadone*
la morfina *morphine*
el opio *opium*

Nombres de algunas drogas en germanía (*Delinquents' slang*)

la marihuana:
una Juanita
la mota
el pasto
el pito
la yerba
la yesca
el zacate

un kilo de marihuana (2.2 lbs.):
el tabique
el ladrillo

la cocaína:
la blanca
la coca
el perico
el polvo

la speed:
el clavo

la heroína:
el caballo
la chiva
la manteca

la heroína negra:
la negra

el crac:
la piedra
la roca
la coca cocinada

Otras palabras relacionadas con el uso de drogas

adicto(a) *addicted*
las alucinaciones *hallucinations*
darse un pase *to snort, to be stoned, to take a drug*
el delírium tremens *DTs*
la desintoxicación *detoxification*
endrogarse *to take drugs, to become addicted to drugs*
la jeringuilla, la jeringa hipodérmica *hypodermic syringe*
pullar (*Caribe*) *to shoot up*
la sobredosis *overdose*

Notas Culturales

According to the United States Census Bureau, out of a total U.S. population of roughly 293.7 million, approximately 41.3 million are Latino. The largest groups are Mexican Americans (66%), Puerto Ricans (9%), Cubans (4%), and Central and South Americans (14%). The states with the highest Latino populations are California, Texas, New York, Florida, Illinois, Arizona, New Jersey, New Mexico, and Colorado. More than half of all Hispanic Americans live in California and Texas alone. The Hispanic population in the United States is now higher than that of Central America. Hispanics are also now the largest minority, followed by African Americans.

© 2017 Cengage Learning

Nombre ______________________ Sección ____________ Fecha ____________

Actividades

Dígame... Answer the following questions, basing your answers on the dialogues.

1. ¿Qué hará la agente Cabrera en la escuela secundaria?

____

2. ¿Por qué habla la agente Cabrera con María?

____

3. ¿Cuándo dice la agente Cabrera que vino a Chicago?

____

4. ¿Qué dice la agente Cabrera de Chicago?

____

5. ¿Qué hacen María y sus amigos para pasarlo bien?

____

6. ¿Cuánto dinero tiene la agente Cabrera?

____

7. ¿Qué dice María que puede hacer su novio?

____

8. Describa el trabajo que se le ha asignado a la agente Rosales esta noche.

____

9. ¿Por qué detiene su carro un hombre?

____

10. ¿Qué le ofrece el hombre a la agente Rosales? ¿Le ofrece algo más?

____

11. Cuando la agente Rosales empieza a leerle la advertencia Miranda, ¿cómo responde el hombre?

____

12. ¿Por qué le dice la agente Rosales al hombre que su situación se ha agravado?

____

© 2017 Cengage Learning

Nombre ______________________ Sección ____________ Fecha ____________

Hablemos Interview a classmate, using the following questions. When you have finished, switch roles.

1. ¿Hay pandillas en la ciudad donde Ud. vive? ¿Son un problema para la policía?
2. ¿Sabe Ud. si se venden drogas en algunas de las escuelas secundarias de su ciudad?
3. ¿Cómo podría conseguir un(a) estudiante drogas o bebidas en su ciudad?
4. ¿Ha trabajado Ud. en la Sección de Servicios Especiales? Describa lo que hizo.
5. ¿Tiene amigos latinos? ¿Cómo son?

Quiz

Vamos a practicar

A Rewrite the following sentences, replacing the underlined verb phrases with the future tense.

MODELO Su situación se va a agravar.
Su situación *se agravará*.

1. Nosotros vamos a tratar de infiltrarnos en la pandilla.

____

2. Mi compañera me va a ayudar con el español.

____

3. Ellos van a ir a Chicago.

____

4. La botella de tequila te va a costar doce dólares.

____

5. Yo te la voy a conseguir.

____

6. Ella no va a venir a la fiesta.

____

7. Nosotros no vamos a poder matricularnos este año.

____

8. Yo voy a tener que demandarlo.

____

© 2017 Cengage Learning

Nombre ______________________ Sección ______________ Fecha ______________

B Answer the questions, using the cues provided.

Modelo ¿Qué dijo María? (su novio poder conseguirle una botella)
María dijo que su novio *podría* conseguirle una botella.

1. ¿Qué dijo la Sra. Santos? (su hija no poder matricularse mañana)

   ____

2. ¿Qué dijo la estudiante? (su amigo salir pronto)

   ____

3. ¿Qué creías tú? (mi tía estar en mi casa en dos horas)

   ____

4. ¿Qué dijo el hombre de negocios? (eso perjudicarle)

   ____

5. ¿Qué pensaba el hombre? (ellos pasar un buen rato)

   ____

6. ¿Qué dijo el sargento? (la agente tener que infiltrarse en la pandilla)

   ____

7. ¿Qué pensaba la agente? (el acusado no decir la verdad)

   ____

Conversaciones breves

Complete the following dialogue, using your imagination and the vocabulary from this lesson.

El agente Gómez, de la Sección de Servicios Especiales, se ha infiltrado en una pandilla que vende drogas en una escuela. Habla con un miembro de la pandilla.

Tomás —Me dice Juana que tú querías hablar conmigo...

Agente Gómez —______________________________

Tomás —Pues, sí. Puedo venderte eso por cincuenta dólares.

Agente Gómez —______________________________

Tomás —¡Hombre, verás que la roca que te voy a conseguir es de primera calidad!

Agente Gómez —______________________________

Tomás —Ven a mi casa a las tres.

Agente Gómez —______________________________

© 2017 Cengage Learning

Tomás —A una cuadra de aquí. Calle Nogales, número 28.

Agente Gómez —______________________________

Tomás —Sí, cómo no. Les diré que vas a traer una botella de tequila para compartirla con nosotros. Nos vemos, ¿eh?

Agente Gómez —______________________________

En estas situaciones

With a partner, act out the following situations in Spanish.

1. You are an undercover agent who has been assigned to infiltrate a gang that has been selling drugs and guns to high school students in the neighborhood. Pretend you just moved to the area and want to get a gun as well as some drugs. Introduce yourself to a gang member at school and ask if he/she could help you get what you want. Mention that money is not a problem, but you're in a hurry to get what you need. Try to arrange to see a dealer later in the day.
2. You are posing as a prostitute in order to arrest people soliciting sex at night in the city. A person approaches you with interest. Ask where he/she wants to take you and discuss the price. After you agree on a price, identify yourself and announce that the person is under arrest. Say that you will read him/her the Miranda warning.

Casos

With you and a partner playing the roles, work through the following scenarios.

1. You are an undercover agent making a drug deal at the high school with a gang member.
2. You arrest a person who tried to solicit sex from a prostitute and who tries to bribe you.

Un paso más

Review the **Vocabulario adicional** in this lesson and place a 1, 2, 3, 4, 5, or 6 next to each of the following terms according to the definition.

1. marihuana
2. hashish
3. cocaína
4. ácido
5. heroína
6. crac

____________ chocolate	____________ sello	____________ piedra
____________ zacate	____________ polvo	____________ roca
____________ coca	____________ grifa	____________ yerba
____________ pegao	____________ kif	____________ pito
____________ mota	____________ pastilla	____________ perico

A joint is a ____________, ____________, or ____________.

© 2017 Cengage Learning

Seguridad doméstica: Robos

Seguridad doméstica: Robos

Read the following information about home burglaries. Try to guess the meaning of all cognates. Then, do the exercise that follows.

Seguridad doméstica: Robos

Más de seis millones de robos residenciales ocurren en los Estados Unidos cada año: ¡uno cada diez segundos!

Prevención: Cuando Ud. salga[1] de la casa...

- siempre cierre con llave las puertas y asegure ventanas. (En casi[2] el 50% de los casos, los ladrones entran en las casas por puertas y ventanas abiertas[3]).
- nunca deje la llave donde se pueda encontrar fácilmente[4] : bajo un felpudo[5], en una maceta de flores[6], etc.
- use un regulador de encendido para que las luces, la radio y el televisor se prendan y se apaguen automáticamente para dar la impresión de que alguien está en casa.
- en caso de viajes[7] extensos, acuérdese de suspender la entrega de la correspondencia y de los periódicos o pídale a un(a) vecino(a) que los recoja.

Si Ud. llega a casa y ve indicaciones de que alguien ha forzado la cerradura de la puerta o de la ventana, no entre. ¡Llame a la policía enseguida!

¡Buenos vecinos!
Si ven algo sospechoso en la casa de un vecino, llamen a la policía enseguida. Nunca traten de detener[8] a un delincuente; puede ser peligroso. Recuerden: ¡Una comunidad que trabaja en cooperación con la policía es la mejor protección contra[9] los delitos!

© Cengage Learning

[1]*leave* [2]*almost* [3]*open* [4]**se...** *can easily be found* [5]*mat* [6]**maceta...** *flower pot* [7]*trips* [8]*to stop* [9]*against*

© 2017 Cengage Learning

Nombre ______________________ Sección ____________ Fecha ____________

Write in Spanish three precautions you would recommend to someone concerned about preventing a robbery at his/her home.

1. ______________________________

2. ______________________________

3. ______________________________

Evite el robo de su automóvil

Read the following list of advice about vehicular security. Again, try to guess the meaning of all cognates. Then, do the exercise item that follows.

EVITE EL ROBO DE SU AUTOMÓVIL HACIENDO LO SIGUIENTE:

1. Cierre su carro con llave y lleve las llaves con Ud.
2. Cierre todas las ventanillas y el maletero (*trunk*) del coche.
3. No deje cosas de valor en los asientos; póngalas en el maletero.
4. Si tiene que dejar su carro en un estacionamiento público por mucho tiempo, asegúrese de que esté atendido.
5. No ponga su nombre y domicilio en el llavero (*keychain*).
6. Por la noche, estacione siempre en un lugar bien iluminado (*illuminated*).
7. Si es posible, utilice aparatos antirrobos (*anti theft*).

Indicate in Spanish the advice you would give to the following people, according to what they do wrong.

1. Javier, who works nights, always parks his car in a dark alley.

   ____

   ____

2. Analía often leaves the car keys in the ignition.

   ____

   ____

3. Daniel's name, address, and telephone number appear on his key ring.

   ____

   ____

© 2017 Cengage Learning

4. Mrs. Agustoni likes to leave her car windows open in the summer so the car won't be too hot when she comes back to it.

____

____

5. When Mrs. Valente goes shopping, you can always look inside her car and see store bags full of interesting things.

____

____

6. Mr. Cota thinks antitheft devices are too expensive and really unnecessary.

____

____

7. Antonio doesn't want to pay for parking, so he leaves his car in unattended parking places.

____

____

© 2017 Cengage Learning

Nombre ______________________ Sección ____________ Fecha ____________

REPASO

Práctica de vocabulario

A Circle the word or phrase that does not belong in each group.

1. chapa placa plata
2. robar encontrar llevarse
3. todo lo posible de nada no hay de qué
4. carril vía valor
5. pasarse la luz roja poner en peligro manejar con cuidado
6. sólo sola solamente
7. mejor atrás cerca
8. carretera autopista venda
9. pierna cara choque
10. apagar chequear examinar
11. collar testigo perla
12. estafar ofrecer perjudicar
13. tía tequila botella
14. agravarse necesitar hacer falta
15. dar responder regalar
16. morir despedir fallecer
17. año oficina jefe
18. próximo pasado rápido

B Circle the word or phrase that best completes each sentence.

1. Ud. (inició / cruzó / evitó) la calle cuando la luz estaba roja.
2. Hay muchos (camiones / caminos / cubiertos) en la carretera.
3. El coche estaba (atrasado / pagado / estacionado) frente a mi casa.
4. Me robaron (la verdad / la computadora / el plazo).
5. No tengo dinero porque (me ofrecieron trabajo / cobré ayer / me quedé sin trabajo).

© 2017 Cengage Learning

Nombre ______________________ Sección ____________ Fecha ____________

6. ¿Es Ud. la madre de este (semáforo / bebé / cruce)?
7. Ella no tiene la culpa; es (inocente / asignada / quieta).
8. Lo vende barato. Es (una ganga / una pandilla / un soborno).
9. Se (matriculó / infiltró / lastimó) la pierna.
10. Yo vi el accidente. Todavía estoy (chocando / aprendiendo / temblando).
11. Necesito el extinguidor de (lados / incendios / pasajeros).
12. Estaba en la (estafa / piedra / cabina) del camión.
13. No estoy al día. (Debo / Entrego / Recobro) como dos meses.
14. Es un Chevrolet azul (rojo / claro / derecho).
15. Es un hombre de (negocios / intento / novios).
16. Tuvimos que pagar (los grados / las cuentas / el jurado).
17. Voy a (abrir / juzgar / infiltrar) la puerta de la calle.
18. La temperatura es muy (roja / alta / atrasada).

C Match the questions in column **A** with the answers in column **B.**

	A		B
1.	____________ ¿Cómo se siente?	a.	Sí, contra todo riesgo.
2.	____________ ¿Dónde está la motocicleta?	b.	Sí, señor. Pero soy inocente.
3.	____________ ¿Qué harán para pasarlo bien?	c.	No, por suerte hace solamente dos días.
4.	____________ ¿Adónde me llevarás?	d.	Sí, una pistola.
5.	____________ ¿Está asegurado tu carro?	e.	No, sólo me dio una advertencia.
6.	____________ ¿Cuándo le robaron el coche?	f.	Debajo del camión.
7.	____________ ¿Se llevaron algún arma?	g.	A un motel.
8.	____________ ¿Son propiedad de Uds.?	h.	No, son de cultivo.
9.	____________ ¿Sabe Ud. de qué se le acusa?	i.	Anoche.
10.	____________ ¿Las perlas son de primera calidad?	j.	Bien.
11.	____________ ¿Hace una semana que lo vio?	k.	No, no son nuestros.
12.	____________ ¿Te impuso una multa?	l.	Iremos a fiestas.

© 2017 Cengage Learning

Nombre ______________________ Sección ____________ Fecha ____________

D Crucigrama

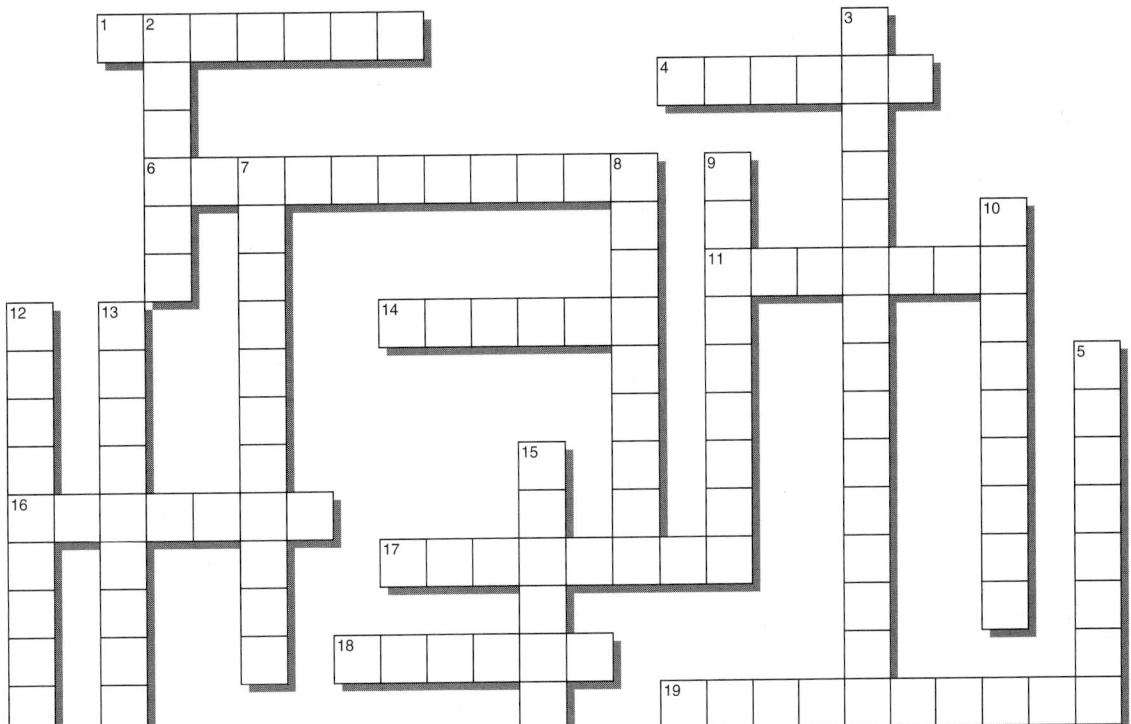

HORIZONTALES

1. pasar
4. opuesto de "primero"
6. *X-ray,* en español
11. ¡Maneje con __________!
14. *jury,* en español
16. *chico,* en México
17. *clerk,* en español
18. Tienes que parar en la línea de __________.
19. daría

VERTICALES

2. vía
3. sin prudencia
5. *gang,* en español
7. acción de describir
8. No es una carretera; es una __________.
9. mucho, mucho
10. persona que conduce (*m.*)
12. camión, carro, etc. (*pl.*)
13. acción de acusar
15. que tiene valor

© 2017 Cengage Learning

Nombre ______________________ Sección ____________ Fecha ____________

Práctica oral Listen to the following exercise on the audio program. The speaker will ask you some questions. Answer the questions, using the cues provided. The speaker will confirm the correct answer. Repeat the correct answer.

1. ¿Cómo se siente Ud. hoy? (bien)
2. ¿Qué hace Ud. para pasarlo bien? (ir al cine)
3. ¿Dónde está estacionado su coche? (frente a la comisaría)
4. ¿Cerró Ud. su coche con llave? (sí)
5. ¿Contra qué está asegurado su coche? (contra todo riesgo)
6. ¿Está Ud. atrasada en los pagos de su coche o está al día? (estoy al día)
7. ¿Llega Ud. tarde al trabajo a veces? (sí)
8. ¿Se pasó Ud. un semáforo con la luz roja alguna vez? (no, nunca)
9. Si alguien cambia de carriles imprudentemente, ¿qué puede causar? (un accidente)
10. ¿Cuándo hubo un accidente? (anoche)
11. ¿Dónde ocurrió el accidente? (en la carretera)
12. ¿Cuántas personas murieron en el accidente? (nadie)
13. ¿Se lastimó alguien? (sí, una señora)
14. ¿Qué usa Ud. si hay un incendio? (un extinguidor de incendios)
15. ¿Prefiere Ud. manejar un coche o una motocicleta? (una motocicleta)
16. Cuando Ud. maneja una motocicleta, ¿qué lleva puesto siempre? (el casco de seguridad)
17. ¿Perdió Ud. el control de su vehículo alguna vez? (no, nunca)
18. ¿Ud. impone multas frecuentemente o prefiere dar advertencias? (dar advertencias)
19. ¿Qué le pasó a la chica que cruzaba la calle? (nada)
20. ¿Qué estaban haciendo muchas pandillas en las escuelas secundarias? (distribuir drogas)
21. ¿Hay a veces robos en su vecindario? (sí, frecuentemente)
22. ¿Ha recobrado Ud. algún objeto robado? (sí, muchos)
23. ¿Ha leído Ud. la advertencia Miranda en español alguna vez? (no, nunca)
24. ¿Se ha quedado Ud. sin trabajo alguna vez? (sí, dos veces)
25. ¿Ha empeñado Ud. algo alguna vez? (no, nunca)

© 2017 Cengage Learning

En una celda de detención preventiva

Objectives

Structures

- The present subjunctive
- The subjunctive with verbs of volition

Communication

- Arresting and booking suspects

iLrn™

En una celda de detención preventiva

El Sr. Bravo acaba de llegar, esposado, a la estación de policía. Después de registrarlo, un policía toma las precauciones necesarias antes de encerrarlo en una celda de detención.

Policía —Quiero que se vacíe los bolsillos por completo y que ponga todas sus cosas en el mostrador.

Sr. Bravo —Solamente tengo la cartera con el dinero, un pañuelo y un peine.

Policía —(*Cuenta el dinero a la vista del detenido.*) Ud. tiene aquí setenta y un dólares y treinta y cuatro centavos. ¿Está de acuerdo?

Sr. Bravo —Sí, señor.

Policía —Ahora quítese el reloj y la cadena que lleva al cuello.

Sr. Bravo —Por favor, anote ahí que el reloj y la cadena son de oro.

Policía —Sí. Todas sus pertenencias serán puestas en un sobre sellado.

Sr. Bravo —Quiero que se las entreguen a mi esposa, por favor.

Policía —Bien, pero es necesario que Ud. lo autorice por escrito. Ahora lo vamos a retratar y a tomarle las huellas digitales.

Sr. Bravo —Yo quiero llamar por teléfono a mi señora.

Policía —Está bien. Ud. tiene derecho a hacer una llamada telefónica. Después de ficharlo le daremos la oportunidad de hacerla.

Sr. Bravo —Está bien.

Policía —Párese allí y mire a la cámara. Bien. Ahora mire hacia la derecha. Bien, ahora hacia la izquierda. No se mueva.

Sr. Bravo —¿Eso es todo?

Policía —Sí. Ahora el técnico le va a tomar las huellas digitales.

Técnico —Deme su mano derecha.

Policía —(*Después de que el técnico terminó de tomarle las huellas digitales*) Ahora quítese el cinto y quíteles los cordones a los zapatos, y me lo entrega todo.

Sr. Bravo —Para eso necesito que me quite las esposas.

Policía —Primero voy a encerrarlo en su celda.

Con el oficial investigador:

Sr. Bravo —¿Qué van a hacer conmigo ahora?

Investigador —Después de terminar todas las investigaciones preliminares, el fiscal lo pondrá a disposición de un juez.

Sr. Bravo —¿Me dejarán salir en libertad bajo palabra?

Investigador —Es posible. Ud. no está acusado de homicidio.

Sr. Bravo —Pero me pondrán en libertad bajo fianza, ¿verdad?

Investigador —Eso lo decidirá el juez, y depende, en buena parte, de si tiene o no antecedentes penales.

Sr. Bravo —Si me ponen una fianza muy alta, yo no voy a tener dinero para pagarla. Entonces me llevarán a la cárcel.

Investigador —Su familia podría comprar un bono pagando una prima.

Sr. Bravo —Necesito un fiancista. ¿A quién me recomienda que llame?

Investigador —Lo siento, pero no nos está permitido recomendar a nadie.

Sr. Bravo —Entonces, ¿qué me aconseja que haga?

Investigador —Yo le sugiero que busque uno en la guía de teléfonos.

¡Escuchemos!

While listening to the dialogue, circle **V (verdadero)** if the statement is true and **F (falso)** if it is false.

1. El Sr. Bravo llegó a la estación de policía esposado.
2. El policía pone el dinero del Sr. Bravo sobre la mesa.
3. Van a encerrar al Sr. Bravo en una celda de detención.
4. El Sr. Bravo tiene más de cien dólares en su cartera.
5. El Sr. Bravo dice que quiere llamar por teléfono a su abogado.
6. Un técnico le va a tomar las huellas digitales al detenido.
7. El detenido puede quitarles los cordones a los zapatos con las esposas puestas.

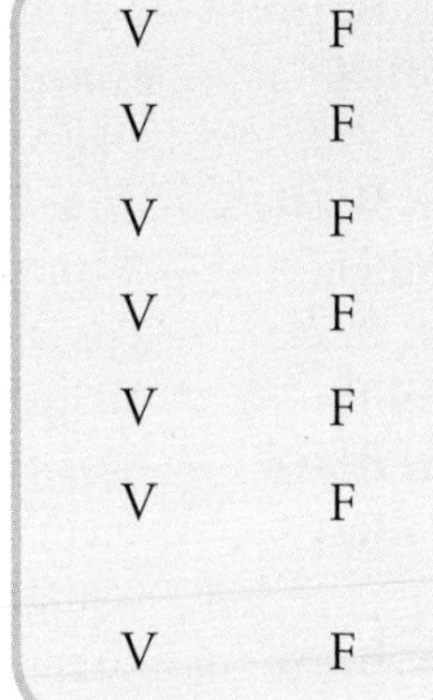

© 2017 Cengage Learning

8. El agente va a quitarle las esposas al detenido después de encerrarlo en su celda. V F
9. No es posible que pongan en libertad bajo fianza al detenido. V F
10. Si le ponen una fianza muy alta el detenido no va a tener dinero para pagarla. V F

VOCABULARIO

Cognados

la detención
la investigación
el (la) investigador(a)
necesario(a)
la oportunidad
preliminar

Nombres

los antecedentes penales *criminal record*
el bono *bond*
la cadena *chain*
la cartera, la billetera *wallet*
la celda *cell*
el centavo *cent*
el cordón (del zapato) *shoelace*
el cuello *neck*
la derecha *right-hand side*
el (la) detenido(a) *person under arrest*
las esposas *handcuffs*
el (la) fiancista *bailor, bail bondsman*
la fianza *bail*
el (la) fiscal *prosecutor, district attorney*
la guía de teléfonos *telephone book*
el homicidio *manslaughter, homicide*
el mostrador *counter*
el oro *gold*
el pañuelo *handkerchief*
el peine *comb*
las pertenencias *belongings*
la prima *premium*
el reloj *watch*
el sobre *envelope*

Verbos

aconsejar *to advise*
autorizar *to authorize, to allow*
depender *to depend*
dudar *to doubt*
encerrar (e:ie) *to lock up*
poner a disposición *to appear before*
quitarse *to take off (clothing)*
recomendar (e:ie) *to recommend*
registrar, fichar *to book, to log in*
retratar *to photograph*
sugerir (e:ie) *to suggest*
vaciar *to empty*

Adjetivos

esposado(a) *handcuffed*
permitido(a) *permitted*
preventivo(a) *preventive*
sellado(a) *sealed*

© 2017 Cengage Learning

Nombre ______________________ Sección ____________ Fecha ____________

Otras palabras y expresiones

a la vista de *in the presence of, in front of*
ahí *there*
en buena parte *to a large extent*
en libertad bajo fianza *out on bail*
en libertad bajo palabra *out on one's own recognizance*
estar de acuerdo *to agree*
por completo *completely*
por escrito *in writing*
tomar las huellas digitales *to fingerprint*

VOCABULARIO ADICIONAL

Para arrestar y fichar

¡Abra las piernas y los brazos! *Spread eagle!*
el alias, el apodo *alias*
avisar *to notify*
la bala *bullet*
el calibre *caliber*
la coartada *alibi*
¿Cómo se escribe? *How do you spell it?*
¡Queda arrestado! *You're under arrest!*
¡Manos arriba! *Hands up!*
el motivo *motive*
¡Párese!, ¡Póngase de pie! *Stand up!*
la pista *clue*
Ponga las manos en la pared. *Put your hands against the wall.*
por poseer drogas *for possession of drugs*
la resistencia a la autoridad *resisting arrest*
Súbase al carro. *Get in the car.*

Notas Culturales

In most Spanish-speaking countries, the police by law must either free a person or bring him or her before a judge within 24 or 48 hours of the arrest, depending on the country. The judge then has 72 hours to indict or release the accused.

Actividades

Dígame... Answer the following questions, basing your answers on the dialogues.

1. ¿Dónde está el Sr. Bravo?

____

2. ¿Qué quiere el policía que haga el Sr. Bravo con sus pertenencias?

____

3. ¿Qué tiene el Sr. Bravo en los bolsillos?

____

© 2017 Cengage Learning

Nombre ______________________ Sección ____________ Fecha ____________

4. Si el Sr. Bravo desea que el policía le entregue sus cosas a su esposa, ¿qué debe hacer?

____

5. ¿Por qué el Sr. Bravo no puede llamar a su esposa en este momento?

____

6. ¿Qué hace el técnico?

____

7. ¿Dónde encerrará el policía al Sr. Bravo?

____

8. ¿De qué no está acusado el Sr. Bravo?

____

9. ¿Qué decidirá el juez?

____

10. ¿Es un hombre muy rico (*rich*) el acusado? ¿Cómo lo sabe?

____

11. ¿Por qué el investigador no puede recomendar un fiancista?

____

12. ¿Qué le sugiere el investigador al Sr. Ramos?

____

Hablemos Interview a classmate, using the following questions. When you have finished, switch roles.

1. ¿Qué es lo primero que Ud. hace cuando ficha a una persona detenida?
2. Cuando Ud. arresta a alguien, ¿le toma las huellas digitales?
3. Si un(a) detenido(a) le pide a Ud. que le dé sus pertenencias a un miembro de su familia, ¿qué responde Ud.?
4. Si una persona detenida le pide a Ud. que le recomiende un buen abogado, ¿qué hace Ud.?
5. ¿Dónde conseguiría Ud. el dinero para una fianza?
6. Necesito un fiancista; ¿qué me aconseja Ud. que haga?

© 2017 Cengage Learning

Nombre ______________________ Sección ______________ Fecha ______________

Quiz

Vamos a practicar

A Complete the following verb chart in the subjunctive mood.

Infinitivo	*Yo*	*Tú*	*Ud., Él, Ella*	*Nosotros(as)*	*Uds., Ellos(as)*
1. trabajar					
2.	diga				
3.		conduzcas			
4.			venga		
5.				vayamos	
6.					entiendan
7. morir					
8.	dé				
9.		estés			
10.			conozca		
11.				sepamos	
12.					sean
13. mover					
14.	ponga				
15.		salgas			
16.			haga		
17.				veamos	
18.					encierren

B Rewrite the following sentences, beginning each one with the cue given.

Modelo: Él pone sus cosas en el mostrador.
Quiero que **él *ponga* sus cosas en el mostrador.**

1. Ella paga la prima del bono.

   Queremos que ______________________________________.

2. Me muestra el sobre con sus pertenencias.

   Necesito que ______________________________________.

3. Ud. habla con un abogado.

   Le recomiendo que ______________________________________.

© 2017 Cengage Learning

4. Yo deseo entregarle el reloj y la cadena a mi esposa.

   Yo deseo que Ud. ______________________________.

5. Le quitan las esposas.

   Necesita que ______________________________.

6. Ellos van a su celda.

   Yo les pido que ______________________________.

7. Me hablas del homicidio.

   No quiero que ______________________________.

8. Ud. me dice la hora y el lugar del accidente.

   Yo le pido que ______________________________.

9. Ellos los ponen en libertad bajo fianza.

   Deseamos que ______________________________.

10. Uds. me dan la información.

    Necesito que ______________________________.

Conversaciones breves

Complete the following dialogue, using your imagination and the vocabulary from this lesson.

El Sr. Paz está en la cárcel.

Sr. Paz —¿Dónde estoy? ¿Por qué me trajeron a la cárcel?

Agente Muñoz —______________________________

Sr. Paz —¿Cuánto tiempo tendré que quedarme aquí?

Agente Muñoz —______________________________

Sr. Paz —¿De mis antecedentes...? ¿Y qué me van a hacer ahora...?

Agente Muñoz —______________________________

Sr. Paz —Esto es todo lo que tengo en los bolsillos... y aquí están mi reloj, mi cinto y los cordones de mis zapatos.

Agente Muñoz —______________________________

Sr. Paz —Huellas digitales... fotografía... ¡pero yo no soy un criminal...!

Agente Muñoz —______________________________

Sr. Paz —¿Y qué pasa si no consigo el dinero para la fianza?

Agente Muñoz —______________________________

© 2017 Cengage Learning

Nombre ______________________ Sección ____________ Fecha ____________

En estas situaciones With a partner, act out the following situations in Spanish.

1. You have just arrested someone. Describe the booking procedure. Explain what to do with personal items.
2. Having booked someone who was arrested, answer his/her questions about the preliminary investigation, the judge, bail, and about being released.

Casos With you and a partner playing the roles, work through the following scenarios.

1. Book someone who has just been charged with homicide.
2. Tell someone who has just been arrested that you need to fingerprint him/her.

Un paso más Review the **Vocabulario adicional** in this lesson and give the Spanish equivalent of the following.

1. Put your hands against the wall.

   ____

2. Stand up!

   ____

3. Spread eagle!

   ____

4. Hands up! You're under arrest!

   ____

5. How do you spell your last name?

   ____

6. Do you have an alias?

   ____

7. You are under arrest for possession of drugs.

   ____

© 2017 Cengage Learning

Una muchacha se escapa de su casa

Objectives

Structures

- The subjunctive to express emotion
- The subjunctive with some impersonal expressions

Communication

- Investigating runaways: talking to parents
- Interrogating a teenager who runs away

iLrn™

Una muchacha se escapa de su casa

El agente Gómez habla con los Sres. Ruiz, padres de una adolescente que se escapó de su casa.

Agente Gómez —¿Cuándo fue la última vez que vieron a su hija?

Sr. Ruiz —Anoche. Nos dijo que iba a estudiar con una compañera.

Agente Gómez —¿Cuándo se dieron cuenta de que se había escapado?

Sra. Ruiz —Ya eran las once de la noche y no había regresado. Entonces llamamos a casa de su amiga y supimos que no había estado allí.

Agente Gómez —Su hija puede haber sido víctima de un secuestro. ¿Por qué piensan que se escapó de la casa?

Sr. Ruiz —Su amiga nos dijo que ella estaba pensando en escaparse.

Agente Gómez —¿Qué edad tiene ella?

Sr. Ruiz —Dieciséis años.

Agente Gómez —Es necesario que me den una descripción completa de su hija.

Sr. Ruiz —Se llama María Elena Ruiz Portillo. Es baja —mide cinco pies y dos pulgadas— delgada, de pelo negro y ojos negros. Tiene un lunar cerca de la boca y una cicatriz en la mejilla derecha.

Agente Gómez —¿Qué ropa tenía puesta?

Sra. Ruiz —Tenía puesta una falda blanca, una blusa roja y un suéter negro... sandalias blancas, y tenía una bolsa blanca.

Agente Gómez —¿Llevaba algunas joyas?
Sra. Ruiz —Sí, una cadena de oro con una cruz, un anillo de plata y unos aretes rojos.
Agente Gómez —Espero que tengan una fotografía reciente de ella.
Sr. Ruiz —Sí, aquí tengo una en la billetera.
Agente Gómez —Esto debe ser muy difícil para Uds., pero ¿tienen idea de por qué se escapó? ¿Ha tenido algún problema con Uds. o en la escuela?
Sr. Ruiz —Bueno... ella estaba saliendo con un muchacho... y nosotros le dijimos que no nos gustaba... Estuvo preso dos veces.
Agente Gómez —¿Creen que su hija se fue con él?
Sra. Ruiz —Yo creo que sí, pero puede ser que esté con otra amiga.
Agente Gómez —¿Qué edad tiene él?
Sra. Ruiz —No sé exactamente. Es dos o tres años mayor que ella.
Agente Gómez —¿Saben cómo se llama y dónde vive?
Sra. Ruiz —Él se llama José Ramírez. No sé dónde vive, pero los dos asisten a la misma escuela secundaria.
Agente Gómez —¿Su hija se había escapado de su casa en alguna otra ocasión?
Sra. Ruiz —No, nunca. Yo creo que él se la llevó contra su voluntad...
Agente Gómez —¿Saben si tenía dinero?
Sra. Ruiz —Sí, tenía unos setenta y cinco dólares, por lo menos.
Agente Gómez —¿Tienen alguna idea de dónde puede estar? Es importante que traten de recordar cualquier detalle.
Sr. Ruiz —No, ninguna, pero tememos que ya esté lejos de aquí.
Agente Gómez —¿Tiene carro?
Sra. Ruiz —No. Nosotros no queremos que maneje. Es muy joven...
Agente Gómez —¿Tiene algún documento de identificación?
Sra. Ruiz —Es posible que lleve la tarjeta de la escuela en la cartera...
Agente Gómez —Bueno. Es necesario que me avisen enseguida si recuerdan algo más o si reciben alguna información.
Sra. Ruiz —Ojalá que puedan encontrarla pronto.
Agente Gómez —Vamos a hacer todo lo posible, señora.

 **¡Escuchemos!** While listening to the dialogue, circle **V (verdadero)** if the statement is true and **F (falso)** if it is false.

1. María Elena, una muchacha de dieciséis años, se escapó de su casa. V F
2. María Elena les dijo a sus padres que iba para la escuela. V F
3. Los padres de María Elena llamaron por teléfono a la escuela. V F
4. Los padres piensan que su hija puede haber sido secuestrada. V F
5. María Elena tenía puesta una blusa azul y una falda gris. V F

© 2017 Cengage Learning

Nombre ______________ Sección ______________ Fecha ______________

		V	F
6.	El Sr. Ruiz tiene una fotografía de su hija en su billetera.	V	F
7.	Ella está saliendo con un muchacho que estuvo preso.	V	F
8.	La madre no cree que la muchacha se fue con su hermano.	V	F
9.	El muchacho es dos o tres años mayor que ella.	V	F
10.	María Elena se había escapado otras veces.	V	F

VOCABULARIO

Cognados

el (la) adolescente
el documento
la ocasión
reciente
la sandalia
el suéter
la víctima

Nombres

el anillo, la sortija *ring*
el arete *earring*
la blusa *blouse*
la boca *mouth*
la cartera, la bolsa, el bolso *purse*
la cicatriz *scar*
el (la) compañero(a) (de clase) *classmate*
la cruz *cross*
el detalle *detail*
la edad *age*
la falda *skirt*
el (la) jovencito(a) *youth, teenager*
el lunar *mole*
la mejilla, el cachete *cheek*
el pelo *hair*
la voluntad *will*

Verbos

asistir (a) *to attend*
escaparse, fugarse *to run away*
estudiar *to study*
medir (e:i) *to measure, to be (amount) tall*
saber *to find out; to know*
salir con *to go out (with), to date*
temer *to fear, to be afraid*
tener puesto(a), llevar puesto(a) *to have on, to wear*

Adjetivos

bajo(a), bajito(a) (*Cuba*) *short*

Otras palabras y expresiones

de pelo (negro) *with (black) hair*
dos veces *twice*
exactamente *exactly*
lejos (de) *far (from)*
ojalá *I hope*
por lo menos *at least*
puede ser *it may be*
los señores[1] **(Ruiz)** *Mr. and Mrs. (Ruiz)*

[1]Abbreviated **Sres.**

© 2017 Cengage Learning

Nombre ______________________ Sección ______________ Fecha ______________

VOCABULARIO ADICIONAL

Para investigar a las personas desaparecidas (*To investigate missing persons*)

abandonar los estudios *to drop out of school*
el alojamiento, el hospedaje *lodging*
el cadáver *corpse*
el (la) conocido(a) *acquaintance*
el (la) delincuente juvenil *juvenile delinquent*
desaparecer *to disappear*
la estación de ómnibus, la estación de autobuses *bus station*
el (la) maestro(a) *teacher*
mayor de edad *of age, adult*
menor de edad *minor*
la morgue *morgue*
el paradero *whereabouts*
pornográfico(a) *pornographic*
la prostitución *prostitution*
refugiarse *to find refuge, shelter*
rescatar *to rescue*
el rescate *ransom*
el tribunal de menores *juvenile court*

Notas Culturales

Latinos in the United States tend to marry within their own groups of origin. Intermarriage between Latinos and Anglos is increasing, however, especially among second-generation individuals.

Actividades

Dígame... Answer the following questions, basing your answers on the dialogue.

1. ¿Por qué habla el agente Gómez con los Sres. Ruiz?

____

2. ¿Cuándo fue la última vez que el Sr. Ruiz vio a su hija?

____

3. ¿Qué les dijo la muchacha a sus padres?

____

4. ¿Qué es necesario que hagan los padres de la muchacha?

____

© 2017 Cengage Learning

Nombre ______________________ Sección __________ Fecha __________

5. ¿La muchacha es alta? ¿Cuánto mide?

____

6. ¿Tiene María Elena algunas marcas visibles?

____

7. ¿Qué ropa tenía puesta?

____

8. ¿Qué joyas llevaba María Elena?

____

9. ¿Qué espera el agente Gómez?

____

10. ¿Cuál es el problema que María Elena ha tenido con sus padres?

____

11. ¿Qué cree la mamá de María Elena? ¿Por qué piensa Ud. que ella cree eso?

____

12. ¿Por qué no tiene carro María Elena?

____

Hablemos Interview a classmate, using the following questions. When you have finished, switch roles.

1. ¿A qué escuela secundaria asistió Ud.?
2. Cuando era estudiante de la escuela secundaria, ¿pensaba en hacerse (*becoming*) policía?
3. Cuando Ud. era adolescente, ¿se escapó alguna vez de su casa?
4. ¿Tiene Ud. una fotografía reciente de su familia?
5. ¿Es importante que una persona siempre traiga consigo (*with him/her*) un documento de identificación? ¿Por qué?
6. ¿Tiene Ud. algún documento de identificación ahora? ¿Puede mostrármelo?
7. ¿Cuánto dinero tenía Ud. cuando salió de su casa hoy?

© 2017 Cengage Learning

Nombre ______________________ Sección ____________ Fecha ____________

Quiz

Vamos a practicar

A Rewrite the following sentences, beginning each one with the cue given.

Modelo Ella tiene documentos.
Espero que **ella *tenga* documentos.**

1. Compran las faldas negras.
   Ojalá que ______________________.
2. Ellos nos traen las fotografías.
   Nos alegramos de que (*We are glad*) ______________________.
3. No están interrogando al acusado.
   Esperamos que ______________________.
4. Ella va a escaparse.
   Temo que ______________________.

B Rewrite the following sentences, beginning each one with the cue given. Make the necessary changes.

1. Ud. nos avisa enseguida.
   Es necesario que ______________________.
2. Ella se escapa con su novio.
   Es posible que ______________________.
3. Asisten a esa escuela.
   Es importante que ______________________.
4. Tú no sales con ese muchacho.
   Es mejor que ______________________.

Conversaciones breves Complete the following dialogue, using your imagination and the vocabulary from this lesson.

El agente Silva y el Sr. Ochoa hablan del hijo del Sr. Ochoa.

Agente Silva —______________________

Sr. Ochoa —Esta mañana supe que él se había escapado porque no durmió (*didn't sleep*) en casa...

Agente Silva —______________________

© 2017 Cengage Learning

Nombre ______________________ Sección ____________ Fecha ____________

Sr. Ochoa —Lo vi ayer por la tarde antes de ir a la oficina.

Agente Silva —____

Sr. Ochoa —Tengo una fotografía de él, pero no es reciente.

Agente Silva —____

Sr. Ochoa —Llevaba puesto un pantalón azul, pero no recuerdo de qué color era la camisa.

Agente Silva —____

Sr. Ochoa —Solamente un anillo de oro.

Agente Silva —____

Sr. Ochoa —No, no ha tenido problemas conmigo.

Agente Silva —____

Sr. Ochoa —Sí, se escapó una vez cuando tenía diez años, pero regresó a casa al día siguiente (*the next day*).

Agente Silva —____

Sr. Ochoa —No, generalmente no lleva ningún documento.

Agente Silva —____

—____

Sr. Ochoa —Sí, si recuerdo algo más, le aviso enseguida. Ojalá que puedan encontrarlo pronto.

Agente Silva —____

En estas situaciones

With two or more partners, act out the following situations in Spanish.

1. You are investigating a runaway. Ask the parents for a description of the child's physical characteristics and the clothing the child was wearing. Question them about his/her friends. Ask for a recent photograph of the child and tell them to notify you immediately if they remember any other details.
2. You are talking to a teenager who ran away from home. Explain that you want to help and ask why he/she ran away. Reassure him/her that if there have been problems with parents or at school, he/she can talk with you.
3. You are investigating a missing person case. Ask the person reporting it to recall when he/she first realized the person wasn't home. Ask for a complete description of the missing person. Promise to do everything possible to find the person.

Casos

With you and a partner playing the roles, work through the following scenarios.

1. You are a police officer speaking with the parents of a child who has run away from home.
2. You are an officer speaking with the best friend of a runaway. Ask for as much information as the friend can—or is willing to—provide.

© 2017 Cengage Learning

Nombre ______________________ Sección ____________ Fecha ____________

Un paso más Review the **Vocabulario adicional** in this lesson and match the questions in column **A** with the answers in column **B.**

	A		B
1.	________ ¿Está muerta (*dead*)?	**a.**	En la morgue.
2.	________ ¿Es Ud. mayor de edad?	**b.**	Cincuenta mil dólares.
3.	________ ¿No está en la escuela?	**c.**	No, solamente conocidos.
4.	________ ¿Se escapó anoche?	**d.**	Sí, la rescataron anoche.
5.	________ ¿Dónde está el cadáver?	**e.**	Sí, y ahora están presos.
6.	________ ¿Consiguió alojamiento?	**f.**	En el tribunal de menores.
7.	________ ¿Son amigos?	**g.**	No, abandonó los estudios.
8.	________ ¿No está aquí?	**h.**	Sí. No conocemos su paradero.
9.	________ ¿Cuánto piden de rescate?	**i.**	Sí, está en un motel.
10.	________ ¿El ladrón tiene 15 años...?	**j.**	Sí, es un delincuente juvenil.
11.	________ ¿Están en la escuela?	**k.**	Sí, la mató su esposo.
12.	________ ¿Dónde estaba el hombre?	**l.**	No... desapareció...
13.	________ ¿Dónde la van a juzgar?	**m.**	No, está lejos.
14.	________ ¿Vendían libros pornográficos?	**n.**	Sí, con la maestra.
15.	________ ¿La víctima del secuestro está en su casa ahora?	**o.**	En la estación de ómnibus.
16.	________ ¿La cárcel está cerca de aquí?	**p.**	No, soy menor de edad.

© 2017 Cengage Learning

Lección 18

Una violación

Objectives

Structures

- The subjunctive to express doubt, disbelief, and denial
- The subjunctive to express indefiniteness and nonexistence

Communication

- Investigating rape: talking to victims on the telephone and in person
- Describing an attacker

iLrn™

Una violación

Una muchacha hispana de dieciséis años llama a la policía, diciendo que acaban[1] de violarla. La muchacha pide que manden a alguien que hable español, porque ella no habla bien el inglés. La agente Rocha está con la víctima ahora.

Víctima —¡Ayúdeme, por favor!
Agente Rocha —¿Tus padres no están en casa...?
Víctima —No, y dudo que lleguen antes de la medianoche.
Agente Rocha —Bueno, cálmate y cuéntame lo que pasó.
Víctima —Yo estaba en mi cuarto, leyendo, cuando tocaron[1] a la puerta... Fui a abrir, y un hombre entró y me empujó... Y me caí... y me golpeó... (*Llora histéricamente.*)
Agente Rocha —Mira, yo comprendo que esto es muy difícil para ti, pero para poder ayudarte y arrestar al hombre que te violó, necesitamos información.
Víctima —Sí, lo sé... pero primero quiero bañarme, quitarme esta ropa... ¡Me siento sucia!
Agente Rocha —Lo siento, pero es mejor esperar. Primero, tiene que examinarte un médico. Además, un baño puede destruir evidencia necesaria. ¿Conocías al hombre que te atacó?

---

[1]The third person is often used (without a subject) to express an indefinite *he, she,* or *they.*

Víctima —No, no, no. Era un extraño.
Agente Rocha —¿Puedes reconocerlo, si lo ves?
Víctima —No creo que pueda olvidar esa cara.
Agente Rocha —¿De qué raza era?
Víctima —Era blanco. Más bien bajo, gordo, de ojos castaños. Tenía barba y bigote, pero era calvo.
Agente Rocha —¿Nunca lo habías visto antes?
Víctima —No, estoy segura de que nunca lo había visto.
Agente Rocha —¿Qué hora era, más o menos?
Víctima —Eran como las nueve y media.
Agente Rocha —¿Te cambiaste de ropa?
Víctima —Todavía no. Llamé en cuanto se fue.
Agente Rocha —Bien, no te cambies. Un médico debe examinarte enseguida. Tenemos que llevarte al hospital. ¿Dónde están tus padres?
Víctima —Están en la casa de mi tía. Su número de teléfono está en aquella libreta.
Agente Rocha —Ahora, ¿el hombre llegó a violarte? Es decir, ¿hubo penetración?
Víctima —Sí. Me amenazó con un cuchillo. Tuve miedo y no hice resistencia.
Agente Rocha —¿Te obligó a realizar algún acto sexual anormal durante la violación?
Víctima —No.
Agente Rocha —¿Se puso un condón?
Víctima —No, y eso me tiene aterrorizada. Tal vez tiene SIDA o una enfermedad venérea...
Agente Rocha —Trata de tranquilizarte. Se te harán las pruebas necesarias. ¿Qué más recuerdas de él? ¿Tenía alguna marca visible? ¿Un tatuaje?
Víctima —Tenía un tatuaje en el brazo izquierdo: un corazón atravesado por una flechita. Además, usaba anteojos.
Agente Rocha —¿Tenía algún acento? ¿Te dijo algo?
Víctima —No, no le noté ningún acento. Sólo me dijo que si gritaba, me mataba.
Agente Rocha —Y no pudiste luchar con él para defenderte, ¿verdad?
Víctima —No. Tenía tanto miedo...
Agente Rocha —Comprendo. ¿Hay alguien que pueda venir a quedarse contigo?
Víctima —No, no conozco a nadie que pueda venir a esta hora.

¡Escuchemos!

While listening to the dialogue, circle **V (verdadero)** if the statement is true and **F (falso)** if it is false.

1. Acaban de violar a una joven hispana de dieciséis años. V F
2. Rocha es el apellido de la muchacha violada. V F
3. Los padres de la joven violada están en su casa. V F
4. La muchacha no se acuerda de lo que pasó. V F
5. La muchacha se cayó y el hombre la golpeó. V F
6. La joven debe esperar a que el médico la examine antes de bañarse. V F
7. Ella no conocía al hombre que la violó. V F

© 2017 Cengage Learning

Nombre ______________________ Sección ____________ Fecha ____________

8. Ella había visto antes al hombre que la violó. V F
9. La muchacha no tuvo miedo e hizo resistencia. V F
10. El hombre le dijo que si gritaba la mataba. V F

VOCABULARIO

Cognados

el acento
el acto
anormal
el condón
la evidencia
la penetración
sexual

Nombres

los anteojos, los lentes, los espejuelos (*Cuba, Puerto Rico*), **las gafas** *eyeglasses*
el baño *bath*
la barba *beard*
el bigote *moustache*
el cuchillo *knife*
la enfermedad venérea *venereal disease*
la flecha, la flechita *arrow, small arrow*
la libreta *address book*
la raza *race*
el SIDA (síndrome de inmunodeficiencia adquirida) *AIDS*
la violación *rape*

Verbos

amenazar *to threaten*
atacar *to attack*
atar *to tie*
bañarse *to bathe*
caerse[1] *to fall*
calmarse *to calm down*
comprender *to understand*
contar (o:ue) *to tell*
defender(se) *to defend (oneself)*
destruir[2] *to destroy*
empujar *to push*
gritar *to scream, to shout*
llorar *to cry*
luchar *to fight, to struggle*
obligar *to obligate, to force*
olvidar *to forget*
ponerse *to put on*
realizar *to perform, to carry out*
violar *to rape*

Adjetivos

aquel, aquella *that*
aterrorizado(a) *terrified, frightened*
atravesado(a) *pierced*
calvo(a), pelado(a) *bald*
castaño, café *brown (ref. to eyes or hair)*
sucio(a) *dirty*

---

[1]Irregular first person present indicative: **me caigo**
[2]Orthographic change in the present indicative, in all forms except the **nosotros** form: **destruyo, destruyes, destruye, destruimos, destruyen**

© 2017 Cengage Learning

Nombre ______________________ Sección ____________ Fecha ____________

Otras palabras y expresiones

cambiarse de ropa *to change clothes*
en cuanto *as soon as*
Eran como las (+ *hora*). *It was about (+ time).*
es decir... *that is to say . . .*
estar seguro(a) *to be certain*
hacer resistencia *to resist*
Hasta mañana. *(I'll) see you tomorrow.*
histéricamente *hysterically*
llegar a (+ *inf.*) *to succeed in (doing something)*
para ti *for you*
¿Qué hora era...? *What time was it . . . ?*
tal vez *perhaps*
¡Tenía tanto miedo! *I was so scared!*

VOCABULARIO ADICIONAL

Más descripciones

La piel (*Skin*)

el acné *acne*
el grano *pimple*
la mancha *spot, mark, blemish*
la peca *freckle*
la verruga *wart*

Los ojos

bizco(a) *cross-eyed*
el ojo de vidrio *glass eye*
los ojos saltones *bulging eyes, bug eyes*

El cuerpo (*Body*)

deforme *deformed*
desfigurado(a) *disfigured*
embarazada *pregnant*
musculoso(a) *muscular*

El pelo

la peluca *wig, hairpiece*
el vello *body hair*
velludo(a) *hairy*

Para describir la ropa

de cuadros *plaid*
de lunares *polka dot*
de rayas *striped*
estampado(a) *print*
mangas cortas *short sleeves*
mangas largas *long sleeves*
ropa interior *underwear*
sin mangas *sleeveless*

Otras palabras

hablar con (la) zeta *to lisp*
tartamudear *to stutter*

Notas Culturales

- Latinos constitute about 10.3% of the population in the United States, yet they account for 14% of the reported AIDS cases, nearly 21% of AIDS cases among women, and 22% of all pediatric AIDS cases. Latinos are at greater risk for HIV infection because of factors such as living in high-prevalence areas and exposure to intravenous drug use, not because of their race and culture. AIDS is most prevalent in large urban centers, with three cities (New York, San Francisco, and Los Angeles) accounting for about 60% of all cases. Nearly half of the Hispanic Americans with AIDS are heterosexuals, and most of the Hispanic AIDS cases in the Northeast are among intravenous drug users. Heterosexual transmission of HIV

© 2017 Cengage Learning

Nombre ______________________ Sección ____________ Fecha ____________

from intravenous drug users to their sexual partners is more prevalent among Latinos because of attitudes regarding the use of condoms. A recent survey indicates that Hispanic Americans know less about HIV and AIDS than non-Latinos. The American Medical Association has recommended that AIDS prevention education programs be tailored to subgroups such as Mexican Americans and Puerto Ricans due to cultural and language differences.

- Like many women, Latina females may feel uncomfortable or embarrassed discussing matters of sex, especially with a male police officer. This reaction may be due in part to cultural taboos, level of education, or both. In some cultures, it is not possible, or it is considered socially unacceptable, to talk about female anatomy or any aspect of sexuality. Therefore, it is important to be sensitive and diplomatic when dealing with these topics.

Actividades

Dígame... Answer the following questions, basing your answers on the dialogue.

1. ¿Cuántos años tiene la muchacha que llama a la policía?

____

2. ¿Qué dice la muchacha y qué pide?

____

____

3. ¿Dónde estaba la víctima y qué estaba haciendo cuando tocaron a la puerta?

____

4. ¿Qué pasó cuando la muchacha abrió la puerta?

____

5. ¿Qué quiere hacer la muchacha antes de hablar con la agente?

____

6. ¿Por qué dice la agente Rocha que es mejor esperar?

____

____

7. ¿Conocía la muchacha al hombre que la atacó?

____

8. Describa al hombre que violó a la muchacha. ¿Tenía alguna marca visible?

____

© 2017 Cengage Learning

9. ¿Se cambió de ropa la muchacha?

____

10. ¿Esperó mucho tiempo la muchacha antes de llamar a la policía?

____

11. ¿El hombre llegó a violar a la muchacha?

____

12. ¿Trató de defenderse la muchacha? ¿Por qué?

____

Hablemos Interview a classmate, using the following questions. When you have finished, switch roles.

1. ¿Qué estaba haciendo Ud. anoche cuando tocaron a la puerta?
2. ¿Se cambió Ud. de ropa antes de ir a trabajar?
3. ¿Solamente las mujeres pueden ser víctimas del abuso sexual?
4. En un caso de violación, ¿qué debe hacer el (la) agente de policía para ayudar a la víctima?
5. ¿Ha investigado Ud. casos de violación?
6. ¿Cómo puede defenderse una mujer si es atacada por un hombre?

Quiz

Vamos a practicar

A Rewrite the following sentences, beginning each one with the cue given.

Modelo Puedo olvidar su cara.
No creo que ***pueda*** **olvidar su cara.**

1. Mis padres llegan mañana.
   No creo que ____.

2. Él la empuja, la golpea y la ata.
   Dudo que ____.

3. Esto es muy difícil.
   No es verdad que ____.

4. Él tiene bigote y barba.
   No estoy segura de que ____.

© 2017 Cengage Learning

Nombre ______________________ Sección ____________ Fecha ____________

B Rewrite the following sentences, beginning each one with the cue given. Make the necessary changes.

1. ¿Habla inglés?
   ¿Hay alguien que ______________________?
2. Un médico puede examinarte.
   Busco un médico que ______________________.
3. Un testigo está seguro de que lo vio allí.
   Necesito encontrar un testigo que ______________________.
4. La fotografía identifica al violador.
   Espero conseguir una fotografía que ______________________.

Conversaciones breves

Complete the following dialogue, using your imagination and the vocabulary from this lesson.

El agente Mena habla con Sara, la víctima de una violación.

Agente Mena —______________________

Sara —No, nunca lo había visto antes.

Agente Mena —______________________

Sara —Era blanco... alto... de pelo negro y ojos azules.

Agente Mena —______________________

Sara —Tenía bigote, pero no tenía barba.

Agente Mena —______________________

Sara —No recuerdo nada más...

Agente Mena —______________________

Sara —No, no usaba lentes.

Agente Mena —______________________

Sara —Sí, me amenazó con un cuchillo.

Agente Mena —______________________

Sara —Sí, traté de defenderme, pero no pude hacer nada.

Agente Mena —______________________

Sara —Sí, llegó a violarme... hubo penetración...

Agente Mena —______________________

Sara —No, nada anormal...

© 2017 Cengage Learning

Nombre ______________________ Sección ____________ Fecha ____________

En estas situaciones With a partner, act out the following situations in Spanish.

1. You answer a call from a hysterical rape victim. Calm her down and ask her to describe what happened. Explain that you know it is difficult for her to talk about it, but that you need to know all the details to find the man who raped her.
2. You are with a rape victim. Advise her not to bathe or change clothes, and help to arrange for a medical examination for her at a hospital. Find out from her if there is anyone else you should call.
3. You are investigating a rape. Ask the victim to describe the man. Help her to remember as many details as possible about the rapist by asking questions about his physical characteristics, clothing, accent, etc.

Casos With you and a partner playing the roles, work through the following scenarios.

1. You are an officer trying to calm down a hysterical rape victim.
2. You are talking to a rape victim, trying to get information about the rapist and what happened.

Un paso más Review the **Vocabulario adicional** in this lesson and match the questions in column **A** with the answers in column **B.**

A		B	
1.	____________ ¿Es una verruga?	a.	Sí, tiene muchos granos.
2.	____________ ¿Es gordo?	b.	No, habla con zeta.
3.	____________ ¿Tiene alguna marca visible?	c.	No, no tiene problemas con los ojos.
4.	____________ ¿Tiene acné?	d.	Sí, algunas, en la nariz.
5.	____________ ¿Tartamudea?	e.	Saltones.
6.	____________ ¿Es velludo?	f.	Sí, tiene mucho vello.
7.	____________ ¿Tiene pecas?	g.	Una es artificial.
8.	____________ ¿Está embarazada?	h.	No, de cuadros.
9.	____________ ¿Es bizco?	i.	Sí, pero usa peluca.
10.	____________ ¿Cómo son los ojos?	j.	No, es musculoso.
11.	____________ ¿Tuvo un accidente?	k.	Porque es sin mangas.
12.	____________ ¿Es calvo?	l.	Sí, una mancha en la cara.
13.	____________ ¿Tiene las dos piernas?	m.	Sí, y ahora está desfigurada.
14.	____________ ¿Es deforme?	n.	No, es perfecto.
15.	____________ ¿Cómo es la camisa?	o.	No, es un lunar.
16.	____________ ¿La falda es de lunares?	p.	Sí, va a tener el bebé en octubre.
17.	____________ ¿Por qué no te gusta la blusa?	q.	De rayas y mangas cortas.

© 2017 Cengage Learning

LECCIÓN 19

UNA TARDE CUALQUIERA

OBJECTIVES

Structures

- The subjunctive after certain conjunctions
- The present perfect subjunctive
- Uses of the present perfect subjunctive

Communication

- Talking to parents of troubled teenagers
- Dealing with attempted suicide
- More on traffic violations

iLrn™

UNA TARDE CUALQUIERA

Una tarde en la vida del agente Cabañas, de la Cuarta Estación de Policía, en Elizabeth, Nueva Jersey.

Las dos de la tarde:
El agente Cabañas habla con el padre de un menor de edad a quien acaban de arrestar.

Padre —Buenos días. Me avisaron que mi hijo estaba detenido aquí.
Agente Cabañas —¿Cómo se llama su hijo?
Padre —Enrique Fernández.
Agente Cabañas —Sí, señor. Está aquí.
Padre —¿Por qué lo arrestaron? ¿De qué lo acusan?
Agente Cabañas —Su hijo está acusado de venderles drogas a sus compañeros, en su escuela.
Padre —¡No es posible! Eso no puede ser cierto. No creo que mi hijo haya hecho tal cosa. ¿Puedo hablar con él?
Agente Cabañas —Sí, señor, pero debe esperar hasta que hayan terminado de interrogarlo.

Las tres y cuarto de la tarde:
El agente Cabañas va a la casa de Felipe Núñez para hablar con él. Habla con la mamá del muchacho.

Agente Cabañas —Necesito hablar con Felipe Núñez, señora. Es urgente.
Sra. Núñez —No está, y no sé a qué hora va a regresar.

Agente Cabañas —Bueno, cuando regrese, dígale que me llame a este número, por favor. Dígale que quiero hacerle unas preguntas.
Sra. Núñez —Muy bien. Se lo diré en cuanto lo vea.

Las cinco de la tarde:
El agente Cabañas va al apartamento de una muchacha que trató de suicidarse.

Agente Cabañas —¿Dónde está la muchacha?
Vecino —Allí, en la cocina. La encontré con la cabeza metida en el horno.
Agente Cabañas —¿Había olor a gas?
Vecino —Sí, por eso llamé al 911 en cuanto llegué. Ya vienen los paramédicos.

Van a la cocina y el agente habla con la muchacha.

Agente Cabañas —¿Puedes oírme? ¿Cómo te sientes?
Muchacha —Mal... Tomé...
Agente Cabañas —¿Qué tomaste? ¿Veneno? ¿Qué veneno tomaste...?
Muchacha —No... calmantes... en el baño... más de diez...

Las seis de la tarde:
El agente Cabañas detiene a una señora que maneja con los faros del carro apagados.

Agente Cabañas —La detuve porque los faros de su carro no están prendidos.
Señora —Sí... parece que están descompuestos...
Agente Cabañas —Bueno, no puede manejar este carro a menos que haga arreglar los faros.
Señora —Muy bien. Mañana, sin falta.
Agente Cabañas —Cuando el carro esté listo, llévelo a esta dirección. Ahí le van a firmar el dorso de esta papeleta para confirmar que Ud. hizo arreglar el desperfecto.

¡Escuchemos!

While listening to the dialogue, circle **V (verdadero)** if the statement is true and **F (falso)** if it is false.

1. Acaban de arrestar a un menor de edad. V F
2. El agente Cabañas está hablando con la madre del joven detenido. V F
3. El joven está acusado de venderles drogas a sus compañeros. V F
4. La mamá de Felipe Núñez no sabe a qué hora va a regresar su hijo. V F
5. Felipe debe llamar al 911 cuando regrese. V F
6. El agente Cabañas va al apartamento de una joven que fue violada. V F
7. Un vecino encontró a la muchacha con la cabeza metida en el horno. V F

© 2017 Cengage Learning

8. La muchacha tomó calmantes en el baño. V F
9. Los faros del carro de la señora están prendidos. V F
10. La señora no puede manejar el carro a menos que haga arreglar los faros. V F

VOCABULARIO

Cognado

intoxicado(a)

Nombres

el calmante, el sedante, el sedativo *sedative*
el desperfecto *(slight) damage, imperfection*
el dorso *back (of paper)*
el faro *headlight*
el frasco *bottle (of pills)*
el gas *gas*
el horno *oven*
el olor *smell*
la papeleta *form*
la pastilla, la píldora *pill*
la rehabilitación *rehab*
el veneno *poison*

Verbos

arreglar *to fix*
confirmar *to confirm*
oír[1] *to hear*
suicidarse *to commit suicide*

Adjetivos

descompuesto(a) *broken, not working*
listo(a) *ready*
metido(a) *inside, inserted in*
prendido(a), encendido(a) *lit, turned on (a lamp)*

Otras palabras y expresiones

a menos que *unless*
en cuanto, tan pronto como *as soon as*
hacer arreglar *to have (something) fixed*
hacer una pregunta *to ask a question*
hasta que *until*
olor a *smell of*
sin falta *without fail*
tal cosa *such a thing*

[1]Irregular present indicative: **oigo, oyes, oye, oímos, oyen**

© 2017 Cengage Learning

Nombre ______________________ Sección ____________ Fecha ____________

VOCABULARIO ADICIONAL

Para responder a una llamada

ahogarse *to drown*
la agresión, el ataque *aggression, attack, assault*
el (la) agresor(a) *aggressor, assailant*
arrancar *to start (a car)*
el (la) asesino(a) *murderer, assassin*
la camilla *stretcher*
dar respiración artificial *to give CPR*
dar una puñalada *to stab*
en defensa propia *in self-defense*
el helicóptero *helicopter*
pegar un tiro, pegar un balazo *to shoot*
la pelea, la riña *fight*
la piscina, la alberca (*Méx.*) *swimming pool*
los primeros auxilios *first aid*
la queja *complaint*
respirar *to breathe*
el ruido *noise*
la silla de ruedas *wheelchair*
tocar la bocina *to honk the horn*

Notas Culturales

Most Latino children are taught from an early age that the family comes first. Knowing one's place in a hierarchical, sometimes authoritarian family structure, and showing appropriate deference and respect to older family members are of great importance, as is recognizing the interdependence of family members and the necessity of placing the family's well-being ahead of one's own needs or desires. Within this context, traditional American values such as individualism, freedom of choice, and self-sufficiency are of secondary importance.

Actividades

Dígame... Answer the following questions, basing your answers on the dialogues.

1. ¿Por qué vino a la estación de policía el padre de un menor de edad?

____

2. ¿De qué está acusado su hijo?

____

3. ¿Qué cree el padre de la acusación?

____

© 2017 Cengage Learning

Nombre ______________________ Sección ______________ Fecha ______________

4. Si el padre quiere ver a su hijo, ¿hasta cuándo tiene que esperar?

____

5. ¿Habla el agente Cabañas con Felipe Núñez? ¿Por qué?

____

6. ¿Para qué quiere hablar con él?

____

7. ¿Cuándo le va a decir la Sra. Núñez a su hijo que el agente quiere hablar con él?

____

8. ¿Dónde está la muchacha que trató de suicidarse?

____

9. ¿Cómo encontró el vecino a la muchacha?

____

10. ¿Qué olor había?

____

11. ¿Esperó mucho tiempo el vecino para llamar a la policía?

____

12. ¿Qué tomó la muchacha?

____

13. ¿Por qué detiene el agente Cabañas a una señora?

____

14. ¿Qué tiene que hacer la señora mañana?

____

15. ¿Qué debe hacer la señora cuando los faros del carro estén listos?

____

© 2017 Cengage Learning

Nombre ______________________ Sección ______________ Fecha ______________

Hablemos

Interview a classmate, using the following questions. When you have finished, switch roles.

1. ¿Qué va a hacer Ud. en cuanto llegue a su casa?
2. ¿A quién quiere Ud. hacerle unas preguntas?
3. ¿Qué le dirá Ud. a su profesor(a) cuando lo (la) vea?
4. ¿Necesita hacer arreglar su coche?
5. ¿Están prendidos o apagados los faros de su carro en este momento?

Quiz

Vamos a practicar

A Complete the following sentences, using the cues in parentheses.

1. Se lo voy a preguntar cuando ___________ (verlos).
2. Yo le avisaré en cuanto el policía ___________ (arrestarlas).
3. Lleve el carro a este lugar tan pronto como el mecánico ___________ (arreglar los faros).
4. No me llame hasta que ellas ___________ (traer al detenido).

B Rewrite the following sentences, beginning each one with the cue given.

Modelo Le leen sus derechos.
Espero que ***le hayan leído*** **sus derechos.**

1. Todos toman pastillas.
   No creo que ______________________________.
2. El joven está intoxicado.
   Ojalá que ______________________________.
3. Tiene que hacer rehabilitación.
   Es posible que ______________________________.
4. Se suicida.
   Ella tiene miedo de que él ______________________________.
5. Lo encuentran.
   Espero que ______________________________.
6. Los frascos han desaparecido.
   Dudo que ______________________________.

© 2017 Cengage Learning

Nombre ______________________ Sección ____________ Fecha ____________

Conversaciones breves Complete the following dialogues, using your imagination and the vocabulary from this lesson.

El agente Ross y el Sr. Soto:

Agente Ross —________________________________

Sr. Soto —Lo siento, pero en este momento no está.

Agente Ross —________________________________

Sr. Soto —No sé. Sólo me dijo que iba a regresar más tarde.

Agente Ross —________________________________

Sr. Soto —Sí, señor. Se lo diré cuando lo vea.

La agente León y la Sra. Torres:

Agente León —¿Qué pasa, señora?

Sra. Torres —________________________________

Agente León —¿Dónde está su hijo ahora?

Sra. Torres —________________________________

Agente León —¿Llamó Ud. a los paramédicos?

Sra. Torres —________________________________

Agente León —Voy a llamarlos. ¿Qué tomó su hijo, señora?

Sra. Torres —________________________________

La agente Suárez y el Sr. Gil:

Agente Suárez —________________________________

Sr. Gil —Buenos días. Busco a mi hijo. Me han dicho que está aquí.

Agente Suárez —________________________________

Sr. Gil —Se llama Alberto Gil Rosas.

Agente Suárez —________________________________

Sr. Gil —Pero, ¿por qué? Alberto es un buen muchacho.

Agente Suárez —________________________________

Sr. Gil —¿Cómo? ¿Mi hijo? ¡No puede ser! Quiero verlo ahora mismo.

Agente Suárez —________________________________

Sr. Gil —Está bien. Voy a esperar, pero primero quiero llamar a mi abogado.

Agente Suárez —________________________________

© 2017 Cengage Learning

Nombre ______________________ Sección ____________ Fecha ____________

En estas situaciones With a partner, act out the following situations in Spanish.

1. Explain to the parent of a minor who has been arrested that he/she can't speak with the child until they've finished booking him/her. Say that the child was arrested for selling drugs at school and for carrying a gun. Tell the parent to take a seat in the waiting room and try to calm him/her down.
2. You want to speak with Mr. Olmedo. Leave this message with his wife: "When your husband returns, have him call me at this number without fail. It is very urgent, because I want to ask him a few questions."
3. Tell a motorist that he/she has to have his/her car fixed. Tell the motorist also that, after the car is ready, he/she has to take it to 125 Flores Street, where someone will sign the back of the form to confirm that the damage has been fixed.

Casos With you and a partner playing the roles, work through the following scenarios.

1. You are talking with the angry and distraught parent of a minor who has just been arrested.
2. You are having difficulty getting in touch with a young woman you need to interrogate, so you leave several messages with her roommate.
3. You talk to a motorist whose car lights are not on and advise him/her on what to do.

Un paso más Review the **Vocabulario adicional** in this lesson and give the Spanish equivalent of the following.

1. There has been a possible drowning.

   a. The child fell in the pool.

   ____

   b. He almost drowned.

   ____

   c. The paramedics gave him CPR.

   ____

2. There has been a complaint.

   a. Is there a fight at this party? There's a lot of noise.

   ____

   b. Who was the aggressor?

   ____

© 2017 Cengage Learning

c. She stabbed him.

____

d. He shot her with a gun.

____

e. She's not breathing. (She doesn't breathe.)

____

f. He killed her in self-defense.

____

3. There has been an accident on the highway.

a. Her car wouldn't start.

____

b. He was honking the horn.

____

c. He crashed into her car.

____

d. Do you know anything about first aid?

____

e. We're going to put her on a stretcher.

____

f. Is there a wheelchair for him?

____

© 2017 Cengage Learning

Otro día, por la mañana

Objectives

Structures

- The imperfect subjunctive
- Uses of the imperfect subjunctive
- *If* clauses

Communication

- More on investigating robberies: asking to search a suspect's car; arresting a pickpocket
- Breaking up an illegal gathering

iLrn™

Otro día, por la mañana

Un día de trabajo para el agente Montero, de la Comisaría Tercera de la ciudad de Albuquerque, Nuevo México.

Las diez y media de la mañana:
El agente Montero investiga un robo en un mercado. Ahora está hablando con el dependiente.

Agente Montero —Cuénteme exactamente lo que pasó.
Dependiente —A eso de las nueve y media vino un hombre y dijo que quería una botella de vino...
Agente Montero —¿Qué pasó entonces?
Dependiente —Me apuntó con una pistola y me obligó a que le diera todo el dinero que había en la caja.
Agente Montero —¿Podría Ud. reconocerlo si lo viera otra vez?
Dependiente —No sé. Tenía barba y bigote... Si se afeitara, no sé si lo reconocería.
Agente Montero —¿Cuánto medía, más o menos? ¿Era como de mi estatura?
Dependiente —No, mucho más alto y más grande. Medía como seis pies y dos pulgadas, y pesaba unas doscientas cincuenta libras.
Agente Montero —¿Cómo estaba vestido?
Dependiente —A ver si recuerdo... Pantalón gris oscuro, camisa azul y una chaqueta de pana café.

Agente Montero —Ud. le dio todo el dinero. ¿Qué pasó después?
Dependiente —Traté de seguirlo, pero me apuntó con la pistola y me dijo que me quedara donde estaba.
Agente Montero —¿Puede describir la pistola?
Dependiente —Una pistola semiautomática, calibre treinta y dos, posiblemente.

Las once y media:
El agente Montero sospecha que hay drogas en el maletero de un carro. Ahora está hablando con la dueña.

Agente Montero —No tengo permiso del juez para registrar su carro, pero me gustaría ver lo que Ud. tiene en el maletero. ¿Quiere darme la llave?
Mujer —Hay un gato y una llanta en el maletero...
Agente Montero —¿Me da Ud. permiso para registrarlo? No la estoy amenazando ni le estoy prometiendo nada. Si Ud. me da permiso, tiene que ser voluntariamente.
Mujer —Consiga una orden del juez si quiere registrar mi carro.

Las dos y media de la tarde:
El agente Montero arresta a un hombre que atacó a una mujer y trató de robarle la cartera.

Agente Montero —Póngase las manos sobre la cabeza y entrelace los dedos. Dese vuelta.
Hombre —¡Hijo de mala madre!
Agente Montero —¡Cállese! Camine hacia el carro patrullero. Súbase. ¡Cuidado con la cabeza...!

Las cuatro y media de la tarde:
El agente Montero ve un grupo de personas que están gritando obscenidades y amenazas frente a un consulado y les ordena dispersarse.

Agente Montero —Soy el agente Montero, de la Policía. Esta reunión queda declarada ilegal y, por lo tanto, les ordeno que se dispersen inmediatamente.

La multitud empieza a dispersarse y algunos murmuran obscenidades.

¡Escuchemos!

While listening to the dialogue, circle **V (verdadero)** if the statement is true and **F (falso)** if it is false.

1.	Hubo un robo en un mercado de la ciudad de Albuquerque.	V	F
2.	Un hombre vino y pidió una botella de vino.	V	F
3.	El hombre se llevó la botella de vino sin pagar.	V	F
4.	La víctima no podría reconocer al ladrón si se afeitara.	V	F

© 2017 Cengage Learning

5. El ladrón era mucho más alto que el agente. V F
6. La víctima no trató de seguir al ladrón. V F
7. El agente Montero tiene permiso del juez para registrar el carro. V F
8. El agente Montero está amenazando a la mujer. V F
9. El hombre debe ponerse las manos sobre la cabeza y entrelazar los dedos. V F
10. La reunión era legal y no tuvieron que dispersarse. V F

VOCABULARIO

Cognados

el calibre
el consulado
la obscenidad
semiautomático(a)
voluntariamente

Nombres

la amenaza *threat*
la caja *cash register*
la chaqueta, la chamarra (*Méx.*) *jacket*
la cerveza *beer*
el (la) dependiente(a) *clerk*
la embajada *embassy*
la estatura *height*
el gato, la gata (*Costa Rica*) *jack*
la libra *pound*
el licor *liquor, spirits*
la llanta, la goma (*Cuba*), **el neumático** *tire*
el maletero, la cajuela (*Méx.*), **el baúl** (*Puerto Rico*) *trunk* (*of a car*)
el mercado *market*
la multitud *crowd*
la pana *corduroy*
el permiso *warrant, permission*
la reunión, la congregación, el mitin *meeting, assembly*
el vino *wine*

Verbos

afeitarse *to shave*
apuntar *to point, to aim* (*a gun*)
dispersarse *to disperse*
entrelazar *to intertwine*
murmurar *to murmur*
ordenar *to order*
pesar *to weigh*
prometer *to promise*

Adjetivos

gris *gray*
liviano(a) *light*
pesado(a) *heavy*

Otras palabras y expresiones

¡Cállese! *Be quiet! Shut up!*
¡Cuidado! *Careful!*
Dese vuelta., Voltéese., Vírese. (*Cuba*) *Turn around.*
por lo tanto *therefore, so*
queda declarado(a) ilegal *is hereby declared illegal*
sobre *on, on top of*

© 2017 Cengage Learning

Nombre ______________________ Sección ____________ Fecha ____________

VOCABULARIO ADICIONAL

Mandatos útiles (*Useful commands*)

¡Acuéstese en el suelo, boca abajo! *Lie down on the floor (ground), face down!*
¡Agáchese! *Bend down!*
¡Aléjese de la ventana! *Get away from the window!*
¡Bájese de allí! *Get down from there!*
¡Levante los brazos! *Lift your arms!*
¡Llame al perro! *Call off the dog!*
¡No dispare! ¡No tire! *Don't shoot!*
¡No salte! *Don't jump!*
¡No se mueva! *Don't move!*
¡Ponga las manos detrás de la espalda! *Put your hands behind your back!*
¡Póngase de rodillas! *Get on your knees!*
¡Salga con las manos en (sobre) la cabeza! *Come out with your hands on top of your head!*
¡Sáquese las manos de los bolsillos! *Take your hands out of your pockets!*
¡Separe los pies! *Spread your feet!*
¡Siga caminando! *Keep walking!*
¡Suelte el arma! *Drop the gun (weapon)!*
¡Suéltelo(la)! *Let go of him (her)!*

Until recently in most Latin American cities, people could walk the streets late at night without running the risk of being assaulted or mugged. Holdups were almost unheard of, and there were few incidents like the one described in this lesson. That is not the case today. Some areas in big Latin American cities have reputations for being rough. Travelers are often warned about increasing crime in most cities.

ACTIVIDADES

Dígame... Answer the following questions, basing your answers on the dialogues.

1. ¿Qué pasó a eso de las nueve y media en el mercado?

____

2. ¿Qué hizo el hombre después de apuntarle al dependiente con una pistola?

____

3. ¿Cómo era el hombre?

____

© 2017 Cengage Learning

Nombre ______________________ Sección ____________ Fecha ____________

4. ¿Qué ropa tenía puesta?

____

5. ¿Qué hizo el hombre cuando el dependiente trató de seguirlo?

____

6. ¿Qué clase de pistola tenía el hombre?

____

7. El agente Montero sospecha que hay drogas en el maletero de un carro. ¿Por qué no le ordena a la dueña que lo abra?

____

8. ¿Le da la mujer permiso al agente Montero para que abra el maletero y lo registre?

____

9. El agente Montero arresta a un hombre. ¿Por qué?

____

10. ¿Qué le ordena el agente Montero al hombre?

____

11. ¿Qué está haciendo la gente que está frente a un consulado?

____

12. ¿Qué les ordena el agente Montero?

____

Hablemos Interview a classmate, using the following questions. When you have finished, switch roles.

1. Si yo le apuntara con una pistola y le pidiera su dinero, ¿me lo daría?
2. José tiene barba y bigote. Si se afeitara, ¿lo reconocería Ud.?
3. Juana mide cinco pies, nueve pulgadas. ¿Cómo es de estatura?
4. ¿Qué ropa tenía Ud. puesta ayer por la tarde?
5. ¿Qué tiene Ud. en el maletero de su coche?
6. ¿Ayer tomó licor u otra bebida alcohólica?
7. Yo no tengo permiso del juez para registrar su casa. ¿Me da Ud. permiso voluntariamente?

© 2017 Cengage Learning

Nombre ______________________ Sección ____________ Fecha ____________

Quiz

Vamos a practicar

A Rewrite each of the following sentences, using the cue given and the appropriate verb tense.

Modelo Es importante que Ud. hable con él.
Era importante **que Ud. *hablara* con él.**

1. Es importante que el agente tenga permiso del juez.
   Era importante ______________________.
2. Quiero que Ud. abra el maletero.
   Quería ______________________.
3. Les digo que me den la llave.
   Les diría ______________________.
4. La mujer no cree que el gato esté en el maletero.
   La mujer no creía ______________________.
5. Les ordeno que se dispersen.
   Les ordenaría ______________________.
6. Ella duda que él ataque a las mujeres.
   Ella dudaba ______________________.
7. La agente nos dice que pongamos las manos en la cabeza.
   La agente nos dijo ______________________.
8. ¡Te digo que vayas a la embajada!
   ¡Te dije ______________________!
9. Es posible que tenga una pistola semiautomática.
   Era posible ______________________.
10. El agente quiere que el dependiente le diga la verdad.
    El agente quería ______________________.

B Answer the following questions, using **si** and the appropriate verb forms.

Modelo ¿Por qué no compras ese carro? (tener dinero)
Si *tuviera* dinero, lo *compraría*.

1. ¿Por qué no me cuentas lo que pasó? (saberlo)

   ____

© 2017 Cengage Learning

2. ¿Por qué no le dices qué ropa tenía puesta? (recordarlo)

____

3. ¿Por qué no lo levantas? (ser liviano)

____

4. ¿Por qué no registra el maletero? (tener permiso del juez)

____

5. ¿Por qué no les ordenas que se dispersen? (hacer algo ilegal)

____

C Change the following commands into statements, using **si** and the expressions in parentheses.

MODELO Venga a verme. (tener tiempo, señor)
Si *tengo* tiempo, *vendré* a verlo, señor.

1. Arreste a este hombre. (hacer algo ilegal, señora)

____

2. Registre el coche. (Ud. darme la llave, señorita)

____

3. Dígale que venga. (verla, señor)

____

4. Quédese aquí. (poder hacerlo, señor)

____

5. Traiga a los niños. (tener el carro, señora)

____

Conversaciones breves

Complete the following dialogue, using your imagination and the vocabulary from this lesson.

El agente Ríos investiga un robo.

Agente Ríos —____

Dependiente —Bueno... no recuerdo mucho... un hombre entró y me apuntó con una pistola...

© 2017 Cengage Learning

Nombre ______________________ **Sección** ____________ **Fecha** ____________

Agente Ríos —______________________

Dependiente —Me dijo que le diera todo el dinero de la caja.

Agente Ríos —______________________

Dependiente —No sé cuánto medía.

Agente Ríos —______________________

Dependiente —No, no era tan alto como Ud... y era muy delgado.

Agente Ríos —______________________

Dependiente —Yo creo que pesaba unas ciento treinta libras...

Agente Ríos —______________________

Dependiente —Tenía pantalón blanco y camisa azul... y sombrero.

Agente Ríos —______________________

Dependiente —No, yo no entiendo nada de armas.

Agente Ríos —______________________

Dependiente —Sí, vi el carro que manejaba. Era un Ford Escort azul.

Agente Ríos —______________________

Dependiente —No, no sé el número de la chapa, pero era de otro estado.

En estas situaciones

With a partner, act out the following situations in Spanish.

1. You are investigating the armed robbery of a food store. Ask the employee to tell you exactly what happened and to describe the robber and his/her weapon. Then ask the employee if he/she would recognize the robber if he/she came into the store again.
2. You want to search somebody's car, but you don't have a warrant. Ask the owner's permission to search it. Make sure the owner knows that you are not threatening him/her.
3. You are arresting a suspect. Tell the person to do the following: "Put your hands on your head. Turn around. Be quiet. Get into the patrol car."
4. You are trying to disperse an unruly crowd. Tell them who you are and order them to disperse immediately.

Casos

With you and a partner playing the roles, work through the following scenarios.

1. You are an officer questioning a shopkeeper whose store was just robbed.
2. You are an officer trying to convince someone to let you search his/her car without a warrant.
3. You are an officer arresting a belligerent suspect.

© 2017 Cengage Learning

Nombre ______________________ Sección ____________ Fecha ____________

Un paso más Review the **Vocabulario adicional** in this lesson and respond to each of the following situations with an appropriate command.

1. You are going to handcuff a prisoner.

 ____

2. Someone is near a window, and this might prove dangerous.

 ____

3. Someone is going to jump off a roof.

 ____

4. You want a suspect to drop his gun.

 ____

5. You want a suspect to walk to the police car, but she stops.

 ____

6. You want to stop someone from shooting.

 ____

7. A suspect has his hands in his pockets.

 ____

8. Someone's dog is running toward you with every intention of biting you.

 ____

9. You want a suspect to lift his arms.

 ____

10. Someone is holding a screaming girl, and you want him to let go of her.

 ____

11. You need to instruct someone to bend over.

 ____

12. You have to tell someone to lie on the floor, face down.

 ____

© 2017 Cengage Learning

13. You are pointing a gun at a suspect. You don't want her to make any sudden moves.

____

14. You want a suspect to get on his knees.

____

15. You want someone to spread his feet.

____

16. Someone has climbed on a roof, and you want her down.

____

17. There is a suspect inside a house, but he is ready to give himself up.

____

© 2017 Cengage Learning

LECTURA 4

EN CASOS DE AGRESIÓN SEXUAL

EN CASOS DE AGRESIÓN SEXUAL

Read the following information from a pamphlet about sexual abuse. Try to guess the meaning of all cognates. Then, do the exercise item on the next page.

EN CASOS DE AGRESIÓN[1] SEXUAL

La violación y el abuso sexual

La violación es un delito en que la víctima es dominada por el uso de la fuerza[2] o la amenaza[3].

- Una de cada cuatro mujeres y uno de cada seis hombres serán víctimas de una agresión sexual durante su vida.
- Cualquier persona puede ser culpable[4] de una agresión sexual: vecinos, compañeros, miembros de la familia, desconocidos[5] o buenos amigos. En más del 50% de los casos, la víctima conoce al agresor.
- La violación es un acto violento en que una persona usa el sexo para humillar y controlar a otra. Es una experiencia violenta, aterrorizadora y brutal.

Si Ud. es víctima de una violación o de otro abuso sexual

1. Recuerde que Ud. no tiene la culpa[6].
2. Vaya a un lugar seguro[7].
3. Busque el apoyo[8] de su familia o de sus amigos o llame a un centro de ayuda para víctimas de violación.
4. Reciba atención médica.
5. Llame a la policía y recuerde que si se ducha[9] o se baña[10] puede destruir evidencia importante.
6. Considere la posibilidad de usar los servicios de un consejero profesional.

¡Recuerde!

Decidir qué hacer después de una agresión sexual es muy difícil. Es normal sentirse confuso. El centro de ayuda para víctimas de violación puede ofrecerle información y apoyo. Los consejeros están a su disposición.

© Cengage Learning

[1]*assault* [2]*force* [3]*threat* [4]*guilty* [5]*strangers* [6]*blame* [7]*safe* [8]*support* [9]**se...** *shower* [10]**se...** *bathe*

© 2017 Cengage Learning

Nombre ______________________ Sección ______________ Fecha ______________

Using the information from the pamphlet, decide what you would say to the following people.

1. Leonardo thinks that, since he is not a girl, he never has to worry about being sexually abused.

____

____

____

2. Liliana thinks that she only has to worry about strangers, but that she is safe with friends, classmates, and acquaintances.

____

____

____

3. Marta was sexually abused, and you are trying to give her some advice about what to do next.

____

____

____

© 2017 Cengage Learning

Nombre ________________ Sección ________ Fecha ________

REPASO

Práctica de vocabulario

A Circle the word or phrase that does not belong in each group.

1. llanta maletero neumático
2. calmante sedante cocina
3. baño descompuesto desperfecto
4. anteojos faros lentes
5. cuchillo bigote barba
6. gritar llorar bañarse
7. pelado sucio calvo
8. anillo blusa sortija
9. cruz cartera bolsa
10. gente mejilla cachete
11. lunar cicatriz arete
12. calmarse escaparse fugarse
13. billetera celda cartera
14. cambiarse de ropa quitarse moverse
15. reloj voluntad cadena
16. sugerir temer aconsejar

B Circle the word or phrase that best completes each sentence.

1. Todas sus pertenencias serán puestas en un (bono / cuello / sobre) sellado.
2. Lo voy a (retratar / vaciar / mirar) porque necesito su fotografía.
3. Ponga todas sus cosas en el (mostrador / centavo / oro).

© 2017 Cengage Learning

Nombre ______________________ Sección ____________ Fecha ____________

4. Es una enfermedad (gris / metida / venérea).
5. Voy a tomarle (la fiscal / el homicidio / las huellas digitales).
6. Su esposa ha sido víctima de (un secuestro / un detalle / una falda).
7. Ponga (las manos / los pies / la cabeza) en la pared.
8. Había (pelo / olor / violación) a gas.
9. Entrelace (la multitud / los dedos / las cajas).
10. Por favor, lea el dorso de (este detenido / esta papeleta / este mercado).
11. Tengo que hacerlo arreglar porque está (listo / prendido / descompuesto).
12. El hombre me (ayudó / afeitó / amenazó) con un revólver.
13. Me caí porque ella me (murmuró / empujó / contó).
14. Tenía (una edad / una cicatriz / una amenaza) en la boca.
15. Ella no tiene (cordones / antecedentes / dependientes) penales.
16. Mi casa no está (cerca / lejos / sellada). Está a una cuadra de aquí.

C Match the questions in column **A** with the answers in column **B.**

A	B
1. ________ ¿Qué van a hacer con él ahora?	a. Sí, acaba de llegar.
2. ________ ¿Le pusieron una fianza muy alta?	b. Sí, por lo menos cien dólares.
3. ________ ¿Ud. va a comprar el bono?	c. Una chaqueta de pana y un suéter negro.
4. ________ ¿Está el Sr. Bravo?	d. No, era una extraña.
5. ________ ¿Necesitas dinero?	e. No, mi familia.
6. ________ ¿A quiénes llamaste?	f. Sí, histéricamente.
7. ________ ¿Qué ropa tenía puesta?	g. Blanco.
8. ________ ¿De qué raza es?	h. Lo pondrán en libertad bajo palabra.
9. ________ ¿Lloraba?	i. Era como de mi estatura.
10. ________ ¿La conocías?	j. Mañana, sin falta.
11. ________ ¿Cuándo arreglarán el horno?	k. A los Sres. Ruiz.
12. ________ ¿Cuánto medía?	l. Sí, y no pudo pagarla.

© 2017 Cengage Learning

Nombre ______________________ Sección ____________ Fecha ____________

D Crucigrama

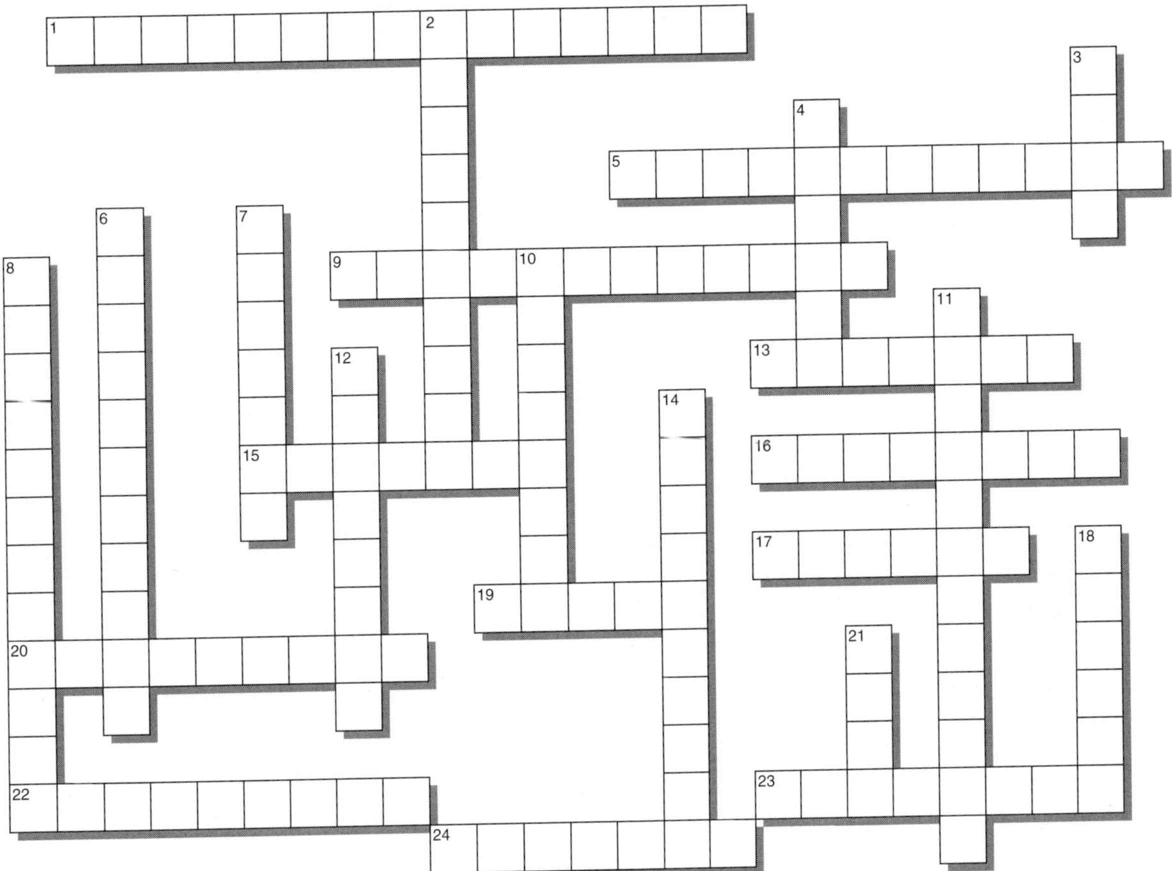

Horizontales

1. sin obligación
5. normalmente
9. Ella no tiene __________ penales.
13. bolsa
15. Tengo su dirección en mi __________.
16. En México lo llaman cajuela.
17. Tomó __________ para suicidarse.
19. Lo necesito para saber la hora.
20. dar autorización
22. fichar
23. chaqueta, en México
24. No hable.

Verticales

2. que tiene importancia
3. Lo necesito para cambiar una llanta.
4. *test,* en español
6. El coche tiene un __________. Tengo que hacerlo arreglar.
7. Quiero comprar una __________ de vino.
8. persona que investiga (*m.*)
10. sedativo
11. *belongings,* en español
12. Está en __________ bajo fianza.
14. anteojos, en Cuba
18. *arrow,* en español
21. Él __________ 180 libras.

© 2017 Cengage Learning

Nombre ______________________ Sección ____________ Fecha ____________

Práctica oral Listen to the following exercise on the audio program. The speaker will ask you some questions. Answer the questions, using the cues provided. The speaker will confirm the correct answer. Repeat the correct answer.

1. ¿Qué tiene Ud. en los bolsillos? (la billetera y un peine)
2. ¿Cuánto dinero tiene Ud. en la cartera? (45 dólares)
3. ¿Se quita Ud. las gafas antes de bañarse? (sí)
4. ¿Tiene todas sus pertenencias con Ud.? (no)
5. ¿Qué lleva Ud. puesto en este momento? (una chaqueta de pana)
6. ¿Necesita Ud. cambiarse de ropa ahora? (no)
7. ¿Qué joya tiene Ud. puesta? (una cadena de oro)
8. ¿Usa Ud. anteojos? (no)
9. ¿Dónde tiene Ud. su libreta de direcciones? (en el bolsillo)
10. ¿De qué calibre es su pistola? (calibre 32)
11. ¿Qué tiene Ud. en el maletero de su carro? (un gato)
12. ¿Ud. necesita hacer arreglar su carro? (sí)
13. ¿Tiene muchos desperfectos su carro? (no)
14. ¿Qué tiene que conseguir Ud. para registrar un carro? (un permiso del juez)
15. Si Ud. viera un grupo de personas gritando obscenidades, ¿qué les ordenaría que hicieran? (dispersarse inmediatamente)
16. ¿Cuándo fue la última vez que Ud. retrató a alguien? (ayer)
17. ¿Le está a Ud. permitido recomendar fiadores? (no)
18. ¿Dónde vivía Ud. cuando era adolescente? (en California)
19. Cuando Ud. era adolescente, ¿se escapó alguna vez de su casa? (no, nunca)
20. Si Ud. viera a un compañero de clase de la escuela, ¿podría reconocerlo? (sí)
21. ¿Le han tomado a Ud. las huellas digitales? (sí)
22. ¿Le han hecho a Ud. alguna prueba este año? (no)
23. ¿Prefiere Ud. defenderse con un cuchillo o con una pistola? (con una pistola)
24. ¿Tiene Ud. una fotografía reciente de sus padres? (no)
25. ¿Tiene Ud. alguna marca visible? (sí, un lunar en la mejilla)

© 2017 Cengage Learning

Introduction to Spanish Sounds and the Alphabet

Sections marked with an audio icon are available on the iLrn that accompanies this text. Repeat each Spanish word after the speaker, imitating as closely as possible the correct pronunciation.

The Alphabet

Letter	Name	Letter	Name	Letter	Name	Letter	Name
a	a	h	hache	ñ	eñe	t	te
b	be (larga)	i	i	o	o	u	u
c	ce	j	jota	p	pe	v	ve, uve
d	de	k	ka	q	cu	w	doble ve, doble uve
e	e	l	ele	r	ere, erre	x	equis
f	efe	m	eme			y	i griega, ye
g	ge	n	ene	s	ese	z	zeta

The Vowels

1. The Spanish **a** has a sound similar to the English *a* in the word *father.* Repeat:

Ana casa banana mala dama mata

2. The Spanish **e** is pronounced like the English *e* in the word *eight.* Repeat:

este René teme deme entre bebe

3. The Spanish **i** is pronounced like the English *ee* in the word *see.* Repeat:

sí difícil Mimí ir dividir Fifí

4. The Spanish **o** is similar to the English *o* in the word *no,* but without the glide. Repeat:

solo poco como toco con monólogo

5. The Spanish **u** is similar to the English *ue* sound in the word *Sue.* Repeat:

Lulú un su universo murciélago

© 2017 Cengage Learning

THE CONSONANTS

1. The Spanish **p** is pronounced like the English *p* in the word *spot.* Repeat:

pan papá Pepe pila poco pude

2. The Spanish **c** in front of **a, o, u, l,** or **r** sounds similar to the English *k.* Repeat:

casa como cuna clima crimen cromo

3. The Spanish **q** is only used in the combinations **que** and **qui,** in which the **u** is silent, and also has a sound similar to the English *k.* Repeat:

que queso Quique quinto quema quiso

4. The Spanish **t** is pronounced like the English *t* in the word *stop.* Repeat:

toma mata tela tipo atún Tito

5. The Spanish **d** at the beginning of an utterance or after **n** or **l** sounds somewhat similar to the English *d* in the word *David.* Repeat:

día dedo duelo anda Aldo

In all other positions, the **d** has a sound similar to the English *th* in the word *they.* Repeat:

medida todo nada Ana dice Eva duda

6. The Spanish **g** also has two sounds. At the beginning of an utterance and in all other positions, except before **e** or **i,** the Spanish **g** sounds similar to the English *g* in the word *sugar.* Repeat:

goma gato tengo lago algo aguja

In the combinations **gue** and **gui,** the **u** is silent. Repeat:

guerra guineo guiso ligue la guía

7. The Spanish **j,** and **g** before **e** or **i,** sounds similar to the English *h* in the word *home.* Repeat:

jamás juego jota Julio gente Genaro gime

8. The Spanish **b** and **v** have no difference in sound. Both are pronounced alike. At the beginning of the utterance or after **m** or **n,** they sound similar to the English *b* in the word *obey.* Repeat:

Beto vaga bote vela también un vaso

Between vowels, they are pronounced with the lips barely closed. Repeat:

sábado yo voy sabe Ávalos Eso vale

9. In most Spanish-speaking countries, the **y** and the **ll** are similar to the English *y* in the word *yet.* Repeat:

yo llama yema lleno ya lluvia llega

© 2017 Cengage Learning

10. The Spanish **r** is pronounced like the English *tt* in the word *gutter.* Repeat:

cara	pero	arena	carie	Laredo	Aruba

The Spanish **r** in an initial position and after **l, n,** or **s,** and **rr** in the middle of a word are pronounced with a strong trill. Repeat:

Rita	Rosa	torre	ruina	Enrique	Israel
perro	parra	rubio	alrededor	derrama	

11. The Spanish **s** sound is represented in most of the Spanish-speaking world by the letters **s, z,** and **c** before **e** or **i.** The sound is very similar to the English sibilant *s* in the word *sink.* Repeat:

sale	sitio	solo	seda	suelo
zapato	cerveza	ciudad	cena	

In most of Spain, the **z,** and **c** before **e** or **i,** is pronounced like the English *th* in the word *think.* Repeat:

zarzuela	cielo	docena

12. The letter **h** is silent in Spanish except when it's preceded by **c** to form the phoneme **ch**. Repeat:

hilo	Hugo	ahora	Hilda	almohada	hermano

13. The Spanish **ch** is pronounced like the English *ch* in the word *chief.* Repeat:

muchacho	chico	coche	chueco	chaparro

14. The Spanish **f** is identical in sound to the English *f.* Repeat:

famoso	feo	difícil	fuego	foto

15. The Spanish **l** is pronounced like the English *l* in the word *lean* except in the combination ***ll*** (see item **9**). Repeat:

dolor	ángel	fácil	sueldo	salgo	chaval

16. The Spanish **m** is pronounced like the English *m* in the word *mother.* Repeat:

mamá	moda	multa	médico	mima

17. In most cases, the Spanish **n** has a sound similar to the English *n.* Repeat:

nada	norte	nunca	entra	nene

The sound of the Spanish **n** is often affected by the sounds that occur around it. When it appears before **b, v,** or **p,** it is pronounced like the English *m.* Repeat:

invierno	tan bueno	un vaso	un bebé	un perro

18. The Spanish **ñ (eñe)** has a sound similar to the English *ny* in the word *canyon.* Repeat:

muñeca	leña	año	señorita	piña	señor

© 2017 Cengage Learning

19. The Spanish **x** has two pronunciations, depending on its position. Between vowels, the sound is similar to the English *ks*. Repeat:

examen   boxeo   exigente   éxito

Before a consonant, the Spanish **x** sounds like the English *s*. Repeat:

expreso   excusa   exquisito   extraño

Linking

In spoken Spanish, the various words in a phrase or sentence are not pronounced as isolated elements, but they are combined. This is called *linking*.

1. The final consonant of a word is pronounced together with the initial vowel of the following word. Repeat:

   Carlos‿anda   un‿ángel   el‿otoño   unos‿estudiantes

2. The final vowel of a word is pronounced together with the initial vowel of the following word. Repeat:
   su‿esposo   la‿hermana   ardua‿empresa   la‿invita

3. When the final vowel of a word and the initial vowel of the following word are identical, they are pronounced slightly longer than one vowel. Repeat:
   Ana‿alcanza   me‿espera   mi‿hijo   lo‿olvida

   The same rule applies when two identical vowels appear within a word. Repeat:
   cooperación   crees   leemos   coordinación

4. When the final consonant of a word and the initial consonant of the following word are the same, they are pronounced as one consonant with slightly longer-than-normal duration. Repeat:

   el‿lado   un‿novio   Carlos‿salta   tienes‿sed   al‿leer

Rhythm

Rhythm is the variation of sound intensity that we usually associate with music. Spanish and English each regulate these variations in speech differently, because they have different patterns of syllable length. In Spanish the length of the stressed and unstressed syllables remains almost the same, while in English stressed syllables are considerably longer than unstressed ones. Pronounce the following Spanish words, enunciating each syllable clearly.

es-tu-dian-te	bue-no	Úr-su-la
com-po-si-ción	di-fí-cil	ki-ló-me-tro
po-li-cí-a	Pa-ra-guay	

© 2017 Cengage Learning

Because the length of the Spanish syllables remains constant, the greater the number of syllables in a given word or phrase, the longer the phrase will be.

Intonation

Intonation is the rise and fall of pitch in the delivery of a phrase or a sentence. In general, Spanish pitch tends to change less than English, giving the impression that the language is less emphatic.

As a rule, the intonation for normal statements in Spanish starts in a low tone, raises to a higher one on the first stressed syllable, maintains that tone until the last stressed syllable, and then goes back to the initial low tone, with still another drop at the very end.

Tu amigo viene mañana. José come pan.
Ada está en casa. Carlos toma café.

Syllable Formation in Spanish

General rules for dividing words into syllables are as follows.

Vowels

1. A vowel or a vowel combination can constitute a syllable.

   a-lum-no a-bue-la Eu-ro-pa

2. Diphthongs and triphthongs are considered single vowels and cannot be divided.

   bai-le puen-te Dia-na es-tu-diáis an-ti-guo

3. Two strong vowels **(a, e, o)** do not form a diphthong and are separated into two syllables.

   em-ple-ar vol-te-ar lo-a

4. A written accent on a weak vowel **(i** or **u)** breaks the diphthong, thus the vowels are separated into two syllables.

   trí-o dú-o Ma-rí-a

Consonants

1. A single consonant forms a syllable with the vowel that follows it.

   po-der ma-no mi-nu-to

   NOTE: **rr** is considered a single consonant: **pe-rro.**

2. When two consonants appear between two vowels, they are separated into two syllables.
   al-fa-be-to cam-pe-ón me-ter-se mo-les-tia

   EXCEPTION: When a consonant cluster composed of **b, c, d, f, g, p,** or **t** with **l** or **r** appears between two vowels, the cluster joins the following vowel: **so-bre, o-tros, ca-ble, te-lé-gra-fo.**

© 2017 Cengage Learning

3. When three consonants appear between two vowels, only the last one goes with following vowel.

ins-pec-tor trans-por-te trans-for-mar

EXCEPTION: When there is a cluster of three consonants in the combinations described in rule 2, the first consonant joins the preceding vowel, and the cluster joins the following vowel: **es-cri-bir, ex-tran-je-ro, im-plo-rar, es-tre-cho.**

Accentuation

In Spanish, all words are stressed according to specific rules. Words that do not follow the rules must have a written accent to indicate the change of stress. The basic rules for accentuation are as follows.

1. Words ending in a vowel, **n,** or **s** are stressed on the next-to-the-last syllable.

hi-jo	**ca**-lle	**me**-sa	fa-**mo**-sos
flo-**re**-cen	**pla**-ya	**ve**-ces	

2. Words ending in a consonant, except **n** or **s,** are stressed on the last syllable.

ma-**yor** a-**mor** tro-pi-**cal** na-**riz** re-**loj** co-rre-**dor**

3. All words that do not follow these rules must have the written accent.

ca-**fé**	**lá**-piz	**mú**-si-ca	sa-**lón**
án-gel	**lí**-qui-do	fran-**cés**	**Víc**-tor
sim-**pá**-ti-co	rin-**cón**	a-**zú**-car	**dár**-se-lo
sa-**lió**	**dé**-bil	e-**xá**-me-nes	**dí**-me-lo

4. Pronouns and adverbs of interrogation and exclamation have a written accent to distinguish them from relative pronouns.

—¿**Qué** comes? *"What are you eating?"*
—La pera que él no comió. *"The pear that he did not eat."*

—¿**Quién** está ahí? *"Who is there?"*
—El hombre a quien tú llamaste. *"The man whom you called."*

—¿**Dónde** está? *"Where is he?"*
—En el lugar donde trabaja. *"At the place where he works."*

5. Words that have the same spelling but different meanings take a written accent to differentiate one from the other.

el	*the*	**él**	*he, him*	**te**	*you*	**té**	*tea*
mi	*my*	**mí**	*me*	**si**	*if*	**sí**	*yes*
tu	*your*	**tú**	*you*	**mas**	*but*	**más**	*more*

© 2017 Cengage Learning

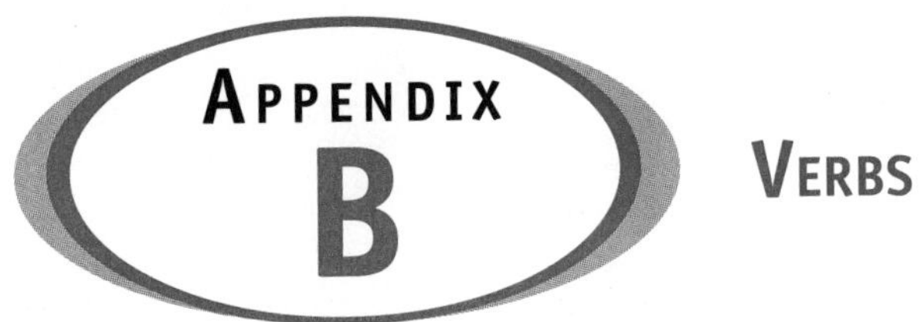

Verbs

Regular Verbs

Model -ar, -er, -ir *verbs*

	INFINITIVE	
amar (*to love*)	**comer** (*to eat*)	**vivir** (*to live*)
	GERUND	
amando (*loving*)	**comiendo** (*eating*)	**viviendo** (*living*)
	PAST PARTICIPLE	
amado (*loved*)	**comido** (*eaten*)	**vivido** (*lived*)

SIMPLE TENSES	*Indicative Mood*	
	PRESENT	
(*I love*)	(*I eat*)	(*I live*)
am**o**	com**o**	viv**o**
am**as**	com**es**	viv**es**
am**a**	com**e**	viv**e**
am**amos**	com**emos**	viv**imos**
am**áis**[1]	com**éis**	viv**ís**
am**an**	com**en**	viv**en**
	IMPERFECT	
(*I used to love*)	(*I used to eat*)	(*I used to live*)
am**aba**	com**ía**	viv**ía**
am**abas**	com**ías**	viv**ías**
am**aba**	com**ía**	viv**ía**
am**ábamos**	com**íamos**	viv**íamos**
am**abais**	com**íais**	viv**íais**
am**aban**	com**ían**	viv**ían**

[1]**Vosotros amáis:** The **vosotros** form of the verb is used primarily in Spain. This form has not been used in this text.

© 2017 Cengage Learning

	PRETERIT	
(*I loved*)	(*I ate*)	(*I lived*)
am**é**	com**í**	viv**í**
am**aste**	com**iste**	viv**iste**
am**ó**	com**ió**	viv**ió**
am**amos**	com**imos**	viv**imos**
am**asteis**	com**isteis**	viv**isteis**
am**aron**	com**ieron**	viv**ieron**

	FUTURE	
(*I will love*)	(*I will eat*)	(*I will live*)
amar**é**	comer**é**	vivir**é**
amar**ás**	comer**ás**	vivir**ás**
amar**á**	comer**á**	vivir**á**
amar**emos**	comer**emos**	vivir**emos**
amar**éis**	comer**éis**	vivir**éis**
amar**án**	comer**án**	vivir**án**

	CONDITIONAL	
(*I would love*)	(*I would eat*)	(*I would live*)
amar**ía**	comer**ía**	vivir**ía**
amar**ías**	comer**ías**	vivir**ías**
amar**ía**	comer**ía**	vivir**ía**
amar**íamos**	comer**íamos**	vivir**íamos**
amar**íais**	comer**íais**	vivir**íais**
amar**ían**	comer**ían**	vivir**ían**

Subjunctive Mood

	PRESENT	
([*that*] *I* [*may*] *love*)	([*that*] *I* [*may*] *eat*)	([*that*] *I* [*may*] *live*)
am**e**	com**a**	viv**a**
am**es**	com**as**	viv**as**
am**e**	com**a**	viv**a**
am**emos**	com**amos**	viv**amos**
am**éis**	com**áis**	viv**áis**
am**en**	com**an**	viv**an**

© 2017 Cengage Learning

	IMPERFECT (two forms: **-ra**, **-se**)	
([*that*] *I* [*might*] *love*)	([*that*] *I* [*might*] *eat*)	([*that*] *I* [*might*] *live*)
am**ara(-ase)**	com**iera(-iese)**	viv**iera(-iese)**
am**aras(-ases)**	com**ieras(-ieses)**	viv**ieras(-ieses)**
am**ara(-ase)**	com**iera(-iese)**	viv**iera(-iese)**
am**áramos (-ásemos)**	com**iéramos (-iésemos)**	viv**iéramos (-iésemos)**
am**arais(-aseis)**	com**ierais(-ieseis)**	viv**ierais(-ieseis)**
am**aran(-asen)**	com**ieran(-iesen)**	viv**ieran(-iesen)**

Imperative Mood (Command Forms)

(*love*)	(*eat*)	(*live*)
am**a** (tú)	com**e** (tú)	viv**e** (tú)
am**e** (Ud.)	com**a** (Ud.)	viv**a** (Ud.)
am**emos** (nosotros)	com**amos** (nosotros)	viv**amos** (nosotros)
am**ad** (vosotros)	com**ed** (vosotros)	viv**id** (vosotros)
am**en** (Uds.)	com**an** (Uds.)	viv**an** (Uds.)

COMPOUND TENSES

	PERFECT INFINITIVE	
haber amado	**haber comido**	**haber vivido**

	PERFECT PARTICIPLE	
habiendo amado	**habiendo comido**	**habiendo vivido**

Indicative Mood

	PRESENT PERFECT	
(*I have loved*)	(*I have eaten*)	(*I have lived*)
he amado	he comido	he vivido
has amado	has comido	has vivido
ha amado	ha comido	ha vivido
hemos amado	hemos comido	hemos vivido
habéis amado	habéis comido	habéis vivido
han amado	han comido	han vivido

© 2017 Cengage Learning

	PLUPERFECT	
(*I had loved*)	(*I had eaten*)	(*I had lived*)
había amado	había comido	había vivido
habías amado	habías comido	habías vivido
había amado	había comido	había vivido
habíamos amado	habíamos comido	habíamos vivido
habíais amado	habíais comido	habíais vivido
habían amado	habían comido	habían vivido

	FUTURE PERFECT	
(*I will have loved*)	(*I will have eaten*)	(*I will have lived*)
habré amado	habré comido	habré vivido
habrás amado	habrás comido	habrás vivido
habrá amado	habrá comido	habrá vivido
habremos amado	habremos comido	habremos vivido
habréis amado	habréis comido	habréis vivido
habrán amado	habrán comido	habrán vivido

	CONDITIONAL PERFECT	
(*I would have loved*)	(*I would have eaten*)	(*I would have lived*)
habría amado	habría comido	habría vivido
habrías amado	habrías comido	habrías vivido
habría amado	habría comido	habría vivido
habríamos amado	habríamos comido	habríamos vivido
habríais amado	habríais comido	habríais vivido
habrían amado	habrían comido	habrían vivido

Subjunctive Mood

	PRESENT PERFECT	
([*that*] *I* [*may*] *have loved*)	([*that*] *I* [*may*] *have eaten*)	([*that*] *I* [*may*] *have lived*)
haya amado	haya comido	haya vivido
hayas amado	hayas comido	hayas vivido
haya amado	haya comido	haya vivido
hayamos amado	hayamos comido	hayamos vivido
hayáis amado	hayáis comido	hayáis vivido
hayan amado	hayan comido	hayan vivido

© 2017 Cengage Learning

	PLUPERFECT (two forms: **-ra, -se**)	
([*that*] *I* [*might*] *have loved*)	([*that*] *I* [*might*] *have eaten*)	([*that*] *I* [*might*] *have lived*)
hubiera(-iese) amado	hubiera(-iese) comido	hubiera(-iese) vivido
hubieras(-ieses) amado	hubieras(-ieses) comido	hubieras(-ieses) vivido
hubiera(-iese) amado	hubiera(-iese) comido	hubiera(-iese) vivido
hubiéramos(-iésemos) amado	hubiéramos(-iésemos) comido	hubiéramos(-iésemos) vivido
hubierais(-ieseis) amado	hubierais(-ieseis) comido	hubierais(-ieseis) vivido
hubieran(-iesen) amado	hubieran(-iesen) comido	hubieran(-iesen) vivido

Stem-Changing Verbs

The -ar *and* -er *stem-changing verbs*

Stem-changing verbs are those that have a change in the root of the verb. Verbs that end in **-ar** and **-er** change the stressed vowel **e** to **ie** and the stressed **o** to **ue.** These changes occur in all persons, except the first and second persons plural of the present indicative, present subjunctive, and command.

INFINITIVE	PRESENT INDICATIVE	IMPERATIVE	PRESENT SUBJUNCTIVE
cerrar (*to close*)	**cie**rro	—	**cie**rre
	cierras	**cie**rra	**cie**rres
	cierra	(Ud.) **cie**rre	**cie**rre
	cerramos	cerremos	cerremos
	cerráis	cerrad	cerréis
	cierran	(Uds.) **cie**rren	**cie**rren

© 2017 Cengage Learning

INFINITIVE	PRESENT INDICATIVE	IMPERATIVE	PRESENT SUBJUNCTIVE
perder (*to lose*)	**pie**rdo **pie**rdes **pie**rde perdemos perdéis **pie**rden	— **pie**rde (Ud.) **pie**rda perdamos perded (Uds.) **pie**rdan	**pie**rda **pie**rdas **pie**rda perdamos perdáis **pie**rdan
contar (*to count, to tell*)	**cue**nto **cue**ntas **cue**nta contamos contáis **cue**ntan	— **cue**nta (Ud.) **cue**nte contemos contad (Uds.) **cue**nten	**cue**nte **cue**ntes **cue**nte contemos contéis **cue**nten
volver (*to return*)	**vue**lvo **vue**lves **vue**lve volvemos volvéis **vue**lven	— **vue**lve (Ud.) **vue**lva volvamos volved (Uds.) **vue**lvan	**vue**lva **vue**lvas **vue**lva volvamos volváis **vue**lvan

Verbs that follow the same pattern include the following.

acertar	*to guess right*
acordarse	*to remember*
acostar(se)	*to go to bed*
almorzar	*to have lunch*
atravesar	*to go through*
cegar	*to blind*
cocer	*to cook*
colgar	*to hang*
comenzar	*to begin*
confesar	*to confess*
costar	*to cost*
demostrar	*to demonstrate, to show*
despertar(se)	*to wake up*
empezar	*to begin*
encender	*to light, to turn on*
encontrar	*to find*
entender	*to understand*
llover	*to rain*
mostrar	*to show*
mover	*to move*
negar	*to deny*
nevar	*to snow*
pensar	*to think, to plan*
probar	*to prove, to taste*
recordar	*to remember*
resolver	*to decide on*
rogar	*to beg*
sentar(se)	*to sit down*
soler	*to be in the habit of*
soñar	*to dream*
tender	*to stretch, to unfold*
torcer	*to twist*

© 2017 Cengage Learning

The -ir *stem-changing verbs*

There are two types of stem-changing verbs that end in **-ir:** one type changes stressed **e** to **ie** in some tenses and to **i** in others and stressed **o** to **ue** or **u;** the second type always changes stressed **e** to **i** in the irregular forms of the verb.

Type I				
		e:ie	or	**i**
	-ir:			
		o:ue	or	**u**

These changes occur as follows.

Present Indicative: all persons except the first and second plural change **e** to **ie** and **o** to **ue.** *Preterit:* third person, singular and plural, changes **e** to **i** and **o** to **u.** *Present Subjunctive:* all persons change **e** to **ie** and **o** to **ue,** except the first and second persons plural, which change **e** to **i** and **o** to **u.** *Imperfect Subjunctive:* all persons change **e** to **i** and **o** to **u.** *Imperative:* all persons except the second person plural change **e** to **ie** and **o** to **ue;** first person plural changes **e** to **i** and **o** to **u.** *Present Participle:* changes **e** to **i** and **o** to **u.**

	Indicative		*Imperative*	*Subjunctive*	
INFINITIVE	PRESENT	PRETERIT		PRESENT	IMPERFECT
sentir	s**ie**nto	sentí	—	s**ie**nta	s**i**ntiera(-iese)
(*to feel*)	s**ie**ntes	sentiste	s**ie**nte	s**ie**ntas	s**i**ntieras
	s**ie**nte	s**i**ntió	(Ud.) s**ie**nta	s**ie**nta	s**i**ntiera
PRESENT	sentimos	sentimos	s**i**ntamos	s**i**ntamos	s**i**ntiéramos
PARTICIPLE	sentís	sentisteis	sentid	s**i**ntáis	s**i**ntierais
s**i**ntiendo	s**ie**nten	s**i**ntieron	(Uds.) s**ie**ntan	s**ie**ntan	s**i**ntieran
dormir	d**ue**rmo	dormí	—	d**ue**rma	d**u**rmiera(-iese)
(*to sleep*)	d**ue**rmes	dormiste	d**ue**rme	d**ue**rmas	d**u**rmieras
	d**ue**rme	d**u**rmió	(Ud.) d**ue**rma	d**ue**rma	d**u**rmiera
PRESENT	dormimos	dormimos	d**u**rmamos	d**u**rmamos	d**u**rmiéramos
PARTICIPLE	dormís	dormisteis	dormid	d**u**rmáis	d**u**rmierais
d**u**rmiendo	d**ue**rmen	d**u**rmieron	(Uds.) d**ue**rman	d**ue**rman	d**u**rmieran

© 2017 Cengage Learning

Other verbs that follow the same pattern include the following.

advertir	*to warn*	**herir**	*to wound, to hurt*
arrepentir(se)	*to repent*	**mentir**	*to lie*
consentir	*to consent, to pamper*	**morir**	*to die*
convertir(se)	*to turn into*	**preferir**	*to prefer*
discernir	*to discern*	**referir**	*to refer*
divertir(se)	*to amuse oneself*	**sugerir**	*to suggest*

Type II **-ir:** **e:i**

The verbs in this second category are irregular in the same tenses as those of the first type. The only difference is that they only have one change: **e:i** in all irregular persons.

	Indicative		*Imperative*	*Subjunctive*	
INFINITIVE	PRESENT	PRETERIT		PRESENT	IMPERFECT
pedir	pido	pedí	—	pida	pidiera(-iese)
(*to ask for,*	pides	pediste	pide	pidas	pidieras
to request)	pide	pidió	(Ud.) pida	pida	pidiera
PRESENT	pedimos	pedimos	pidamos	pidamos	pidiéramos
PARTICIPLE	pedís	pedisteis	pedid	pidáis	pidierais
pidiendo	piden	pidieron	(Uds.) pidan	pidan	pidieran

Verbs that follow this pattern include the following.

competir	*to compete*	**reír(se)**	*to laugh*
concebir	*to conceive*	**reñir**	*to fight*
despedir(se)	*to say good-bye*	**repetir**	*to repeat*
elegir	*to choose*	**seguir**	*to follow*
impedir	*to prevent*	**servir**	*to serve*
perseguir	*to pursue*	**vestir(se)**	*to dress*

© 2017 Cengage Learning

ORTHOGRAPHIC-CHANGING VERBS

Some verbs undergo a change in the spelling of the stem in certain tenses in order to maintain the original sound of the final consonant. The most common verbs of this type are those with the consonants **g** and **c.** Remember that **g** and **c** have a soft sound in front of **e** or **i** and a hard sound in front of **a, o,** or **u.** In order to maintain the soft sound in front of **a, o,** and **u, g** and **c** change to **j** and **z,** respectively. And in order to maintain the hard sound of **g** and **c** in front of **e** and **i, u** is added to the **g** (**gu**) and **c** changes to **qu.**

The following important verbs undergo spelling changes in the tenses listed below.

1. Verbs ending in **-gar** change **g** to **gu** before **e** in the first person of the preterit and in all persons of the present subjunctive.

   pagar (*to pay*)
   Preterit: pa**gu**é, pagaste, pagó, etc.
   Pres. Subj.: pa**gu**e, pa**gu**es, pa**gu**e, pa**gu**emos, pa**gu**éis, pa**gu**en

   Verbs that follow the same pattern: **colgar, jugar, llegar, navegar, negar, regar, rogar.**

2. Verbs ending in **-ger** and **-gir** change **g** to **j** before **o** and **a** in the first person of the present indicative and in all persons of the present subjunctive.

   proteger (*to protect*)
   Pres. Ind.: prote**j**o, proteges, protege, etc.
   Pres. Subj.: prote**j**a, prote**j**as, prote**j**a, prote**j**amos, prote**j**áis, prote**j**an

   Verbs that follow the same pattern: **coger, corregir, dirigir, elegir, escoger, exigir, recoger.**

3. Verbs ending in **-guar** change **gu** to **gü** before **e** in the first person of the preterit and in all persons of the present subjunctive.

   averiguar (*to find out*)
   Preterit: averi**gü**é, averiguaste, averiguó, etc.
   Pres. Subj.: averi**gü**e, averi**gü**es, averi**güe,** averi**güemos,** averi**gü**éis, averi**gü**en

   The verb **apaciguar** follows the same pattern.

4. Verbs ending in **-guir** change **gu** to **g** before **o** and **a** in the first person of the present indicative and in all persons of the present subjunctive.

   conseguir (*to get*)
   Pres. Ind.: consi**g**o, consigues, consigue, etc.
   Pres. Subj.: consi**g**a, consi**g**as, consi**g**a, consi**g**amos, consi**g**áis, consi**g**an

   Verbs that follow the same pattern: **distinguir, perseguir, proseguir, seguir.**

© 2017 Cengage Learning

5. Verbs ending in **-car** change **c** to **qu** before **e** in the first person of the preterit and in all persons of the present subjunctive.

tocar (*to touch, to play [a musical instrument]*)
Preterit: to**qu**é, tocaste, tocó, etc.
Pres. Subj.: to**qu**e, to**qu**es, to**qu**e, to**qu**emos, to**qu**éis, to**qu**en

Verbs that follow the same pattern: **atacar, buscar, comunicar, explicar, indicar, pescar, sacar.**

6. Verbs ending in **-cer** and **-cir** preceded by a consonant change **c** to **z** before **o** and **a** in the first person of the present indicative and in all persons of the present subjunctive.

torcer (*to twist*)
Pres. Ind.: tuer**z**o, tuerces, tuerce, etc.
Pres. Subj.: tuer**z**a, tuer**z**as, tuer**z**a, tor**z**amos, tor**z**áis, tuer**z**an

Verbs that follow the same pattern: **convencer, esparcir, vencer.**

7. Verbs ending in **-cer** and **-cir** preceded by a vowel change **c** to **zc** before **o** and **a** in the first person of the present indicative and in all persons of the present subjunctive.

conocer (*to know, to be acquainted with*)
Pres. Ind.: cono**zc**o, conoces, conoce, etc.
Pres. Subj.: cono**zc**a, cono**zc**as, cono**zc**a, cono**zc**amos, cono**zc**áis, cono**zc**an

Verbs that follow the same pattern: **agradecer, aparecer, carecer, entristecer, establecer, lucir, nacer, obedecer, ofrecer, padecer, parecer, pertenecer, reconocer, relucir.**

8. Verbs ending in **-zar** change **z** to **c** before **e** in the first person of the preterit and in all persons of the present subjunctive.

rezar (*to pray*)
Preterit: re**c**é, rezaste, rezó, etc.
Pres. Subj.: re**c**e, re**c**es, re**c**e, re**c**emos, re**c**éis, re**c**en

Verbs that follow the same pattern: **abrazar, alcanzar, almorzar, comenzar, cruzar, empezar, forzar, gozar.**

9. Verbs ending in **-eer** change the unstressed **i** to **y** between vowels in the third person singular and plural of the preterit, in all persons of the imperfect subjunctive, and in the present participle.

creer (*to believe*)
Preterit: creí, creíste, cre**y**ó, creímos, creísteis, cre**y**eron
Imp. Subj.: cre**y**era(ese), cre**y**eras, cre**y**era, cre**y**éramos, cre**y**erais, cre**y**eran
Pres. Part.: cre**y**endo

Leer and **poseer** follow the same pattern.

© 2017 Cengage Learning

10. Verbs ending in **-uir** change the unstressed **i** to **y** between vowels (except **-quir,** which has the silent **u**) in the following tenses and persons.

huir (*to escape, to flee*)
Pres. Part.: hu**y**endo
Past Part.: huido
Pres. Ind.: hu**y**o, hu**y**es, hu**y**e, huimos, huís, hu**y**en
Preterit: huí, huiste, hu**y**ó, huimos, huisteis, hu**y**eron
Imperative: hu**y**e, hu**y**a, hu**y**amos, huid, hu**y**an
Pres. Subj.: hu**y**a, hu**y**as, hu**y**a, hu**y**amos, hu**y**áis, hu**y**an
Imp. Subj.: hu**y**era(ese), hu**y**eras, hu**y**era, hu**y**éramos, hu**y**erais, hu**y**eran

Verbs that follow the same pattern: **atribuir, concluir, constituir, construir, contribuir, destituir, destruir, disminuir, distribuir, excluir, incluir, influir, instruir, restituir, sustituir.**

11. Verbs ending in **-eír** lose one **e** in the third person singular and plural of the preterit, in all persons of the imperfect subjunctive, and in the present participle.

reír(se) (*to laugh*)
Preterit: reí, reíste, r**i**ó, reímos, reísteis, r**i**eron
Imp. Subj.: r**i**era(ese), r**i**eras, r**i**era, r**i**éramos, r**i**erais, r**i**eran
Pres. Part.: r**i**endo

Freír and **sonreír** follow the same pattern.

12. Verbs ending in **-iar** add a written accent to the **i,** except in the first and second persons plural of the present indicative and subjunctive.

fiar(se) (*to trust*)
Pres. Ind.: f**í**o, f**í**as, f**í**a, fiamos, fiáis, f**í**an
Pres. Subj.: f**í**e, f**í**es, f**í**e, fiemos, fiéis, f**í**en

Verbs that follow the same pattern: **ampliar, criar, desviar, enfriar, enviar, esquiar, guiar, telegrafiar, vaciar, variar.**

13. Verbs ending in **-uar** (except **-guar**) add a written accent to the **u,** except in the first and second persons plural of the present indicative and subjunctive.

actuar (*to act*)
Pres. Ind.: act**ú**o, act**ú**as, act**ú**a, actuamos, actuáis, act**ú**an
Pres. Subj.: act**ú**e, act**ú**es, act**ú**e, actuemos, actuéis, act**ú**en

Verbs that follow the same pattern: **acentuar, continuar, efectuar, exceptuar, graduar, habituar, insinuar, situar.**

© 2017 Cengage Learning

14. Verbs ending in **-ñir** remove the **i** of the diphthongs **ie** and **ió** in the third person singular and plural of the preterit and in all persons of the imperfect subjunctive. They also change the **e** of the stem to **i** in the same persons.

teñir (*to dye*)
Preterit: teñí, teñiste, **tiñó,** teñimos, teñisteis, **tiñeron**
Imp. Subj.: **tiñe**ra(ese), **tiñe**ras, **tiñe**ra, **tiñé**ramos, **tiñe**rais, **tiñe**ran

Verbs that follow the same pattern: **ceñir, constreñir, desteñir, estreñir, reñir.**

Some Common Irregular Verbs

Only those tenses with irregular forms are given below.

adquirir (*to acquire*)
Pres. Ind.: adquiero, adquieres, adquiere, adquirimos, adquirís, adquieren
Pres. Subj.: adquiera, adquieras, adquiera, adquiramos, adquiráis, adquieran
Imperative: adquiere, adquiera, adquiramos, adquirid, adquieran

andar (*to walk*)
Preterit: anduve, anduviste, anduvo, anduvimos, anduvisteis, anduvieron
Imp. Subj.: anduviera (anduviese), anduvieras, anduviera, anduviéramos, anduvierais, anduvieran

avergonzarse (*to be ashamed, to be embarrassed*)
Pres. Ind.: me avergüenzo, te avergüenzas, se avergüenza, nos avergonzamos, os avergonzáis, se avergüenzan
Pres. Subj.: me avergüence, te avergüences, se avergüence, nos avergoncemos, os avergoncéis, se avergüencen
Imperative: avergüénzate, avergüéncese, avergoncémonos, avergonzaos, avergüéncense

caber (*to fit, to have enough room*)
Pres. Ind.: quepo, cabes, cabe, cabemos, cabéis, caben
Preterit: cupe, cupiste, cupo, cupimos, cupisteis, cupieron
Future: cabré, cabrás, cabrá, cabremos, cabréis, cabrán
Conditional: cabría, cabrías, cabría, cabríamos, cabríais, cabrían
Imperative: cabe, quepa, quepamos, cabed, quepan
Pres. Subj.: quepa, quepas, quepa, quepamos, quepáis, quepan
Imp. Subj.: cupiera (cupiese), cupieras, cupiera, cupiéramos, cupierais, cupieran

caer (*to fall*)
Pres. Ind.: caigo, caes, cae, caemos, caéis, caen
Preterit: caí, caíste, cayó, caímos, caísteis, cayeron
Imperative: cae, caiga, caigamos, caed, caigan
Pres. Subj.: caiga, caigas, caiga, caigamos, caigáis, caigan
Imp. Subj.: cayera (cayese), cayeras, cayera, cayéramos, cayerais, cayeran
Past Part.: caído

© 2017 Cengage Learning

conducir (*to guide, to drive*)

Pres. Ind.: conduzco, conduces, conduce, conducimos, conducís, conducen
Preterit: conduje, condujiste, condujo, condujimos, condujisteis, condujeron
Imperative: conduce, conduzca, conduzcamos, conducid, conduzcan
Pres. Subj.: conduzca, conduzcas, conduzca, conduzcamos, conduzcáis, conduzcan
Imp. Subj.: condujera (condujese), condujeras, condujera, condujéramos, condujerais, condujeran

(All verbs ending in **-ducir** follow this pattern.)

convenir (*to agree*) See **venir.**

dar (*to give*)

Pres. Ind.: doy, das, da, damos, dais, dan
Preterit: di, diste, dio, dimos, disteis, dieron
Imperative: da, dé, demos, dad, den
Pres. Subj.: dé, des, dé, demos, deis, den
Imp. Subj.: diera (diese), dieras, diera, diéramos, dierais, dieran

decir (*to say, to tell*)

Pres. Ind.: digo, dices, dice, decimos, decís, dicen
Preterit: dije, dijiste, dijo, dijimos, dijisteis, dijeron
Future: diré, dirás, dirá, diremos, diréis, dirán
Conditional: diría, dirías, diría, diríamos, diríais, dirían
Imperative: di, diga, digamos, decid, digan
Pres. Subj.: diga, digas, diga, digamos, digáis, digan
Imp. Subj.: dijera (dijese), dijeras, dijera, dijéramos, dijerais, dijeran
Pres. Part.: diciendo
Past Part.: dicho

detener (*to stop, to hold, to arrest*) See **tener.**

entretener (*to entertain, to amuse*) See **tener.**

errar (*to err, to miss*)

Pres. Ind.: yerro, yerras, yerra, erramos, erráis, yerran
Imperative: yerra, yerre, erremos, errad, yerren
Pres. Subj.: yerre, yerres, yerre, erremos, erréis, yerren

estar (*to be*)

Pres. Ind.: estoy, estás, está, estamos, estáis, están
Preterit: estuve, estuviste, estuvo, estuvimos, estuvisteis, estuvieron
Imperative: está, esté, estemos, estad, estén
Pres. Subj.: esté, estés, esté, estemos, estéis, estén
Imp. Subj.: estuviera (estuviese), estuvieras, estuviera, estuviéramos, estuvierais, estuvieran

haber (*to have*)

Pres. Ind.: he, has, ha, hemos, habéis, han
Preterit: hube, hubiste, hubo, hubimos, hubisteis, hubieron
Future: habré, habrás, habrá, habremos, habréis, habrán
Conditional: habría, habrías, habría, habríamos, habríais, habrían

© 2017 Cengage Learning

Imperative: he, haya, hayamos, habed, hayan
Pres. Subj.: haya, hayas, haya, hayamos, hayáis, hayan
Imp. Subj.: hubiera (hubiese), hubieras, hubiera, hubiéramos, hubierais, hubieran

hacer (*to do, to make*)
Pres. Ind.: hago, haces, hace, hacemos, hacéis, hacen
Preterit: hice, hiciste, hizo, hicimos, hicisteis, hicieron
Future: haré, harás, hará, haremos, haréis, harán
Conditional: haría, harías, haría, haríamos, haríais, harían
Imperative: haz, haga, hagamos, haced, hagan
Pres. Subj.: haga, hagas, haga, hagamos, hagáis, hagan
Imp. Subj.: hiciera (hiciese), hicieras, hiciera, hiciéramos, hicierais, hicieran
Past Part.: hecho

imponer (*to impose, to deposit*) See **poner.**

introducir (*to introduce, to insert, to gain access*) See **conducir.**

ir (*to go*)
Pres. Ind.: voy, vas, va, vamos, vais, van
Imp. Ind.: iba, ibas, iba, íbamos, ibais, iban
Preterit: fui, fuiste, fue, fuimos, fuisteis, fueron
Imperative: ve, vaya, vayamos, id, vayan
Pres. Subj.: vaya, vayas, vaya, vayamos, vayáis, vayan
Imp. Subj.: fuera (fuese), fueras, fuera, fuéramos, fuerais, fueran

jugar (*to play*)
Pres. Ind.: juego, juegas, juega, jugamos, jugáis, juegan
Imperative: juega, juegue, juguemos, jugad, jueguen
Pres. Subj.: juegue, juegues, juegue, juguemos, juguéis, jueguen

obtener (*to obtain*) See **tener.**

oír (*to hear*)
Pres. Ind.: oigo, oyes, oye, oímos, oís, oyen
Preterit: oí, oíste, oyó, oímos, oísteis, oyeron
Imperative: oye, oiga, oigamos, oíd, oigan
Pres. Subj.: oiga, oigas, oiga, oigamos, oigáis, oigan
Imp. Subj.: oyera (oyese), oyeras, oyera, oyéramos, oyerais, oyeran
Pres. Part.: oyendo
Past Part.: oído

oler (*to smell*)
Pres. Ind.: huelo, hueles, huele, olemos, oléis, huelen
Imperative: huele, huela, olamos, oled, huelan
Pres. Subj.: huela, huelas, huela, olamos, oláis, huelan

poder (*to be able*)
Pres. Ind.: puedo, puedes, puede, podemos, podéis, pueden

© 2017 Cengage Learning

Preterit: pude, pudiste, pudo, pudimos, pudisteis, pudieron
Future: podré, podrás, podrá, podremos, podréis, podrán
Conditional: podría, podrías, podría, podríamos, podríais, podrían
Imperative: puede, pueda, podamos, poded, puedan
Pres. Subj.: pueda, puedas, pueda, podamos, podáis, puedan
Imp. Subj.: pudiera (pudiese), pudieras, pudiera, pudiéramos, pudierais, pudieran
Pres. Part.: pudiendo

poner (*to place, to put*)
Pres. Ind.: pongo, pones, pone, ponemos, ponéis, ponen
Preterit: puse, pusiste, puso, pusimos, pusisteis, pusieron
Future: pondré, pondrás, pondrá, pondremos, pondréis, pondrán
Conditional: pondría, pondrías, pondría, pondríamos, pondríais, pondrían
Imperative: pon, ponga, pongamos, poned, pongan
Pres. Subj.: ponga, pongas, ponga, pongamos, pongáis, pongan
Imp. Subj.: pusiera (pusiese), pusieras, pusiera, pusiéramos, pusierais, pusieran
Past Part.: puesto

querer (*to want, to wish, to like*)
Pres. Ind.: quiero, quieres, quiere, queremos, queréis, quieren
Preterit: quise, quisiste, quiso, quisimos, quisisteis, quisieron
Future: querré, querrás, querrá, querremos, querréis, querrán
Conditional: querría, querrías, querría, querríamos, querríais, querrían
Imperative: quiere, quiera, queramos, quered, quieran
Pres. Subj.: quiera, quieras, quiera, queramos, queráis, quieran
Imp. Subj.: quisiera (quisiese), quisieras, quisiera, quisiéramos, quisierais, quisieran

resolver (*to decide on*)
Past Part.: resuelto

saber (*to know*)
Pres. Ind.: sé, sabes, sabe, sabemos, sabéis, saben
Preterit: supe, supiste, supo, supimos, supisteis, supieron
Future: sabré, sabrás, sabrá, sabremos, sabréis, sabrán
Conditional: sabría, sabrías, sabría, sabríamos, sabríais, sabrían
Imperative: sabe, sepa, sepamos, sabed, sepan
Pres. Subj.: sepa, sepas, sepa, sepamos, sepáis, sepan
Imp. Subj.: supiera (supiese), supieras, supiera, supiéramos, supierais, supieran

salir (*to leave, to go out*)
Pres. Ind.: salgo, sales, sale, salimos, salís, salen
Future: saldré, saldrás, saldrá, saldremos, saldréis, saldrán
Conditional: saldría, saldrías, saldría, saldríamos, saldríais, saldrían
Imperative: sal, salga, salgamos, salid, salgan
Pres. Subj.: salga, salgas, salga, salgamos, salgáis, salgan

© 2017 Cengage Learning

ser (*to be*)

Pres. Ind.: soy, eres, es, somos, sois, son
Imp. Ind.: era, eras, era, éramos, erais, eran
Preterit: fui, fuiste, fue, fuimos, fuisteis, fueron
Imperative: sé, sea, seamos, sed, sean
Pres. Subj.: sea, seas, sea, seamos, seáis, sean
Imp. Subj.: fuera (fuese), fueras, fuera, fuéramos, fuerais, fueran

suponer (*to assume*) See **poner.**

tener (*to have*)

Pres. Ind.: tengo, tienes, tiene, tenemos, tenéis, tienen
Preterit: tuve, tuviste, tuvo, tuvimos, tuvisteis, tuvieron
Future: tendré, tendrás, tendrá, tendremos, tendréis, tendrán
Conditional: tendría, tendrías, tendría, tendríamos, tendríais, tendrían
Imperative: ten, tenga, tengamos, tened, tengan
Pres. Subj.: tenga, tengas, tenga, tengamos, tengáis, tengan
Imp. Subj.: tuviera (tuviese), tuvieras, tuviera, tuviéramos, tuvierais, tuvieran

traducir (*to translate*) See **conducir.**

traer (*to bring*)

Pres. Ind.: traigo, traes, trae, traemos, traéis, traen
Preterit: traje, trajiste, trajo, trajimos, trajisteis, trajeron
Imperative: trae, traiga, traigamos, traed, traigan
Pres. Subj.: traiga, traigas, traiga, traigamos, traigáis, traigan
Imp. Subj.: trajera (trajese), trajeras, trajera, trajéramos, trajerais, trajeran
Pres. Part.: trayendo
Past Part.: traído

valer (*to be worth*)

Pres. Ind.: valgo, vales, vale, valemos, valéis, valen
Future: valdré, valdrás, valdrá, valdremos, valdréis, valdrán
Conditional: valdría, valdrías, valdría, valdríamos, valdríais, valdrían
Imperative: vale, valga, valgamos, valed, valgan
Pres. Subj.: valga, valgas, valga, valgamos, valgáis, valgan

venir (*to come*)

Pres. Ind.: vengo, vienes, viene, venimos, venís, vienen
Preterit: vine, viniste, vino, vinimos, vinisteis, vinieron
Future: vendré, vendrás, vendrá, vendremos, vendréis, vendrán
Conditional: vendría, vendrías, vendría, vendríamos, vendríais, vendrían
Imperative: ven, venga, vengamos, venid, vengan
Pres. Subj.: venga, vengas, venga, vengamos, vengáis, vengan
Imp. Subj.: viniera (viniese), vinieras, viniera, viniéramos, vinierais, vinieran
Pres. Part.: viniendo

© 2017 Cengage Learning

ver (*to see*)

Pres. Ind.:	veo, ves, ve, vemos, veis, ven
Imp. Ind.:	veía, veías, veía, veíamos, veíais, veían
Preterit:	vi, viste, vio, vimos, visteis, vieron
Imperative:	ve, vea, veamos, ved, vean
Pres. Subj.:	vea, veas, vea, veamos, veáis, vean
Imp. Subj.:	viera (viese), vieras, viera, viéramos, vierais, vieran
Past. Part.:	visto

volver (*to return*)

Past Part.:	vuelto

© 2017 Cengage Learning

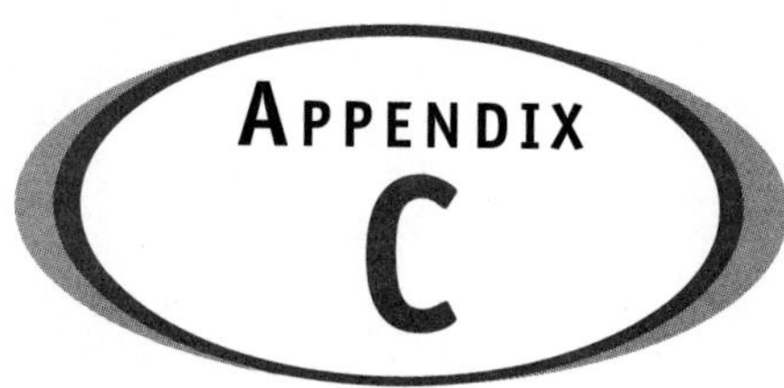

Appendix C — Useful Classroom Expressions

You will hear your teacher use the following directions and general terms in class. Take time to familiarize yourself with them.

- When the teacher is speaking to the whole class:

Abran sus libros, por favor.	*Open your books, please.*
Cierren sus libros, por favor.	*Close your books, please.*
Escriban, por favor.	*Write, please.*
Escuchen, por favor.	*Listen, please.*
Estudien la lección...	*Study Lesson . . .*
Hagan el ejercicio número...	*Do exercise number . . .*
Levanten la mano.	*Raise your hands.*
Repasen el vocabulario.	*Review the vocabulary.*
Repitan, por favor.	*Repeat, please.*
Siéntense, por favor.	*Sit down, please.*
Vayan a la página...	*Go to page . . .*

- When the teacher is speaking to one student:

Continúe, por favor.	*Go on, please.*
Lea, por favor.	*Read, please.*
Vaya a la pizarra, por favor.	*Go to the chalkboard, please.*

- Some other words used in the classroom:

diccionario	*dictionary*	**palabra**	*word*
dictado	*dictation*	**presente**	*present, here*
examen	*exam*	**prueba**	*quiz*
horario de clases	*class schedule*	**tarea**	*homework*

© 2017 Cengage Learning

Weights and Measures

Length

la pulgada = *inch*
el pie = *foot*
la yarda = *yard*
la milla = *mile*

1 centímetro (cm) = .3937 pulgadas (*less than 1/2 inch*)
1 metro (m) = 39.37 pulgadas (*1 yard, 3 inches*)
1 kilómetro (km) (1.000 metros) = .6214 millas (*5/8 mile*)

Weight

la onza = *ounce*
la libra = *pound*
la tonelada = *ton*

1 gramo (g) = .03527 onzas
100 gramos = 3.527 onzas (*less than 1/4 pound*)
1 kilogramo (kg) (1.000 gramos) = 2.2 libras

Liquid Measure

la pinta = *pint*
el cuarto (de galón) = *quart*
el galón = *gallon*

1 litro (l) = 1.0567 cuartos (de galón) (*slightly more than a quart*)

Surface

el acre = *acre*
1 hectárea = 2.471 acres

Temperature

°C = Celsius (*Celsius*) or centigrade (*centígrado*); °F = Fahrenheit (*Fahrenheit*)
0 °C = 32 °F (*freezing point of water*)
37 °C = 98.6 °F (*normal body temperature*)
100 °C = 212 °F (*boiling point of water*)

Conversión de grados Fahrenheit a grados centígrados °C = 5/9 (°F −32)
Conversión de grados centígrados a grados Fahrenheit °F = 9/5 (°C) + 32

© 2017 Cengage Learning

Spanish-English Vocabulary

The Spanish-English and English-Spanish vocabularies contain all active and passive vocabulary that appears in the manual. Active vocabulary includes words and expressions appearing in the **Vocabulario** lists. These items are followed by a number indicating the lesson in which each word is introduced in the dialogues. Passive vocabulary consists of words and expressions included in the **Vocabulario adicional** lists and those that are given an English gloss in the readings, exercises, activities, and authentic documents.

The following abbreviations are used in the vocabularies.

adj.	adjective	*L.A.*	Latin America
adv.	adverb	*m.*	masculine noun
col.	colloquial	*Méx.*	Mexico
f.	feminine noun	*pl.*	plural
form.	formal	*sing.*	singular noun
inf.	infinitive		

A

a to, at, on, 2
— **cargo de** in charge of, 8
— **eso de** at about (with time), 14
— **esta hora** at this time (hour), 3
— **la derecha** to the right, 2
— **la fuerza** by force, 8
— **la izquierda** to the left, 2
— **la vista de** in the presence of, in front of, 16
— **los costados** on the sides, 9
— **mediados de mes (semana)** about the middle of the month (week)
— **medianoche** at midnight
— **menos que** unless, 19
— **menudo** often, 6
— **pie** on foot, 2
— **plazos** in installments, on time (payments), 10
— **sus órdenes** at your service, any time, 3
— **tiempo** on time, 13; just in time, 13
— **una cuadra (dos cuadras, etc.) de aquí** a block (two blocks, etc.) from here, 2
— **veces** sometimes, 2
— **ver** let's see, 6
abandonar los estudios to drop out of school
abecedario (*m.*) alphabet, 9
abierto(a) open, 5
abogado(a) (*m., f.*) lawyer, 6
— **defensor(a)** (*m., f.*) counsel for the defense
abrigo (*m.*) coat
— **de piel** fur coat
abrir las piernas y los brazos to spreadeagle
absuelto(a) acquitted
abuelo(a) (*m., f.*) grandfather; grandmother
abusar de to abuse, 8
acabar de (+ *inf.*) to have just (done something), 13
accidente (*m.*) accident, 1
aceite (*m.*) oil
acelerador (*m.*) accelerator
acento (*m.*) accent, 18
aceptar to accept, 8
acera (*f.*) sidewalk, 9
ácido (*m.*) LSD (*col.*)
acné (*m.*) acne
acompañar to accompany, to go (come) with, 7
aconsejar to advise, 16
acordarse (o:ue) (de) to remember, 10
acostarse (o:ue) to lie down
actividad (*f.*) activity, 5
acto (*m.*) act, 18
actuar to act
acumulador (*m.*) battery
acusación (*f.*) accusation, 14
acusado(a) (*m., f.*) defendant
acusar to accuse, 8
además besides, 2
adentro inside, 8
adicional additional
adicto(a) addicted
adiós good-bye, P
adjetivo (*m.*) adjective
adolescente (*m., f.*) adolescent, teenager, 17
¿adónde? where (to)?, 5
advertencia warning, 12
— **Miranda** (*f.*) Miranda warning, 6
afeitarse to shave, 20
agacharse to bend down
agarrar to get hold of, to grab, 9
agente (*m., f.*) officer, P
agravarse to get worse, to worsen, 15
agresión (*f.*) aggression; attack; assault
agresor(a) (*m., f.*) aggressor; assailant
Agte. (*abbreviation for* **Agente**) officer
aguardiente (*m.*) a type of liquor
aguja (*f.*) needle, 6
agujerito (*m.*) peephole, 5
ahí there, 16
ahijado(a) (*m., f.*) godson; goddaughter
ahogarse to drown
ahora now, 1
ahorcar to suffocate, 8
al (a + el) to the, 3
— **amanecer** at dawn; at daybreak
— **anochecer** at dusk
— **contado** in cash, 10
— **día** up to date, 11
— **día siguiente** the next day
— **mediodía** at noon
alarma (*f.*) alarm
alberca (*f.*) (*Méx.*) swimming pool
alcohol (*m.*) alcohol, 9
alcohólico(a) alcoholic, 9
alegrarse de to be glad
alejarse to get away
alérgico(a) allergic
alfabeto (*m.*) alphabet, 9
alfombra (*f.*) carpet, 10
algo something, 5; anything, 8
¿— más? Anything else?, 7
alguien someone, 4
algún, alguno(a) some, any, 6
alguna vez ever
alias (*m.*) alias
aliento (*m.*) breath, 9
aló (*Puerto Rico*) hello (on the telephone)
allá there, 2
allí there, 2
alojamiento (*m.*) lodging
alto(a) tall, 4; high, 12
¡alto! halt!, stop!, 3
alucinaciones (*f. pl.*) hallucinations

© 2017 Cengage Learning

amarillo(a) yellow, 7
ambulancia (*f.*) ambulance, 13
amenaza (*f.*) threat, 20
amenazar to threaten, 18
ametralladora (*f.*) machine gun
amigo(a) (*m., f.*) friend, 3
amortiguador (de ruido) (*m.*) muffler
— **de choque** (*m.*) shock absorber
anciano(a) old, 1
andar to walk, 2
anfetamina (*f.*) amphetamine
anillo (*m.*) ring, 17
anoche last night, 10
anormal abnormal, 18
anotar to write down, to take note of, 10
anteanoche the night before last
anteayer the day before yesterday
antecedente penal (*m.*) criminal record, 16
anteojos (*m. pl.*) eyeglasses, 18
antes (de) before, 3
— **de anoche** the night before last
— **de ayer** the day before yesterday
— **de que lo interroguen** before they question you, 6
anular (*m.*) ring finger
año (*m.*) year, 11
el — pasado last year
el — próximo next year
el — que viene next year
apagado(a) out, off (light), 9
apagar to turn off, 9; to put out (*a fire*), 13
apartamento (*m.*) apartment, 1
apelación (*f.*) appeal
apelar to appeal
apellido (*m.*) last name, surname, P
apodo (*m.*) alias
apoyo (*m.*) support
aprender to learn, 15
aproximadamente approximately
aproximado(a) approximate, 11
apuntar to point, to aim, 20
aquel that, 18
aquello(a) that, 18
aquí here, 1
área (*f. but* **el área**) area
arete (*m.*) earring, 17
arma (*f. but* **el arma**) weapon, 8
— **de fuego** firearm, 4
— **blanca** blade
arrancar to start (*a car*)
arranque (*m.*) starter
arreglar to fix, 19; to arrange
arrestado(a) arrested, 6
arrestar to arrest, 3
arrimar to pull over (*a car*), to place nearby, 9
artículo (*m.*) article, 14
asaltante (*m., f.*) assailant
asaltar to assault; to mug; to hijack
asalto (*m.*) assault; mugging; holdup; hijacking
asegurado(a) insured, 11
asesinar to murder
asesinato (*m.*) murder
asesino(a) (*m., f.*) murderer; assassin, 1
así like this, 9
asiático(a) Asian
asiento (*m.*) seat
— **para el niño** child's car seat
asignado(a) assigned, 15
asistir (a) to attend, 17
atacar to attack, 18
ataque (*m.*) aggression, attack, assault
— **al corazón** heart attack, 7
atar to tie
aterrorizado(a) terrified, frightened, 18
atrás behind, 12
atrasado(a) behind, 11
atravesado(a) pierced, 18
aunque although, 15; even though
autobús (*m.*) bus
automático(a) automatic
automóvil (*m.*) automobile, 6
automovilístico(a) car-related
autopista (*f.*) highway, 12
autoridad (*f.*) authority, 8
autorizar to authorize, to allow, 16
¡auxilio! help!
avenida (*f.*) avenue, P
averiguación (*f.*) investigation, 10
averiguar to find out, 10
avisar de (que) to inform, to give notice, to report, 1; to notify
¡Ay, Dios mío! Oh, goodness gracious!, 2
ayer yesterday, 8
ayuda (*f.*) help, 1
ayudar to help, 5
azul blue, 4

B

bajarse to get out (off), 9; to get down
bajito(a) (*Cuba*) short, 4
bajo under
— **juramento** under oath
— **los efectos (de)** under the influence (of), 6
bajo(a) short (*in height*), 4; low
bala (*f.*) bullet
balazo (*m.*) shot
baliza (*f.*) hazard light
banco (*m.*) bank, 2
— **de sangre** blood bank, 6
banqueta (*f.*) (*Méx.*) sidewalk, 9
bañadera (*f.*) bathtub
bañarse to bathe, 18
baño (*m.*) bath, 18; bathroom
bar (*m.*) bar, 8
barba (*f.*) beard, 18
barbilla (*f.*) chin
barra (*f.*) bar, 8
barrio (*m.*) neighborhood, district, 5
barro (*m.*) mud, 10
bastante quite, rather, 8
basura (*f.*) trash, garbage, 10
batería (*f.*) battery, 9
baúl (*m.*) (*Puerto Rico*) trunk (*of a car*), 20
bebé (*m.*) baby, 12
bebida (*f.*) drinking, drink, 8
beber to drink, 8
bicicleta (*f.*) bicycle, 2
bien fine, well, P
bigote (*m.*) moustache, 18
billetera (*f.*) wallet, 16
bizco(a) cross-eyed
blanca (*col.*) cocaine, 15
blanco(a) white, 4; Caucasian
blusa (*f.*) blouse, 17
boca (*f.*) mouth, 17
— **abajo** face down
bocina (*f.*) horn
bofetada (*f.*) slap
bolsa (*f.*) purse, 17
bolsillo (*m.*) pocket, 6
bolso (*m.*) purse, 17
bomba (*f.*) bomb
— **de agua** water pump
— **de tiempo** time bomb
bombero(a) (*m., f.*) firefighter
bono (*m.*) bond, 16
borracho(a) drunk, 6
bota (*f.*) boot
botar to throw away, 10
botella (*f.*) bottle, 15
botica (*f.*) drugstore
botón (*m.*) button
brazo (*m.*) arm, 6
breve brief, P
bueno(a) okay, P; good; (*Méx.*) hello (*on the telephone*)
buenas noches good evening, good night, P
buenas tardes good afternoon, P
buenos días/buen día good morning, good day, P
bujía (*f.*) spark plug
buscar to look for, 2

C

caballo (*m.*) heroin (*col.*)
cabello (*m.*) hair
cabeza (*f.*) head, 9
cabina (*f.*) cab (*of a truck*), 13
cachete (*m.*) cheek, 17
cada each, every, 6
cadáver corpse
cadena (*f.*) chain, 16
cadera (*f.*) hip
caerse to fall, 9
café (*adj.*) brown, 18
caja (*f.*) cash register, 20
cajero(a) (*m., f.*) cashier
cajuela (*f.*) (*Méx.*) trunk (*of a car*), 20
calibre (*m.*) caliber, 20
callado(a) silent, quiet, 6
callarse to be quiet
¡cállese! be quiet!, shut up!, 20
calle (*f.*) street, 1
calmante (*m.*) sedative, 19
calmarse to calm down, 18
calvo(a) bald, 18
cámara de vídeo (*f.*) video camera, 10
cambiar to change, 12
cambiarse de ropa to change clothes, 18

© 2017 Cengage Learning

cambio de velocidad (*m.*) gearshift
camilla (*f.*) stretcher
caminar to walk, 2
camino (*m.*) road, 13
camión (*m.*) truck, 13; bus (*Méx.*)
camisa (*f.*) shirt, 4
camiseta (*f.*) T-shirt
canoso(a) gray-haired
cansado(a) tired, 8
cantina (*f.*) bar, 8
capó (*m.*) hood (*of a car*)
capucha (*f.*) hood (*of a garment*)
cara (*f.*) face, 13
característica (*f.*) characteristic
carburador (*m.*) carburetor
cárcel (*f.*) jail
caro(a) expensive
carretera (*f.*) highway, 13
carril (*m.*) lane, 12
carro (*m.*) car, 6
  — deportivo sports car
  — patrullero patrol car, 1
cartera (*f.*) wallet, 16; purse, 17
casa (*f.*) house, home, 1
casado(a) married, P
casco de seguridad (*m.*) safety (bike) helmet, 2
casi almost, 5
caso (*m.*) case, 6
castaño(a) brown (*eyes or hair*), 18
castigar to punish, 8
castigo corporal (*m.*) corporal punishment
causar to cause, 12
  — daño a to hurt
ceda el paso yield
ceja (*f.*) eyebrow
celda (*f.*) cell, 16
cena (*f.*) dinner, 5
centavo (*m.*) cent, 16
central central, 1
centro comercial (*m.*) shopping mall, 2
centro de reclusión de menores (*m.*) juvenile hall
cerca (de) close, 12; near
cercano(a) close, 5; near, nearby, 10
cerrado(a) closed, locked, 11
cerradura (*f.*) lock, 10
cerrar (e:ie) to close, to shut, 5
  — con llave to lock, 5
cerrojo (*m.*) lock
  — de seguridad deadbolt, 5
cerveza (*f.*) beer, 20
césped (*m.*) lawn, 5
chamaco(a) (*m., f.*) (*Méx.*) boy, girl, 13
chamarra (*f.*) (*Méx.*) jacket, 20
chantaje (*m.*) blackmail
chantajear to blackmail
chantajista (*m., f.*) blackmailer, 1
chapa (*f.*) license plate, 11
chaparro(a) (*Méx.*) short, 4
chaqueta (*f.*) jacket, 20
chequear to examine, 10
chico(a) (*m., f.*) boy, girl, 13
chiva (*f.*) heroin (*col.*)
chocar to collide, to run into, to hit, 13
chocolate (*m.*) hashish (*col.*)
chofer (*m.*) driver, 6
choque (*m.*) collision, crash, 13
cicatriz (*f.*) scar, 17
ciego(a) blind
cierto(a) certain, 8
cigarrillo (*m.*) cigarette, 7
cine (*m.*) (movie) theatre, movies, 15
cinto (*m.*) belt, 8
cintura (*f.*) waist, 13
  nivel de la — waist-high
cinturón (*m.*) belt, 8
  — de seguridad safety belt
ciudad (*f.*) city, 2
claro(a) light, 11
  claro que sí of course, 10
clase (*f.*) kind, type, class, 7
clavo (*m.*) speed (drugs) (*col.*)
cliente (*m., f.*) customer, 7
clínica (*f.*) clinic
coartada (*f.*) alibi
cobrar to charge, to collect, 14
coca (*f.*) cocaine (*col.*)
  — cocinada crack cocaine (*col.*)
cocaína (*f.*) cocaine
coche (*m.*) car, 6
cocina (*f.*) kitchen, 5
codo (*m.*) elbow
coger to get hold of, to grab, 9
cognado (*m.*) cognate
cojo(a) lame
collar (*m.*) necklace, 14
colocar to place, to put
colonia (*f.*) (*Méx.*) neighborhood, district, 5
color (*m.*) color
colorado(a) red
comadre (*f.*) godmother or mother (*in relation to each other*)
comedor (*m.*) dining room
comenzar (e:ie) to begin, 5
  comienza la autopista begin freeway
cometer to commit, 6
comisaría (*f.*) police station, P
como about, approximately, 11; as, like, 14; since, being that, 10
¿cómo? how?, 2
  ¿— es? what does he/she/you look like?, 4
  ¿— está Ud.? how are you?, P
  ¡— no! certainly!, gladly!, sure!, 7
  ¿— se escribe? how do you spell it?
compadre (*m.*) godfather or father (*in relation to each other*)
compañero(a) (*m., f.*) pal, peer
  — de clase classmate, 17
comparecer to appear
  — ante un juez to appear in court
completar to complete, 9
completo(a) complete, 5
complexión (*f.*) build
cómplice (*m., f.*) accomplice
comprar to buy, 10
comprender to understand, 18
computadora (*f.*) computer, 10
común common
comunicar to communicate, 5
con with, P
  — cuidado carefully, 12
  — él with him, 6
condena (*f.*) sentence
condición (*f.*) condition, 6
condón (*m.*) condom, 18
conducir to drive, 6
  — a cincuenta millas por hora to drive fifty miles per hour, 9
conductor(a) (*m., f.*) driver, 12
confesar (e:ie) to confess
confesión (*f.*) confession
confirmar to confirm, 19
confuso(a) confused
congregación (*f.*) meeting, assembly, 20
conmigo with me, 6
conocer to know, 7
conocido(a) (*m., f.*) acquaintance
conseguir (e:i) to get, to obtain, 8; to manage
consejero(a) (*m., f.*) counsellor
conserve su derecha keep right
consigo with him/her
considerar to consider
consulado (*m.*) consulate, 20
contar (o:ue) to count, 9; to tell, 18
contenido (*m.*) content, 9
contestación (*f.*) answer
contestar to answer, 5
contigo with you, 15
continuar to continue, 10
contra against, 11
contrabandear to smuggle
contrabandista (*m., f.*) smuggler, 1
contrabando (*m.*) contraband; smuggling
contrato (*m.*) contract, 10
control (*m.*) control, 13
conversación (*f.*) conversation, P
  — breve brief conversation, P
conversar to talk
cooperación (*f.*) cooperation, 3
copia (*f.*) copy, 11
corazón (*m.*) heart, 7; middle finger
corbata (*f.*) tie
cordón (del zapato) (*m.*) shoelace, 16
correa (*f.*) belt, 8
correo (*m.*) post office, 2; mail, 5
correr to run, 7
correo electrónico (*m.*) e-mail, P
correspondencia (*f.*) mail, 5
cortar (el césped) to mow, to cut (the lawn)
cortavidrios (*m.*) glass cutter
corte (*f.*) court (of law), 14
cortesía (*f.*) courtesy
corto(a) short (*in length*)
cosa (*f.*) thing, 6
costar (o:ue) to cost, 15
crac (*m.*) crack cocaine, 15
creer to believe, to think, 4
  — que sí to think so, 7
crespo(a) curly (*hair*)

© 2017 Cengage Learning

criminal criminal
cruce (*m.*) crossing, intersection, 12
— **de niños** school crossing
cruz (*f.*) cross, 17
cruzar to cross, 12
cuadra (*f.*) block, 2
¿cuál? which?, what?, 4
cualquier(a) any, any (one), either, 5
cualquier cosa que diga anything you say, 6
cuando when, 5
¿cuándo? when?, 4
¿cuánto(a)? how much?
¿cuánto tiempo? how long?, 5
¿cuántos(as)? how many?, 2
cuarto (*m.*) room, 10
cuarto(a) fourth, 4
cubierta (*f.*) hood
cubiertos (*m. pl.*) silverware, 11
cucaracha (*f.*) joint (*col.*)
cuchillo (*m.*) knife, 18
cuello (*m.*) neck, 13, 16; collar
cuenta (*f.*) bill, 11
cuerpo (*m.*) body, 8
¡cuidado! careful!, 20
cuidar to take care of, 5
culpa (*f.*) blame, 12
culpable guilty
cultural cultural
cuñado(a) (*m., f.*) brother-in-law; sister-in-law
curva peligrosa (*f.*) dangerous curve
cuyo(a) whose, 15

D

daga (*f.*) dagger
dar to give, 3
— **respiración artificial** to give CPR
— **un paso** to take a step, 9
— **un tiro (balazo)** to shoot
— **una puñalada** to stab
darse to give (oneself)
— **cuenta de** to realize, to become aware of, 13
— **preso(a)** to be under arrest
— **un pase** to snort, to be stoned, to take a drug
— **vuelta** to turn around, 20
dato personal (*m.*) personal data (information), 1
de of, 1; from, about
— **al lado** next-door (*neighbor, house*), 10
— **cuadros** plaid
— **cultivo** cultured (pearl), 14
— **estatura mediana** of medium height, 4
— **este modo** in this way
— **la mano** hand in hand, 2
— **lunares** polka dot
— **madrugada** at dawn; at daybreak
— **mangas cortas** short-sleeved
— **mangas largas** long-sleeved
— **nada** you're welcome, don't mention it, P
— **nuevo** over, again, 9
— **ojos (azules)** with (blue) eyes, 7
— **pelo (negro)** with (black) hair, 17
— **primera calidad** first class, top quality, 14
— **rayas** striped
— **vacaciones** on vacation, 4
debajo de under, underneath, below, 13
deber must, should, 2; to owe, 11
decidir to decide, 6
décimo(a) tenth, P
decir (e:i) to say, to tell, 7
declaración falsa (*f.*) false statement
declarar culpable to convict
dedo (*m.*) finger, 9
— **del pie** toe
defender(se) to defend (oneself), 18
defensa propia (*f.*) self-defense
deforme deformed
dejar to leave (behind), 2; to allow; to let, 9
— **de** (+ *inf.*) to fail (to do something); to stop (doing something), 6
— **encendido(a), prendido(a)** to leave on (*a light*)
del (de + el) of the, to the, 3
deletrear to spell, 1
delgado(a) thin, 7
delincuente juvenil (*m., f.*) juvenile delinquent
delírium tremens (*m.*) DTs
delito (*m.*) crime, misdemeanor, 5
— **mayor (grave)** felony, 14
demanda (*f.*) lawsuit
demandar to sue
demasiado(a) excessive, too much, 12
dentro inside, 4
— **de** in, within, 6
denuncia (*f.*) report (*of a crime*), 4
denunciar to report (*a crime*), 1
departamento (*m.*) department, 4
depender to depend, 16
dependiente(a) (*m., f.*) clerk, 20
derecha (*f.*) right-hand side, 16
derecho (*m.*) right 6; (*adv.*) straight ahead
derecho(a) right, 13; straight ahead, 2
desaparecer to disappear
desaparecido(a) missing
descanso (*m.*) rest, vacation
— **de primavera** spring break, 10
descompuesto(a) broken, not working, 19
desconocido(a) (*m., f.*) stranger
describir to describe, 7
descripción (*f.*) description, 11
desde from, 8
— **luego** of course, 2
¡dese vuelta! turn around!, 20
desear to want, to wish, 1
desfigurado(a) disfigured
desintoxicación (*f.*) detoxification
desmayado(a) unconscious, 13
desocupado(a) vacant, empty, 3
despacio slowly, 1; slow
despedida (*f.*) farewell
despedir (e:i) to fire (*from a job*), 12
desperfecto (*m.*) (slight) damage; imperfection, 19
después (de) later, 6; after, 7
destruir to destroy, 18
desviarse to swerve, 13
desvío (*m.*) detour
detalle (*m.*) detail, 17
detective (*m., f.*) detective, 14
detención (*f.*) detention, 16
detener to detain, to stop, 6
detenido(a) arrested, 6; (*m., f.*) person under arrest, 16
determinar to determine, 9
detrás de la espalda behind your back
diabetes (*f.*) diabetes, 6
diario (*m.*) newspaper, 5
dictar sentencia to sentence
diente (*m.*) tooth
diestro(a) right-handed, 7
diga (*Cuba y España*) hello (*on the telephone*)
dinamita (*f.*) dynamite
dinero (*m.*) money, 8
dirección (*f.*) address, P
disciplinar to discipline, 8
disco compacto (*m.*) compact disc, 10
disparar to shoot, 3
dispersarse to disperse, 20
dispuesto(a) willing, 8
distribuir to distribute, 15
distrito (*m.*) area
división (*f.*) section, division, 1
divorciado(a) divorced, P
doblar to turn, 2
doble double
— **circulación** (*f.*) two-way traffic
— **vía** (*f.*) divided road
doctor(a) (*m., f.*) doctor, 8
documento (*m.*) document, 17
— **de identidad** ID, 3
— **falso** forged document
dólar (*m.*) dollar, 10
doler (o:ue) to hurt, to ache, 8
domicilio (*m.*) address, P; domicile, P
¿dónde? where?, 1
dormir (o:ue) to sleep, 6
dormitorio (*m.*) bedroom, 8
dorso (*m.*) back (*of paper*), 19
dos veces twice, 17
droga (*f.*) drug, 6
drogadicto(a) (*m., f.*) drug addict, 6
ducharse to shower
dudar to doubt, 16
dueño(a) (*m., f.*) owner, 3
durante during, 5
— **el día (la noche)** during the day (night)

E

echar to throw
— **la cabeza hacia atrás** to tilt one's head back, 9
edad (*f.*) age, 17
edificio (*m.*) building, 6
elegido(a) chosen, 9
elegir (e:i) to choose, 9

© 2017 Cengage Learning

embajada (*f.*) embassy, 20
embarazada pregnant
embrague (*m.*) clutch
emergencia (*f.*) emergency, 4
empeñar to pawn, 14
empezar (e:ie) to begin, 5
empleado(a) (*m., f.*) employee, clerk, 14
empleo (*m.*) job, 11
empujar to push, 18
en in, on, at, 1
— **bicicleta** on a bike, 2
— **buena parte** to a large extent, 16
— **casa** at home, 5
— **contra de** against, 6
— **cuanto** as soon as, 18
— **defensa propia** in self-defense
— **efectivo** in cash, 10
— **libertad bajo fianza** out on bail, 16
— **libertad bajo palabra** out on one's own recognizance, 16
— **lugar de** instead of, 8
— **persona** personally, in person, 1
— **primer lugar** in the first place, 5
¿— qué puedo (podemos) servirle? what can I (we) do for you?, P
— **sentido contrario** in the opposite direction, 13
encender (e:ie) to turn on (a light), 5
encendido(a) on (a light, a TV set), 5
encerrado(a) locked up, closeted, 8
encerrar (e:ie) to lock up, 16
encontrar (o:ue) to find, 11
endrogado(a) on drugs, 6
endrogarse to take drugs, to become addicted to drugs
enfermedad (*f.*) disease
— **venérea** venereal disease, 18
enfrente de across the street from, 5
engañar to cheat, to deceive, 14
enojado(a) angry, 8
enseguida right away, 1
enseñar to show, 9
entender (e:ie) to understand, 6
entonces then, 4
entrada (*f.*) entrance
entrar (en) to go in, 4
no entre do not enter; wrong way
entre between, 1; among
entrega (*f.*) delivery, 5
entregar to give, to turn over (something to someone), 11
entrelazar to interlace; to intertwine, 20
entremeterse to meddle, to butt in, 8
entrenado(a) trained, 4
entrometerse to meddle, to butt in, 8
enviar to send, 1
epiléptico(a) epileptic
equipo (*m.*) equipment, 10
es it is
— **de unos...** it's about . . .
— **decir...** that is to say . . . , 18
— **que...** it's just that . . . , 9
escala de soga (*f.*) rope ladder
escalera de mano (*f.*) hand ladder
escaparse to run away, 17
escopeta (*f.*) shotgun
escribir to write, 6
escuela (*f.*) school, 7; school crossing
— **primaria (elemental)** grade school
— **secundaria** junior high school, high school, 15
escusado (*m.*) (*Méx.*) bathroom
ése(a) (*m., f.*) that one, 8
eso (*m.*) that, 8
espalda (*f.*) back
español (*m.*) Spanish (language), 1
especial special, 5
espejo (*m.*) mirror
espejuelos (*m. pl.*) (*Cuba, Puerto Rico*) eyeglasses, 18
esperar to wait (for), 7
esposado(a) handcuffed, 16
esposas (*f. pl.*) handcuffs, 16
esposo(a) (*m., f.*) husband, 4; wife, 4
esquina (*f.*) corner, 3
esta this
— **noche** tonight, 5
— **vez** this time, 8
ésta (*f.*) this one, 8
establecer to establish, 5
estación (*f.*) station; season
— **de bomberos** fire department
— **de ómnibus (autobuses)** bus station
— **de policía** police station, P
— **de servicio** gas station
estacionado(a) parked, 11
estacionamiento de emergencia solamente emergency parking only
estacionamiento para residentes resident parking
estado (*m.*) state, 2
— **civil** marital status
estafa (*f.*) swindle, fraud, 14
estafar to swindle, 14
estampado(a) print
estar to be, 3
— **a la vista** to be visible
— **apurado(a)** to be in a hurry, 9
— **bien** to be okay, 3
— **de acuerdo** to agree, 16
— **de regreso** to be back, 5
— **de vuelta** to be back, 5
— **en condiciones de** (+ *inf.*) to be in a condition to (do something), 6
— **equivocado(a)** to be wrong, 8
— **preso(a)** to be under arrest, to be in jail
— **seguro(a)** to be certain, 18
estatal (*adj.*) of or pertaining to the state, 9
estatua (*f.*) statue
estatura (*f.*) height, 20
de — mediana medium height, 4
este (*m.*) east
este(a) this, 2
éste(a) (*m., f.*) this one, 8
estómago (*m.*) stomach
estos(as) these, 6
estudiante (*m., f.*) student, 7
estudiar to study, 17
evidencia (*f.*) evidence, 18
evitar to avoid, 5
exactamente exactly, 17
examinar to examine, 13
excusa (*f.*) excuse, 12
excusado (*m.*) (*Méx.*) bathroom
exigir to demand, 2
explosivo (*m.*) explosive
expresión (*f.*) expression
extender (e:ie) to stretch out, to spread, 9
extinguidor de incendios (*m.*) fire extinguisher, 13
extintor de incendios (*m.*) (*España*) fire extinguisher, 13
extraño(a) strange, 4; (*m., f.*) stranger, 5

F

fácilmente easily
falda (*f.*) skirt, 17
falsificación (*f.*) falsification; counterfeit; forgery
falsificador(a) forger, 1
falsificar to falsify; to counterfeit; to forge
falso(a) forged; fake
faltar to be missing, 10
fallecer to die, to pass away, 11
fallo (*m.*) decision; verdict
familia (*f.*) family, 8
fango (*m.*) mud, 10
farmacia (*f.*) pharmacy
faro (*m.*) headlight, 19
felpudo (*m.*) mat
ferrocarril (*m.*) railroad
fiancista (*m., f.*) bailor, bail bondsman, 16
fianza (*f.*) bail, 16
fichar to book, to log in, 16
fiesta (*f.*) party, 10
filtro (*m.*) filter
final (*m.*) end, 9
firmar to sign, 12
fiscal (*m., f.*) prosecutor, district attorney, 16
flaco(a) thin, skinny
flecha, flechita (*f.*) arrow, 18
floreado(a) flowered
foco (*m.*) light
fondo (*m.*) back
en el — in the back
forma (*f.*) way, 8
forzar (o:ue) to force, 10
fotografía (*f.*) photograph, 3
frasco (*m.*) bottle (*of pills*), 19
frecuentemente frequently, 8
freno (*m.*) brake
frente (*f.*) forehead
— **a** in front of, 1
fuego (*m.*) fire, 5
— **intencional** arson
fuera outside, 4
fugarse to run away, 17
fumar to smoke, 7
futuro (*m.*) future

© 2017 Cengage Learning

G

gafas (*f. pl.*) eyeglasses, 18
galleta (*f.*) (*Cuba y Puerto Rico*) slap
ganga (*f.*) bargain, 14
ganzúa (*f.*) skeleton key, picklock
garaje (*m.*) garage
gas (*m.*) gas, 19
gasoil (*m.*) Diesel
gasolina (*f.*) gasoline
gasolinera (*f.*) gas station
gata (*f.*) (*Costa Rica y España*) jack, 20
gato (*m.*) jack, 20
generalmente generally, 5
gente (*f.*) people, 20
girar to turn, 13
golpear to hit, to strike, 18
goma (*f.*) tire, 20
  — ponchada flat tire
gordo(a) fat, 7
gorra (*f.*) cap, 4
grabadora (*f.*) tape recorder, 11
gracias thank you, P
grado (*m.*) degree, 12
grafiti (*m.*) graffiti
gran great, 14
granada de mano (*f.*) hand grenade
grande big, large, 2
grano (*m.*) pimple
grave serious, 1
grifa (*f.*) hashish (*col.*)
gris gray, 20
gritar to scream, to shout, 18
grueso(a) portly
grupo (*m.*) group, 5
guagua (*f.*) (*Cuba y Puerto Rico*) bus
guante (*m.*) glove
guantera (*f.*) glove compartment, 7
guardado(a) put away, saved, 10
guardafangos (*m.*) fender
guardar to keep
güero(a) (*Méx.*) blond(e), fair skinned, 7
guía de teléfonos (*f.*) telephone book, 16
gustar to be pleasing, to like, 8

H

habitación (*f.*) room, 10
hablar to speak, to talk, 1
  — con (la) zeta to lisp
hace un mes (una semana) a month ago, 13; (a week ago); 14
hacer to do, to make, 3
  — arreglar to have (something fixed, 19
  — buen tiempo to have good weather
  — (mucho) calor to be (very) hot
  — caso (a) to pay attention (to), 8
  — falta to need, 8
  — fresco to be cool
  — (mucho) frío to be (very) cold
  — mal tiempo to have bad weather
  — resistencia to resist, 18
  — una pregunta to ask a question, 19
  — (mucho) sol to be (very) sunny
  — (mucho) viento to be (very) windy
hacerse to become
hacia toward, 7
hachich, hachís (*m.*) hashish
hasta until, 2
  — la... up to . . .
  — luego so long, see you later, P
  — mañana I'll see you tomorrow, P
  — que until, 19
hay there is, there are, 1
  — de todo you can find everything, 15
  no — de qué you're welcome, don't mention it, P
helicóptero (*m.*) helicopter
herido(a) (*adj.*) hurt, injured, 1; (*m., f.*) injured person
hermanastro(a) (*m., f.*) stepbrother; stepsister
hermano(a) (*m., f.*) brother; sister
heroína (*f.*) heroin
hijastro(a) (*m., f.*) stepson; stepdaughter
hijo(a) (*m., f.*) son; daughter, 2
hijos (*m. pl.*) children, 4; sons
hispánico(a) Hispanic
hispano(a) Hispanic, 2
histéricamente hysterically, 18
hola hello, hi, P
hombre (*m.*) man, 3
  — de negocios businessman, 15
hombro (*m.*) shoulder
homicida (*m., f.*) murderer, 1
homicidio (*m.*) manslaughter, homicide, 16
hora (*f.*) time, hour, 3
horno (*m.*) oven, 19
hospedaje (*m.*) lodging
hospital (*m.*) hospital, 4
hotel (*m.*) hotel
hoy today, P
hubo there was, (were), 11
huella (*f.*) footprint, 10
  — digital fingerprint, 10
hueso bone, 13
humedad humidity
humillar to humiliate
humo (*m.*) smoke, 5

I

idea (*f.*) idea, 5
identificación (*f.*) identification, ID, 3
  — falsa fake identification, forged ID
identificar to identify, 5
iglesia (*f.*) church
impermeable (*m.*) raincoat
imponer una multa to impose a fine, to give a ticket, 12
importante important, 5
imprudentemente imprudently, recklessly, 12
incendiar to set on fire
incendio (*m.*) fire, 5
  — intencional arson
incómodo(a) uncomfortable, 2
índice (*m.*) index (finger), 9
infiltrar(se) to infiltrate, 15
información (*f.*) information, P
informe (*m.*) report, 1
infracción de tránsito (*f.*) traffic violation, 6
inglés (*m.*) English (language), 1
ingresado(a) admitted (to), 8
ingresar to be admitted (to), to enter, 8
iniciar to begin, 12
inmediatamente immediately, 5
inocente innocent, 14
instalar to install, 5
intento (*m.*) attempt, 15
intérprete (*m., f.*) interpreter
interrogar to question, to interrogate, 6
interrogatorio (*m.*) interrogation, questioning, 6
intoxicado(a) intoxicated, 19
inválido(a) disabled, crippled
investigación (*f.*) investigation, 16
investigador(a) (*adj.*) investigating, 16
investigar to investigate, 8
invierno (*m.*) winter
ir to go, 3
  — a (+ *inf.*) to be going (to do something), 5
irse to go away, to leave, 10
izquierdo(a) left, 7

J

jardín (*m.*) garden
jardinero(a) (*m., f.*) gardener, 3
jefatura de policía (*f.*) police station, P
jefe(a) (*m., f.*) boss, 12
jeringa hipodérmica (*f.*) hypodermic syringe
jeringuilla (*f.*) hypodermic syringe
joven young, 4; (*m., f.*) young man, young woman, 6
jovencito(a) (*m., f.*) adolescent, teenager, 17
joya (*f.*) jewel, jewelry, 10
juanita (*f.*) marijuana (*col.*)
juez(a) (*m., f.*) judge, 8
juicio (*m.*) trial, 6
junta (*f.*) meeting, 5
juntos(as) together, 9
jurado (*m.*) jury, 14
juramento (*m.*) oath
jurar to take an oath, to swear
juzgado (*m.*) court (of law), 14
juzgar to judge, 14

K

kif (*m.*) hashish (*col.*)

L

labio (*m.*) lip
lacio(a) straight (*hair*)
lado (*m.*) side, 13

© 2017 Cengage Learning

ladrillo (*m.*) one-kilo brick of marijuana (*col.*)
ladrón(ona) (*m., f.*) thief, burglar, 3
largo(a) long
lastimado(a) hurt, injured, 7
lastimarse to get hurt, 13
latino(a) Latin, Hispanic, 15
leer to read, 6
lejos far, 17
  — de far from
lengua (*f.*) tongue; language
lentes (*m. pl.*) eyeglasses, 18
leño (*m.*) joint (*col.*)
lesión (*f.*) injury, 8
lesionado(a) injured, 8
levantar to lift
levantarse to get up, 13
ley (*f.*) law, 2
libra (*f.*) pound, 20
librería (*f.*) bookstore
libreta (de teléfonos) (*f.*) address book, 18
licencia (*f.*) license
  — de conducir driver's license, 3
  — para manejar (conducir) driver's license, 3
licor (*m.*) liquor, spirits, 20
licorería (*f.*) liquor store, 7
límite (*m.*) limit, 9
  — de velocidad speed limit, 9
limpiaparabrisas (*m.*) windshield wiper
limpiar to clean, 10
línea (*f.*) line, 9
  — de parada stop line, 12
linterna (*f.*) flashlight, 4
lista (*f.*) list, 11
listo(a) ready, 19
liviano(a) light, 20
llamada (*f.*) call, 4
  — telefónica telephone call, 5
llamar to call, 1
  — al perro to call off the dog
llamarse to be named, to be called, 9
llanta (*f.*) (*Mex.*) tire, 20
  — pinchada flat tire
llave (*f.*) key, 5
  — falsa skeleton key; picklock
llegar (a) to arrive (at), to reach, 2
  — a (+ *inf.*) to succeed in (doing something), 18
  — tarde to be late, 12
llenar to fill out, 1
llevar to take, to carry, to wear, 2
  — puesto(a) to wear, 2
llevarse to steal, 11
llorar to cry, 18
llover (o:ue) to rain
lluvia (*f.*) rain
lo you, him, it, 6
  — demás the rest, 6
  — más importante the most important thing, 5
  — primero the first thing, 5
  — que what, that which, 8
  — siento I'm sorry, 6
  — único the only thing, 8
local local, 8
los (las) demás the others, 5; the remaining ones, 10
luchar to fight, to struggle, 18
luego later, afterwards, 10
lugar (*m.*) place, 5
lunar (*m.*) mole, 17
  de lunares polka dot
luz (*f.*) light, 4
  — de giro turn signal

M

maceta de flores (*f.*) flower pot
madrastra (*f.*) stepmother, 3
madre (*f.*) mother, mom, 2
madrina (*f.*) godmother
madrugada (*f.*) early morning, 9
maestro(a) (*m., f.*) teacher
maletero (*m.*) trunk (*of a car*), 20
malo(a) bad, 6
maltratar to abuse, 8
maltrato (*m.*) abuse, 8
mamá (*f.*) mom, mother, 2
mancha (*f.*) spot, mark, blemish
mandar to send, 1
  mande (*Mex.*) hello (*on the telephone*)
manejar to drive, 6
  ¡maneje con cuidado! drive safely!, 12
manera (*f.*) way, 5
mangas (*f. pl.*) sleeves
  de — cortas short-sleeved
  de — largas long-sleeved
  sin — sleeveless
mano (*f.*) hand, 6
  ¡manos arriba! hands up!
manteca (*f.*) (*Caribe*) heroin (*col.*)
mantener to keep
  mantenga su derecha keep right
manzana (*f.*) city block
mañana (*f.*) morning, 10; (*adv.*) tomorrow
  a la — in the morning
máquina (*f.*) (*Cuba*) car, 6
marca (*f.*) mark, 6; brand, 10; make (car)
mareado(a) dizzy, 13
marido (*m.*) husband, 4
mariguana, marihuana, marijuana (*f.*) marijuana
más more
  — bien rather, 7
  — o menos more or less, 8
  — ... que (de) more . . . than, 4
  — tarde later, 2
máscara (*f.*) mask
matar to kill, 8
matricularse to register, to enroll (*in a school*), 15
mayor older, oldest, 3
  — de edad of age, adult
  dedo — (*m.*) middle finger
mécanico (*m.*) mechanic
mediano(a) medium; average
medianoche (*f.*) midnight, 3
medicina (*f.*) medicine, 7
médico (*m., f.*) doctor, 8
medio (*adv.*) rather, 7
medir (e:i) to measure, 7; to be (amount) tall, 17
mejilla (*f.*) cheek, 17
mejor better, best, 12
  — que nunca better than ever, 6
menor younger, 4; minor
  — de edad (*m., f.*) minor, 3
menos de (que) less than, fewer than, 4
mensaje (*m.*) message, 7
mentira (*f.*) lie, 8
meñique (*m.*) little finger
mercado (*m.*) market, 20; supermarket
  — al aire libre (*m.*) open-air market
mes (*m.*) month
  el — pasado (próximo) last (next) month
  el — que viene next month
mestizo(a) mixed (any of two or more races)
metadona (*f.*) methadone
metido(a) inside, inserted in, 19
mi my, 1
miembro (*m., f.*) member, 3
  — del jurado jury member
mientras while, 5
milla (*f.*) mile, 9
mirando watching
mirar to look at, 5; to watch
mire look, 6
mismo(a) same, 9
  por sí — by himself, by herself
mitin (*m.*) meeting, assembly, 20
modelo (*m.*) model, 11
modo (*m.*) way, 5
momento (*m.*) moment, P
moneda (*f.*) coin, 9
monumento (*m.*) monument
mordaza (*f.*) gag
mordida (*f.*) bite
morfina (*f.*) morphine
morgue (*f.*) morgue
morir (o:ue) to die, to pass away, 11
morocho(a) dark-haired, 7
mostrador (*m.*) counter, 16
mostrar (o:ue) to show, 7
mota (*f.*) marijuana (*col.*)
motel (*m.*) motel, 15
motivo (*m.*) motive
motocicleta (*f.*) motorcycle, 13; motor-driven cycle
motor (*m.*) engine, motor, 9
  — de arranque starter
mover(se) (o:ue) to move, 6
  ¡no se mueva(n)! don't move!, freeze!, 6
muchacho(a) (*m., f.*) boy, girl, 2
muchísimo very much, 15
mucho (*adv.*) much, 4
muchos(as) many, 2
  muchas gracias thank you very much, P
mudo(a) mute
muerto(a) dead, 1

© 2017 Cengage Learning

mujer (*f.*) woman, 1; wife, 4
 — de negocios businesswoman, 15
mulato(a) mixed race (black and white)
multa (*f.*) ticket, fine, 6
multitud (*f.*) crowd, 20
municipal municipal
muñeca (*f.*) wrist
murmurar to murmur, 20
musculoso(a) muscular
muy very, P

N

nacimiento (*m.*) birth
nada nothing, P
nadie nobody, 8
nalgada (*f.*) spanking, slap on the buttocks
nariz (*f.*) nose, 9
navaja (*f.*) switchblade, razor, 8
neblina (*f.*) fog
necesario(a) necessary, 5
necesitar to need, 1
negarse (e:ie)(a) to refuse to, 6
 — a hablar to refuse to speak, 6
negro(a) black, 4
 negra (*f.*) black heroin (*col.*)
neumático (*m.*) tire, 20
nevar (e:ie) to snow
niebla (*f.*) fog
nieto(a) (*m., f.*) grandson; granddaughter
nieve (*f.*) snow
ninguno(a) not any
niño(a) (*m., f.*) child, 1
no no
 ¡— dispare! don't shoot!
 — entre do not enter; wrong way
 — hay de qué you're welcome, don't mention it, P
 — me hace caso. He/She doesn't pay attention to me.
 — pasar do not pass
 — rebasar (*Mex.*) do not pass
 ¡— salte! don't jump!
 ¡— se mueva! don't move!, freeze!, 6
 ¡— tire! don't shoot!
 ¡— tire basura! don't litter!
¿Nos va a llevar presos? Are you going to arrest us?, 6
noche (*f.*) night, 5
 a la — in the evening
nombrar to appoint
nombre (*m.*) name, P; noun
noreste (*m.*) northeast
noroeste (*m.*) northwest
norte (*m.*) north
nota (*f.*) note
notar to notice, 5
notificar to inform, to give notice, to report, 1
novio(a) (*m., f.*) boyfriend, 15; girlfriend, 15
nuera (*f.*) daughter-in-law
nuestro(a) our, 5
nuevo(a) new, fresh, 6
número (*m.*) number, 5
 — de serie serial number, 10
 — de teléfono (celular) (cell) telephone number, P
nunca never, 6
 — antes never before, 11

O

o or, 3
objeto (*m.*) object, item, 11
obligar to obligate, to force, 18
obligatorio(a) compulsory, 13
obscenidad (*f.*) obscenity, 20
observar to observe, 5
ocasión (*f.*) occasion, 17
ocurrir to occur, 14; to happen
oeste (*m.*) west
oficina (*f.*) office, 12
 — de correos post office
ofrecer to offer, 14
oído (*m.*) inner ear
Oigo. (*Cuba*) Hello. (on the telephone)
oír to hear, 19
ojalá I hope, 17
ojo (*m.*) eye
 — de vidrio glass eye
 de ojos (azules) with (blue) eyes, 7
 ojos saltones (*m. pl.*) bulging eyes, bug eyes
olor (*m.*) smell, 19
 — a smell of, 19
olvidar to forget, 18
ómnibus (*m.*) bus
operador(a) (*m., f.*) telephone operator, dispatcher, 1
opio (*m.*) opium
oportunidad (*f.*) opportunity, 16
opuesto(a) opposite
orden (*f.*) warrant, order, 8
ordenador (*m.*) (*España*) computer, 10
ordenar to order, 20
organizar to organize, 5
oreja (*f.*) outer ear
orina (*f.*) urine, 9
oro (*m.*) gold, 16
oscuro(a) dark, 4
otoño (*m.*) autumn, fall
otro(a) other, another, 4
 otra vez again, once again, 6

P

padrastro (*m.*) stepfather, 3, 8
padre (*m.*) father, dad, 5
padres (*m. pl.*) parents, 3
 — de crianza/adoptivos (*m. pl.*) foster parents
padrino (*m.*) godfather
pagado(a) paid (for), 11
pagar to pay (for), 6
pago (*m.*) payment, 11
país (*m.*) country, 8
palabra (*f.*) word
palanca de cambio de velocidades (*f.*) gearshift lever
paliza (*f.*) beating
pana (*f.*) corduroy, 20
pandilla (*f.*) gang, 3
pantalón, (*m.*) **pantalones** (*m. pl.*) pants, trousers, 4
 — corto(s) shorts, 4
pañuelo (*m.*) handkerchief, 16
papá (*m.*) dad, father, 5
papeleta (*f.*) form, 19
par: un — de a couple of, 6
para for, 1; to, in order to, 5
 — allá there, over there, 1
 — mí for me, 14
 — que so that
 — que lo represente to represent you, 6
 — servirle at your service, P
 — ti for you, 18
parada (*f.*) stop
 — de autobuses, de guaguas (*Cuba y Puerto Rico*), **de camiones** (*Mex.*) bus stop
paradero (*m.*) whereabouts
parado(a) standing, 7
paralítico(a) disabled, crippled
paramédico (*m., f.*) paramedic, 1
parar to stop, 12
 ¡pare! stop!
pararse to stand (up), 9
 ¡párese! stand up!
parecer to seem, 4
pared (*f.*) wall, 6
pariente (*m., f.*) relative
 parientes políticos (*m. pl.*) in-laws
parpadear to blink, 6
parque (*m.*) park
parte (*f.*) part
pasado (*m.*) past
pasado(a) last, 11
 pasado mañana the day after tomorrow
pasajero(a) (*m., f.*) passenger, 13
pasar to come in, P; to happen, 2; to pass (a car), 13; to spend (time)
 no — do not pass
 no pase wrong way; do not enter
 — un buen rato to have a good time, 15
 pasarlo bien to have a good time, 15
pase come in, P
pasarse la luz roja to go through a red light, 12
pasillo (*m.*) hall(way)
paso (*m.*) steps, 9
 — de peatones pedestrian crossing
pastilla (*f.*) pill, 19; LSD (*col.*)
pasto (*m.*) marijuana (*col.*)
pata de cabra (*f.*) crowbar
patada (*f.*) kick
patio (*m.*) yard, 3
patrulla (*f.*) patrol, 5
patrullero(a) (*adj.*) patrol
peatón (*m., f.*) pedestrian
peca (*f.*) freckle, 7
pecho (*m.*) chest
pedir (e:i) to ask (for), 7
 — prestado(a) to borrow, 11

© 2017 Cengage Learning

pegao (*m.*) LSD (*col.*)
pegar to beat, 8
— **un tiro (un balazo)** to shoot
peine (*m.*) comb, 16
pelado(a) bald, 18
pelea (*f.*) fight
peligro (*m.*) danger
peligroso(a) dangerous, 4
pelirrojo(a) red haired, 7
pelo (*m.*) hair, 17
pelón(ona) bald
peluca (*f.*) wig; hairpiece
penetración (*f.*) penetration, 18
pensar (e:ie) to think, 5
— (+ *inf.*) to plan (to do something), 5
pequeño(a) little, small, 1
perder (e:ie) to lose, 6
perdido(a) lost, 2
perdón (*m.*) pardon, forgiveness, 8
perdonar to forgive, 8
perico (*m.*) cocaine (*col.*)
periódico (*m.*) newspaper, 5
perito (*m., f.*) expert
perjudicar to cause damage, to hurt, 14
perla (*f.*) pearl, 14
permanecer to stay, to remain, 6
permiso (*m.*) permission, warrant, 20
permitido(a) permitted, 16
pero but, 1
persona (*f.*) person, 1
pertenencias (*f. pl.*) belongings, 16
pesado(a) heavy, 20
pesar to weigh, 20
peso (*m.*) weight
pestaña (*f.*) eyelash
pie (*m.*) foot, 7
piedra (*f.*) rock (crack cocaine) (*col.*), 15; stone, rock
piel (*f.*) skin
pierna (*f.*) leg, 13
pieza (*f.*) bedroom, 8
píldora (*f.*), 19
piscina (*f.*) swimming pool
pista (*f.*) clue
pistola (*f.*) pistol, 4
pito (*m.*) marijuana (*col.*)
placa (*f.*) license plate, 11
plata (*f.*) silver, 11
playa (*f.*) beach, 10
plazo (*m.*) installment, 11
poco little
un — de a little, 1
podar arbustos (árboles) to trim bushes (trees)
poder (o:ue) can, to be able, 6
no se puede escribir... you (one) cannot write . . . , 6
puede usarse can be used, 6
policía (*f.*) police (force), (*m., f.*) police officer, 1
— **secreta** (*f.*) undercover police, 15
pollera (*f.*) skirt, 4
polvo (*m.*) cocaine (*col.*)

poner to put, 9
a disposición to appear before, 16
— **en peligro** to endanger, 12
ponerse to put on, 18
— **de pie** to stand up
— **de rodillas** to get on one's knees
por for, P; on (by way of), 2; through, 2
— **completo** completely, 16
— **ejemplo** for example, 5
— **escrito** in writing, 16
— **favor** please, P
— **la mañana** in the morning, 7
— **la noche** in the evening, at night, 7
— **la tarde** in the afternoon, 7
— **lo menos** at least, 17
— **lo tanto** therefore, so, 20
— **poseer drogas** for possession of drugs
¿— qué? why?, 2
— **sí mismo(a)** by himself/herself
— **suerte** fortunately, 13
— **teléfono** on the telephone, by telephone, 1
pornográfico(a) pornographic
porque because, 3
porqué (*m.*) reason, 8
porro (*m.*) joint (*col.*)
portaequipajes (*m.*) trunk (*of a car*)
portaguantes (*m.*) glove compartment
portal (*m.*) porch, 5
posible possible, 5
practicar to practice
precaución (*f.*) precaution, 13
preferir (e:ie) to prefer, 5
pregunta (*f.*) question
preguntar to ask, 8
preliminar preliminary, 16
prender to arrest, 3; to turn on (*a light*), 4
prendido(a) (turned) on (*a light, a TV set*), 5; lit, 19
presentar to introduce, 15
— **una apelación** to file an appeal
presente present, 6
preso(a) arrested, 6
prestar to lend
— **atención** to pay attention, 9
prevenir to prevent, 5
preventivo(a) preventive, 16
prima (*f.*) premium, 16
primavera (*f.*) spring
primero (*adv.*) first, 1
primero(a) first, 5
primeros auxilios (*m. pl.*) first aid
primo(a) (*m., f.*) cousin
prisión (*f.*) prison, jail
problema (*m.*) problem, 3
procesado(a) indicted
programa (*m.*) program, 5
prohibido(a) forbidden, 6; prohibited
— **estacionar** no parking
— **girar en rojo** no turn on red
— **pasar** no trespassing
prometer to promise, 20
prometido(a) (*m., f.*) fiancé(e)

pronto soon, 4
propiedad (*f.*) property, 11
— **privada** private property
prostitución (*f.*) prostitution
prostituto(a) (*m., f.*) prostitute, 15
proteger to protect, 5
protestar to complain, to protest, 3
próximo(a) next, 4
prueba (*f.*) test, 9; evidence
— **del alcohol** sobriety test, 9
pueblo (*m.*) town, 10
puede ser it may be, 17
puerta (*f.*) door, 5
— **blindada** armored door, 5
— **de la calle** front door, 5
— **de salida** exit (door)
pulgada (*f.*) inch, 7
pulgar (*m.*) thumb
pullar (*Caribe*) to shoot up (drugs)
punta (*f.*) end, tip, 9
puñal (*m.*) dagger
puñalada: dar una — to stab
puñetazo (*m.*) punch

Q

que that, what, who, 2
¿qué? what?, 1
¿— hay de nuevo? what's new?, P
¿— hora era (es)? what time was (is) it?, 18
¿— más? what else?, 7
¿— tiene? what's wrong?, 7
¿— se le ofrece? what can I (we) do for you?, P
quebrado(a) broken, 13
¡Queda arrestado(a)! You are under arrest!
quedar to be located, 2
— **declarado(a) ilegal** to be hereby declared illegal, 20
quedarse to stay, 10
— **callado(a)** to remain silent, 6
— **sin trabajo** to lose one's job, 14
queja (*f.*) complaint
querer (e:ie) to want, to wish, 5
¿quién? ¿quiénes? who?, 1
quieto(a) still, quiet, calm, 13
¡quieto(a)! freeze!, 3
químico(a) (*adj.*) chemical, 9
quitar to take away, 8
quitarse to take off (*clothing*), 16

R

radiografía (*f.*) X-ray, 13
rápido (*adj.*) quick, quickly, fast, 12
raza (*f.*) race, 18
realizar to perform, to carry out, 18
rebasar (*Méx.*) to pass (a car), 13
recámara (*f.*) (*Méx.*) bedroom, 8
recibir to receive, 4
reciente recent, 17
recientemente recently
recitar to recite, 9

© 2017 Cengage Learning

recobrar to recover, 11
recoger to pick up, 5
recomendar (e:ie) to recommend, 16
reconocer to recognize, 7
recordar (o:ue) to remember, 6
refugiarse to find refuge (shelter)
regalar to give (*a gift*), 15
registrado(a) registered, 11
registrar to book, to log in, 16
registro (*m.*) registration, 6
regresar to return, 2
rehabilitación (*f.*) rehab, 19
reloj (*m.*) watch, 16
reo(a) (*m., f.*) defendant
reporte (*m.*) report, 1
representar to represent
reproductor de DVD DVD player
reproductor MP3 MP3 player
rescatar to rescue
rescate (*m.*) ransom
residencial residential, 9
resistencia a la autoridad (*f.*) resisting arrest
respirar to breathe
responder to respond, 15
respuesta (*f.*) answer
restaurante (*m.*) restaurant
retratar to photograph, 16
reunión (*f.*) meeting, assembly, 5
revisar to review, to check, 10
revólver (*m.*) revolver, 4
rico(a) rich
riego (*m.*) watering, 5
riesgo (*m.*) risk, 11
rifle (*m.*) rifle
rincón (*m.*) corner
riña (*f.*) fight
rizado(a) curly
rizo(a) curly
robado(a) stolen, 10
robar to rob, to steal from, 10
robo (*m.*) robbery, burglary, 1
roca (*f.*) crack cocaine (*col.*)
rodilla (*f.*) knee
rojo(a) red, 4
rondar to prowl, 10
ropa (*f.*) clothes, 4
— **interior** underwear
rubio(a) blond(e), 7
rueda (*f.*) wheel
ruido (*m.*) noise

S

saber to know, 5; to find out (*pret.*), 17
sacar to take out, 6
saco (*m.*) jacket
sala (*f.*) living room
— **de estar** family room
salida (*f.*) exit
salir to get out, 5; to leave, 5; to come out
— **con** to go out with, to date, 17
saltar to jump, 13
¡salud! to your health!
saludar to greet, 15
saludo (*m.*) greeting
salvar to save, 2
sandalia (*f.*) sandal, 17
sangre (*f.*) blood, 9
sargento (*m.*) sergeant, P
sección (*f.*) section, division, 1
secreto(a) secret, 15
secuestrador(a) kidnapper, 1
secuestrar to kidnap, 12
secuestro (*m.*) kidnapping, 5
sedante (*m.*) sedative, 19
sedativo (*m.*) sedative, 19
seguir (e:i) to follow
— **caminando** to keep walking
— **derecho** to go straight ahead, 2
según according to
seguro (*m.*) lock (*cars*)
seguro(a) safe
Seguro Social Social Security, 7
sellado(a) sealed, 16
sello (*m.*) LSD (*col.*)
semáforo (*m.*) traffic light, 12
semana (*f.*) week, 4
la — pasada (próxima) last (next) week
la — que viene next week
semiautomático(a) semiautomatic, 20
sentarse (e:ie) to sit down
siéntese sit down, 8
sentencia (*f.*) sentence
sentenciar to sentence
sentimental sentimental, 14
sentirse (e:ie) to feel, 13
señal de tránsito (*f.*) traffic sign
señor (Sr.) (*m.*) Mr., sir, gentleman, P
los señores (Ruiz) (*m. pl.*) Mr. and Mrs. (Ruiz), 17
señora (Sra.) (*f.*) Mrs., lady, Ma'am, Madam, P
señorita (Srta.) (*f.*) Miss, young lady, P
separar los pies to separate (spread) your feet
ser to be, P
— **como las (+ *time*)** to be about (+ *time*), 18
— **culpable (de)** to be at fault, to be guilty (of), 12
serie (*f.*) series, 10
serio(a) serious, 13
serrucho de mano (*m.*) handsaw
servicio (*m.*) service, 15
servir (e:i) to serve
sexo (*m.*) sex, 15
sexual sexual, 18
Sgto. (*abbrev. of* **Sargento**) sergeant
shorts (*m. pl.*) shorts
si if, 4
sí yes, 1
sí mismo(a) yourself; himself; herself
SIDA (síndrome de inmunodeficiencia adquirida) (*m.*) AIDS, 18
siempre always, 3
siéntese sit down, 8
sierra de mano (*f.*) handsaw
siguiente following
silenciador (*m.*) muffler
silla de ruedas (*f.*) wheelchair
sin without, 3
— **embargo** nevertheless, however, 14
— **falta** without fail, 19
— **mangas** sleeveless
sinceramente sincerely, 14
sistema (*m.*) system, 5
situación (*f.*) situation
soborno (*m.*) bribe, 15
sobre (*m.*) envelope, 16
sobre (*prep.*) about; on, on top of, 20
sobredosis (*f.*) overdose
sobrino(a) (*m., f.*) nephew; niece
¡socorro! help!
soga (*f.*) rope
solamente only, 5
solicitar to ask for, 2; to solicit, 15
solo(a) alone, 2
sólo only, 5
soltar (o:ue) to let go of
— **el arma** to drop the gun (weapon)
soltero(a) single, P
sombrero (*m.*) hat, 4
someterse a to submit (oneself) to, 9
son las (+ *time*) it's (+*time*)
sordo(a) deaf
sortija (*f.*) ring, 17
sospecha (*f.*) suspicion, 8
sospechar to suspect, 7
sospechoso(a) suspicious, 5
sótano (*m.*) basement
su your, 1; his, her, 3
subir to get in (*a car, etc.*), 3
súbase al carro get in the car
suceder to happen, 2
sucio(a) dirty, 18
suegro(a) (*m., f.*) father-in-law; mother-in-law
suelo (*m.*) floor, 7
suéter (*m.*) sweater, 17
suficiente sufficient, enough, 15
sugerir (e:ie) to suggest, 16
suicidarse to commit suicide, 19
supermercado (*m.*) supermarket, market
suspender (la entrega) to stop (delivery)
— **la entrega de la correspondencia** to stop mail delivery
— **la entrega del periódico** to stop newspaper delivery
sur (*m.*) south
sureste (*m.*) southeast
suroeste (*m.*) southwest
suyo(a) yours

T

tabique (*m.*) 1-kilo brick of marijuana (*col.*)
tablero (*m.*) instrument panel
tal such
— **cosa** such a thing, 19
— **vez** perhaps, 18
talón (*m.*) heel, 9
tamaño (*m.*) size
también also, too, 5

© 2017 Cengage Learning

tan so, 12
— **...como** as . . . as, 4
— **pronto como** as soon as, 19
tanque (*m.*) tank
tapicería (*f.*) upholstery
taquígrafo(a) (*m., f.*) court reporter, stenographer
tarde (*f.*) afternoon, 1; (*adv.*) late, 2
a la — in the afternoon
tarjeta verde (*f.*) green card, 3
tartamudear to stutter
tartamudo(a) (*m., f.*) person who stutters
tatuaje (*m.*) tattoo, 7
teatro (*m.*) (movie) theater
técnico(a) (*m., f.*) technician, 10
techo (de tejas) (*m.*) (tile) roof
telefónico(a) (*adj.*) related to the telephone, 4; telephonic
telefonista (*m., f.*) operator, dispatcher, 1
teléfono (*m.*) telephone, 1
televisor (*m.*) television set, 10
temblar (e:ie) to shake, to tremble, to shiver, 13
temer to fear, to be afraid, 17
temperatura (*f.*) temperature, 12
temprano early, 2
tener to have, 4
— **a su cargo** to be in charge of, 15
— **...años** to be . . . years old, 4
— **el derecho de** to have the right to, 6
— **la culpa (de)** to be at fault, to be guilty, 12
— **(mucho) miedo** to be (very) afraid, scared, 4
— **(mucho) sueño** to be (very) sleepy, 6
— **prisa** to be in a hurry, 9
— **puesto(a)** to have on, to wear, 17
— **que** (+ *inf.*) to have to (do something), 4
— **razón** to be right, 12
— **tanto miedo** to be so scared, 18
teniente lieutenant, P
tequila (*f.*) tequila, 15
tercero(a) third, 8
terminar to finish, 10; to end
— **de** (+ *inf.*) to finish (doing something), 10
terraza (*f.*) terrace
testigo (*m., f.*) witness, 14
tianguis (*m.*) (*Méx.*) open-air market
tiempo (*m.*) time, 5
tienda (*f.*) store
timón (*m.*) (*Cuba*) steering wheel
tío(a) (*m., f.*) uncle 9; aunt, 9
tirar to throw away, 10; to shoot
título (*m.*) title
tobillo (*m.*) ankle
tocar to touch, 9
— **a la puerta** to knock at the door, 8
— **el timbre** to ring the doorbell, 5
— **la bocina** to honk the horn
todavía still, yet, 2
todo (*m.*) everything
— **lo posible** everything possible, 11
todo(a) whole, 8; all, 11
— **el (la)...** the whole . . .
todos(as) all, every(body), 5
todos los días every day, 8
tomar to take, 6; to drink, 6
— **asiento** to take a seat, P
— **las huellas digitales** to fingerprint, 16
— **medidas** to take measures, 5
tontería (*f.*) foolishness, nonsense, 10
toque de queda (*m.*) curfew, 3
totalmente totally, 11
trabajo (*m.*) work, job, 8
traer to bring, 7
traficante (*m., f.*) drug pusher
tráfico (*m.*) traffic
trago (*m.*) drink, 6
traje (*m.*) suit
tránsito (*m.*) traffic
— **lento** slow traffic
tratar (de) to try (to), 4; to treat, 8
tribunal (*m.*) court
— **de menores** (*m.*) juvenile court
— **supremo** supreme court
trompada (*f.*) punch
Tte. (*abbreviation of* **Teniente**) lieutenant
tu your, 2

U

últimamente lately, 6
último(a) last (*in a series*), 11
un par de a couple of, 6
unido(a) united, 5
unos(as) about, around, 2
urgente urgent, 4
urgentemente urgently, 14
usado(a) used
usar to use, 4
se usará will be used, 6
uso (*m.*) use, 2
usual usual, 5
no — unusual, 5

V

vacaciones (*f. pl.*) vacation, 10
de — on vacation, 4
— **de primavera** spring break, 10
vaciar to empty, 16
válido(a) valid, 12
valor (*m.*) value, 11
vamos let's go, 2
— **a** (+ *inf.*) let's (+ *verb*)
vandalismo (*m.*) vandalism, 6
varios(as) several, 5
vecindario (*m.*) neighborhood, 5
vecino(a) (*m., f.*) neighbor, 5
vehículo (*m.*) vehicle, 13
velocidad (*f.*) speed, 9
— **máxima** speed limit, 9
vello (*m.*) body hair
velludo(a) hairy
venda (*f.*) bandage, 13
vender to sell, 3
veneno (*m.*) poison, 19
venir (e:ie) to come, 4
ventana (*f.*) window, 5
— **con rejas** window with bars, 5
ventanilla (*f.*) window (*of a car*)
ver to see, 2
verano (*m.*) summer
verbo (*m.*) verb
verdad (*f.*) truth, 11
¿verdad? right?, true?, 2
verde green, 3
veredicto (*m.*) verdict
verruga (*f.*) wart
vestido (*m.*) dress
vestido(a) dressed, 4
veterinario(a) (*m. f.*) veterinary
vez (*f.*) time, 8
vía (*f.*) lane, 12
viaje (*m.*) trip
víctima (*f.*) victim, 17
vida (*f.*) life, 2
videocámara (*f.*) video camera, 10
videojuego videogame
viejo(a) old, 7
vigilancia del barrio (*f.*) neighborhood watch, 5
vino (*m.*) wine, 20
violación (*f.*) rape, 18
violador(a) rapist, 1
violar to rape, 18
violento(a) violent, 8
virarse (*Cuba*) to turn around, 20
visible visible, 5
visto(a) seen
viudo(a) widower; widow
vivir to live, 2
vocabulario (*m.*) vocabulary
volante (*m.*) steering wheel
voltear(se) (*Méx.*) to turn (around)
voluntad (*f.*) will, 17
voluntariamente voluntarily, 20
volver (o:ue) to come (go) back, to return, 6

Y

y and, P
ya already, 2; at last, finally, 8
— **están en camino** they are (already) on their way, 4
yerba (*f.*) marijuana (*col.*), 15
yerno (*m.*) son-in-law
yesca (*f.*) marijuana (*col.*)

Z

zacate (*m.*) (*Méx.*) lawn, 5; marijuana (*col.*)
zapatilla (*f.*) tennis shoe, sneaker, 4
zapato (*m.*) shoe
— **de tenis** tennis shoe
zona (*f.*) zone, 9
— **de estacionamiento** parking lot, 7
— **de grúa** tow zone
zurdo(a) left-handed, 7

© 2017 Cengage Learning

English-Spanish Vocabulary

A

a little un poco, 1
a week ago hace una semana, 14
abnormal anormal, 18
about unos(as), 2; como, 11; (*with time*) a eso de, 14; sobre
abuse maltrato (*m.*), 8; maltratar, abusar, 8
accelerator acelerador (*m.*)
accent acento (*m.*), 18
accept aceptar, 8
accident accidente (*m.*), 1
accompany acompañar, 7
accomplice cómplice (*m., f.*)
according to según
accusation acusación (*f.*), 14
accuse acusar, 8
ache doler (o:ue), 8
acid (LSD) pegao (*m.*) (*col.*)
acne acné (*m.*)
acquaintance conocido(a) (*m., f.*)
acquitted absuelto(a)
across the street from enfrente de, 5
act acto (*m.*), 18; actuar
activity actividad (*f.*), 5
addicted adicto(a)
additional adicional
address dirección (*f.*), domicilio (*m.*), P
  — book libreta de direcciones (*f.*), 18
adjective adjetivo (*m.*), 1
admitted (to) ingresado(a), 8
adolescent adolescente (*m., f.*), jovencito(a) (*m., f.*), 17
adult mayor de edad
advise aconsejar, 16
after después (de), 7
afternoon tarde (*f.*), 1
  in the — por la tarde, a la tarde, 7
afterwards luego, 10
again otra vez, 6; de nuevo, 9
against en contra de, 6; contra, 11
age edad (*f.*), 17
ago: a week — hace una semana, 14
agree estar de acuerdo, 16
aggression agresión (*f.*); ataque (*m.*)
aggressor agresor(a) (*m., f.*)
AIDS SIDA (síndrome de inmunodeficiencia adquirida) (*m.*), 18
aim (a gun) apuntar, 20
alarm alarma (*f.*)
alcohol alcohol (*m.*), 9
alcoholic alcohólico(a), 9
alias alias (*m.*)
alibi coartada (*f.*)
all todo(a), 11; todos(as)
allergic alérgico(a)
allow dejar, 9; autorizar, 16
almost casi, 5
alone solo(a), 2
alphabet abecedario (*m.*), alfabeto (*m.*), 9
already ya, 2
also también, 5
although aunque, 15
always siempre, 3
ambulance ambulancia (*f.*), 13
among entre
amphetamine amfetamina (*f.*)
and y, P
angry enojado(a), 8
ankle tobillo (*m.*)
another otro(a), 4
answer contestar, 5; respuesta (*f.*), contestación (*f.*)
any cualquier, alguno(a), 5
  — one cualquier(a)
  — time a sus órdenes, 3
  not — ninguno(a)
anything algo (*m.*), 8; cualquier cosa (*f.*)
  — else? ¿algo más?, 7
  — you say cualquier cosa que diga, 6
apartment apartamento (*m.*), 1
appeal apelación (*f.*); 1 apelar
appear comparecer
  — before poner a disposición, 16
  — in court comparecer ante un juez
appoint nombrar
approximate aproximado(a), 11
approximately como, 11; aproximadamente
area distrito (*m.*), área (*f. but* el área)
arm brazo (*m.*), 6
armored door puerta blindada (*f.*), 5
around unos(as), 2
arrange arreglar
arrest arrestar, prender, 3; llevar preso(a)
  person under — detenido(a) (*m., f.*), 16
arrested arrestado(a), detenido(a), preso(a), 6
arrive (at) llegar (a), 2
arrow flecha (*f.*), 18
arson fuego intencional (*m.*), incendio intencional (*m.*)
article artículo (*m.*), 14
as como, 14
  — (big, small, etc.) as tan (grande, pequeño, etc.) como, 4
  — soon as en cuanto, 18; 1 tan pronto como, 19
Asian asiático(a)
ask (a question) preguntar, 8
  — a question hacer una pregunta, 19
  — for solicitar, 2; pedir (e:i), 7
assailant agresor(a) (*m., f.*), asaltante (*m., f.*)
assassin asesino(a) (*m., f.*), 1
assault asaltar; asalto (*m.*), agresión (*f.*), ataque (*m.*)
assembly reunión (*f.*), congregación (*f.*), mitin (*m.*), 20
assigned asignado(a), 15
at en, 1; a, 2
  — dawn (daybreak) al amanecer; de madrugada
  — dusk al anochecer
  — home en casa, 5
  — least por lo menos, 17
  — midnight a medianoche
  — night por la noche
  — noon a mediodía
  — this time (hour) a esta hora, 3
  — your service para servirle, P; a sus órdenes, 3
attack atacar, 18; ataque (*m.*), agresión (*f.*)
attempt intento (*m.*), 15
attend asistir, 17
aunt tía (*f.*), 9
authority autoridad (*f.*), 8
authorize autorizar, 16
automatic automático(a)
automobile automóvil (*m.*), 6
avenue avenida (*f.*), P
average mediano(a)
avoid evitar, 5

B

baby bebé (*m.*), 12
back (*of paper*) dorso (*m.*); (*part of body*) espalda (*f.*)
  in the — (of) en el fondo (de)
bad malo(a), 6
bail fianza (*f.*), 16
  — bondsman fiancista (*m., f.*), 16
bailor fiancista (*m., f.*), 16
bald calvo(a), pelado(a), 18; pelón(ona)
bandage venda (*f.*), 13
bank banco (*m.*), 2
bar bar (*m.*), cantina (*f.*), barra (*f.*), 8
bargain ganga (*f.*), 14
basement sótano (*m.*)
bath baño (*m.*), 18
bathe bañarse, 18
bathroom baño (*m.*); escusado (excusado) (*m.*) (*Méx.*)
bathtub bañadera (*f.*), tina (*f.*) (*Mex.*)
battery batería (*f.*), acumulador (*m.*), 9
be ser, P; estar, 3
  — able to poder (o:ue), 6
  — about (+ *time*) ser como las (+ *time*), 18
  — admitted (to) ingresar, 8
  — afraid tener miedo, 5; temer
  — at fault tener la culpa (de), ser culpable (de), 12
  — back estar de vuelta, estar de regreso, 5
  — called llamarse, 9
  — certain estar seguro(a), 18
  — (very) cold hacer (mucho) frío
  — cool hacer fresco
  — free on bail estar en libertad bajo fianza
  — glad alegrarse
  — going (to do something) ir a (+ *inf.*), 5

© 2017 Cengage Learning

— **guilty** tener la culpa (de), ser culpable (de), 12
— **hereby declared illegal** quedar declarado(a) ilegal, 20
— **(very) hot** hacer (mucho) calor
— **in a condition to (do something)** estar en condiciones de (+ *inf.*), 6
— **in a hurry** estar apurado(a), tener prisa, 9
— **in charge** tener a su cargo, 15
— **in jail** estar preso(a)
— **late** llegar tarde, 12
— **located** quedar, 2
— **missing** faltar, 10
— **named** llamarse, 9
— **okay** estar bien, 3
— **on the way** estar en camino, 4
— **pleasing** gustar, 8
— **quiet!** ¡cállese!, 20
— **right** tener razón, 12
— **(very) sleepy** tener (mucho) sueño, 6
— **(very) scared** tener (mucho) miedo, 4
— **so scared** tener tanto miedo, 18
— **stoned** darse un pase
— **(very) sunny** hacer (mucho) sol
— (*amount*) **tall** medir (e:i) (*amount*), 17
— **under arrest** darse preso(a)
— **visible** estar a la vista
— **(very) windy** hacer (mucho) viento
— **wrong** estar equivocado(a), 8
— **. . . years old** tener... años, 4
beach playa (*f.*), 10
beard barba (*f.*), 18
beat pegar, 8
beating paliza (*f.*)
because porque, 3
become hacerse
— **addicted to drugs** endrogarse
— **aware of** darse cuenta de, 13
bedroom dormitorio (*m.*), pieza, recámara (*f.*) (*Méx.*), 8
beer cerveza (*f.*), 20
before antes (de), 3
— **they question you** antes de que lo interroguen, 6
begin comenzar (e:ie), 5; empezar (e:ie), 5; iniciar, 12
behind atrasado(a), 11; atrás, 12
— **your back** detrás de la espalda
believe creer, 4
belongings pertenencias (*f. pl.*), 16
below debajo de, 13
belt cinto (*m.*), cinturón (*m.*), correa (*f.*), 8
bend down agacharse
besides además, 2
best mejor, 12
better mejor, 12
— **than ever** mejor que nunca, 6
between entre, 1
bicycle bicicleta (*f.*), 2
big grande, 2
bill cuenta (*f.*), 11
birth nacimiento (*m.*)
bite mordida (*f.*)
black negro(a), 4
— **heroin** negra (*f.*) (*col.*)
blackmail chantaje (*m.*,); chantajear
blackmailer chantajista (*m. f.*), 1
blade arma blanca (*f. but* el arma blanca)
blame culpa (*f.*); culpar
blemish mancha (*f.*)
blind ciego(a)
blink parpadear, 6
block cuadra (*f.*), 2; manzana (*f.*)
a — **from here** a una cuadra de aquí, 2
blonde rubio(a), güero(a) (*Méx.*), 7
blood sangre (*f.*), 9
— **bank** banco de sangre (*m.*), 6
blouse blusa (*f.*), 17
blue azul, 4
body cuerpo (*m.*), 8; (*corpse*) cadáver (*m.*)
— **hair** vello (*m.*)
bomb bomba (*f.*)
time — bomba de tiempo (*f.*)
bond bono (*m.*), 16
bone hueso, 13
book registrar, fichar, 16
bookstore librería (*f.*)
boot bota (*f.*)
borrow pedir (e:i) prestado, 11
boss jefe (a) (*m., f.*), 12
bottle botella (*f.*), 15; frasco (*m.*), 19
boy muchacho (*m.*), 2; chico (*m.*), chamaco (*m.*) (*Mex.*), 13
boyfriend novio (*m.*), 15
brake freno (*m.*)
brand marca (*f.*), 10
breath aliento (*m.*), 9
breathe respirar
bribe soborno (*m.*), 15
brief breve, P
— **conversation** conversación breve (*f.*), P
bring traer, 7
broken quebrado(a), 13; descompuesto(a), 19
brother hermano (*m.*)
— **in-law** cuñado (*m.*)
brown (*hair, eyes*) castaño(a), café, 18
bug-eyes (bulging eyes) ojos saltones (*m. pl.*)
build complexión (*f.*)
building edificio (*m.*), 6
bullet bala (*f.*)
burglar ladrón(ona), (*m., f.*), 3
burglary robo (*m.*), 1
bus camión (*Mex.*) (*m.*), autobús (*m.*), guagua (*f.*) (*Cuba*)
— **station** estación de ómnibus (autobuses) (*f.*)
— **stop** parada de autobuses (*f.*), 1
parada de guaguas (*f.*) (*Cuba y Puerto Rico*), 1
parada de camiones (*Méx.*) (*f.*)
businessman(woman) hombre (mujer) de negocios (*m., f.*), 15
but pero, 1
butt in entremeterse, entrometerse, 8
button botón (*m.*)
buy comprar, 10
by
— **force** a la fuerza, 8
— **himself/herself** por sí mismo(a)
— **telephone** por teléfono, 1

C

cab (*of a truck*) cabina (*f.*), 13
caliber calibre (*m.*), 20
call llamar, 1; llamada (*f.*), 4
— **off the dog** llamar al perro
calm quieto(a), 13
— **down** calmarse, 18
can poder (o:ue), 6
cannot: you (one) — write . . . no se puede escribir..., 6
cap gorra (*f.*), 4
car carro (*m.*), coche (*m.*), máquina (*f.*) (*Cuba*), 6
— **related** automovilístico(a)
carburetor carburador (*m.*)
card tarjeta (*f.*), 3
careful! ¡cuidado!, 20
carefully con cuidado, 12
carpet alfombra (*f.*), 10
carry llevar, 2
— **out** realizar, 18
case caso (*m.*), 6
cash: in — en efectivo, 10
— **register** caja (*f.*), 20
cashier cajero(a) (*m., f.*)
Caucasian blanco(a)
cause causar, 12
— **damage** perjudicar, 14
cell celda (*f.*), 16
cell phone number número de teléfono celular, 3
cent centavo (*m.*), 16
central central, 1
certain cierto(a), 8
certainly! ¡cómo no!, 7
chain cadena (*f.*), 16
change cambiar, 12
— **clothes** cambiarse de ropa, 18
characteristic característica (*f.*)
charge acusación (*f.*), 14; cobrar, 14
cheat engañar, 14
check revisar, 10
cheek mejilla (*f.*), cachete (*m.*), 17
chemical químico(a), 9
chest pecho (*m.*)
child niño(a) (*m., f.*), 1
—**'s car seat** asiento para el niño (*m.*)
children hijos (*m. pl.*), 4
chin barbilla (*f.*)
choose elegir (e:i), 9
chosen elegido(a), 9
church iglesia (*f.*)
cigarette cigarrillo (*m.*), 7
city ciudad (*f.*), 2
class clase (*f.*), 7
classmate compañero(a) de clase (*m., f.*), 17

© 2017 Cengage Learning

clean limpiar, 10
clerk empleado(a) (*m., f.*), 14; dependiente(a) (*m., f.*), 20
clinic clínica (*f.*)
close cerrar (e:ie), 5
close (*adj.*) cercano (a), 5; cerca (de), 12
closed cerrado(a), 11
closeted encerrado(a), 8
clothes ropa (*f.*), 4
clothing ropa (*f.*), 4
clue pista (*f.*)
clutch embrague (*m.*)
coat abrigo (*m.*)
cocaine coca (*f.*), cocaína (*f.*); *col.:* perico (*m.*), polvo (*m.*); *col.:* blanca (*f.*), 15
cognate cognado (*m.*)
coin moneda (*f.*), 9
collar cuello (*m.*)
collect cobrar, 14
collide chocar, 13
collision choque (*m.*), 13
color color (*m.*)
comb peine (*m.*), 16
come venir, 4
  — back volver (o:ue), 6
  — in pasar, P; entrar (en)
  — out salir
  — with acompañar, 7
commit cometer, 6
  — suicide suicidarse, 19
common común
communicate comunicar, 5
compact disc disco compacto (*m.*), 10
complain protestar, 3
complaint queja (*f.*)
complete completo(a), 5; completar, 9
completely por completo, 16
compulsory obligatorio(a), 13
computer computadora (*f.*), ordenador (*m.*) (*España*), 10
condition condición (*f.*), 6
condom condón (*m.*), 18
confess confesar (e:ie)
confession confesión (*f.*)
confirm confirmar, 19
confused confuso(a)
consider considerar
consulate consulado (*m.*), 20
content contenido (*m.*), 9
continue continuar, 10
contraband contrabando (*m.*)
contract contrato (*m.*), 10
control control (*m.*), 13
conversation conversación (*f.*)
convict declarar culpable
cooperation cooperación (*f.*), 3
copy copia (*f.*), 11
corduroy pana (*f.*), 20
corner esquina (*f.*), 3; rincón (*m.*)
corporal punishment castigo corporal (*m.*)
corpse cadáver
cost costar (o:ue), 15
counsel for the defense abogado(a) defensor(a) (*m., f.*)
counsellor consejero(a) (*m., f.*)
count contar (o:ue), 9
counter mostrador (*m.*), 16
counterfeit falsificar; falsificación
country país (*m.*), 8
couple: a — of un par de, 6
court (of law) corte (*f.*), tribunal (*m.*), juzgado (*m.*), 6, 14
  — reporter taquígrafo(a) (*m., f.*)
courtesy cortesía (*f.*)
cousin primo(a) (*m., f.*)
crack cocaine crac (*m.*); *col.:* piedra (*f.*), roca (*f.*), coca cocinada (*f.*), 15
crash choque (*m.*), 13
crime delito (*m.*), 6
criminal criminal
  — record antecedentes penales (*m. pl.*), 16
crippled inválido(a); paralítico(a)
cross cruzar, 12; cruz (*f.*), 17
cross-eyed bizco(a)
crossing cruce (*m.*), 12
crowbar pata de cabra (*f.*)
crowd multitud (*f.*), 20
cry llorar, 18
cultural cultural
curfew toque de queda (*m.*), 3
curly rizado(a), rizo(a), crespo(a)
customer cliente (*m., f.*), 7
cut cortar, 5

D

dad papá (*m.*), 5
dagger puñal (*m.*); daga (*f.*)
damage: slight — desperfecto (*m.*), 19
danger peligro (*m.*)
dangerous peligroso(a), 4
  — curve curva peligrosa (*f.*)
dark oscuro(a), 4
dark-haired morocho(a), 7
date fecha (*f.*); salir con, 17
daughter hija (*f.*)
  — in-law nuera (*f.*)
day día (*m.*)
  during the — durante el día
  the — after tomorrow pasado mañana
  the — before yesterday anteayer, antes de ayer
dead muerto(a), 1
deadbolt cerrojo de seguridad (*m.*), 5
deaf sordo(a)
deceive engañar, 14
decide decidir, 6
decision fallo (*m.*)
defend (oneself) defender(se), 18
defendant acusado(a) (*m., f.*), reo(a) (*m., f.*)
deformed deformado(a)
degree grado (*m.*), 12
delivery entrega (*f.*), 5
demand exigir, 2
department departamento (*m.*), 4
depend depender, 16
describe describir, 7
description descripción (*f.*), 11
destroy destruir, 18
detail detalle (*m.*), 17
detain detener, 6
detective detective (*m., f.*), 14
detention detención (*f.*), 16
determine determinar, 9
detour desvío (*m.*)
detoxification desintoxicación (*f.*)
diabetes diabetes (*f.*), 6
die fallecer, 11; morir (o:ue), 13
diesel gasoil (*m.*)
dining room comedor (*m.*)
dinner cena (*f.*), 5
dirty sucio(a), 18
disabled inválido(a); paralítico(a)
disappear desaparecer
discipline disciplinar, 8
disease enfermedad (*f.*)
disfigured desfigurado(a)
dispatcher operador(a) (*m., f.*), telefonista (*m., f.*), 1
disperse dispersar(se), 20
distribute distribuir, 15
district barrio (*m.*), colonia (*f.*) (*Méx.*), 5
  — attorney fiscal (*m., f.*), 16
divided road doble vía (*f.*)
division división (*f.*), 1; sección, 1
divorced divorciado(a), P
dizzy mareado(a), 13
do hacer, 3
do not (don't) no
  — enter no entre, no pase
  — jump! ¡no salte!
  — litter no tire basura
  — mention it no hay de qué
  — move! ¡no se mueva!
  — pass no pasar, no rebasar (*Méx.*)
  — shoot! ¡no dispare!, ¡no tire!
doctor médico(a) (*m., f.*), doctor(a) (*m., f.*), 8
document documento (*m.*), 17
dollar dólar (*m.*), 10
domicile domicilio (*m.*)
door puerta (*f.*), 5
double doble
doubt dudar, 16
dress vestido (*m.*)
dressed vestido(a), 4
drink trago (*m.*), 6; bebida (*f.*); 8; tomar, 6; beber, 8
drinking bebida (*f.*), 8
drive manejar, conducir, 6
  — fifty miles per hour conducir a cincuenta millas por hora, 9
  — safely! ¡maneje con cuidado!, 12
driver chofer (*m.*), 6; conductor(a) (*m., f.*), 12
  —'s license licencia para manejar (*f.*), licencia de conducir (*f.*), 3
drop soltar (o:ue)
  — out of school abandonar los estudios
  — the gun (weapon) soltar el arma
drown ahogarse
drug droga (*f.*), 6
  — addict drogadicto(a) (*m., f.*)
  — pusher traficante (*m., f.*)
  on drugs endrogado(a), 6
drugstore farmacia (*f.*), botica (*f.*)

© 2017 Cengage Learning

drunk borracho(a), 6
DTs delírium tremens (*m.*)
during durante, 15
DVD player reproductor de DVD
dynamite dinamita (*f.*)

E

each cada, 6
ear (inner) oído (*m.*); (outer) oreja (*f.*)
early temprano, 2
earring arete (*m.*), 17
east este (*m.*)
easy fácil
either cualquiera, 9
elbow codo (*m.*)
e-mail correo electrónico (*m.*)
embassy embajada (*f.*), 20
emergency emergencia (*f.*), 4
 — parking only estacionamiento de emergencia solamente
employee empleado(a) (*m., f.*), 14
empty desocupado(a), 3; vaciar, 16
end final (*m.*), punta (*f.*), 9; terminar
endanger poner en peligro, 12
engine motor (*m.*), 9
English (language) inglés (*m.*), 1
enough suficiente, 15
enroll (in a school) matricularse, 15
enter ingresar, 8
 do not — no entre; no pase
entrance entrada (*f.*)
envelope sobre (*m.*), 16
epileptic epiléptico(a)
equipment equipo (*m.*), 10
establish establecer, 5
even though aunque
evening noche (*f.*)
 in the — por la noche, a la noche, 7
ever alguna vez
every cada, 6, todos(as)
 — day todos los días, 8
everything possible todo lo posible, 11
evidence evidencia (*f.*), 18; prueba (*f.*)
exactly exactamente, 17
examine examinar, chequear, 13
example: for — por ejemplo, 7
excessive demasiado(a), 12
excuse excusa (*f.*), 12
expensive caro(a)
expert perito(a) (*m., f.*)
explosive explosivo (*m.*)
expression expresión (*f.*)
 — of courtesy expresión de cortesía (*f.*)
extent: to a large — en buena parte, 16
exit salida (*f.*)
 — door puerta de salida (*f.*)
eye ojo (*m.*)
 with (blue) eyes de ojos (azules), 7
eyebrow ceja (*f.*)
eyeglasses anteojos (*m. pl.*), lentes (*m. pl.*), espejuelos (*m. pl.*) (*Cuba, Puerto Rico*), gafas (*f. pl.*), 18
eyelashes pestañas (*f. pl.*)

F

face cara (*f.*), 13
 — down boca abajo
fake falso(a)
 — identification identificación falsa (*f.*)
fall caerse, 9; (*autumn*) otoño (*m.*)
false statement declaración falsa (*f.*)
falsification falsificación (*f.*)
falsify falsificar
family familia (*f.*), 8
 — room sala de estar (*f.*)
far lejos, 17
 — from lejos de
farewell despedida (*f.*)
fast rápido, 5
fat gordo(a), 7
father padre (*m.*), papá (*m.*), 5
 — in-law suegro (*m.*)
fear temer
feel sentir(se) (e:ie), 13
felony delito mayor (*m.*), delito grave (*m.*), 14
fender guardafangos (*m.*)
fewer than menos de, 4
fiancé(e) prometido(a) (*m., f.*)
fight luchar, 18; pelea (*f.*), riña (*f.*)
file an appeal presentar una apelación
fill out llenar, 1
filter filtro (*m.*)
finally ya, 8
find encontrar (o:ue), 11; hallar
 — out averiguar, 10; saber (*pret.*), 17
 — refuge (shelter) refugiarse
fine (*adv.*) bien, P; multa (*f.*), 6
finger dedo (*m.*), 9
fingerprint huella digital (*f.*), 10; tomar las huellas digitales, 16
finish terminar, 10
 — (doing something) terminar de (+ *inf.*), 10
fire fuego (*m.*), incendio (*m.*), 5; despedir (e:ie), 12
 — department estación de bomberos (*f.*)
 — extinguisher extinguidor de incendios (*m.*), extintor de incendios (*m.*) (*España*) 13
 — fighter bombero(a) (*m., f.*), 5
firearm arma de fuego (*f. but* el arma de fuego), 4
first (*adv.*) primero, 1; (*adj.*) primero(a)
 — aid primeros auxilios (*m. pl.*)
 — class de primera calidad, 14
 the — thing lo primero, 5
fix arreglar, 19
flashlight linterna (*f.*), 4
flat tire goma ponchada (*f.*), llanta pinchada (*f.*)
floor piso (*m.*), 7
flower flor (*f.*)
 — pot maceta de flores (*f.*)
flowered floreado(a)
following siguiente
fog niebla (*f.*), neblina (*f.*)
foolishness tontería (*f.*), 10
foot pie (*m.*), 7
footprint huella (*f.*), 10
for por, P; para, 1
 — example por ejemplo, 5
 — me para mí, 14
 — possession of drugs por poseer drogas
 — you para ti, 18
forbidden prohibido (a), 6
force forzar (o:ue), 10; obligar, 18; fuerza (*f.*)
 by — a la fuerza, 8
forehead frente (*f.*)
forge falsificar
forger falsificador(a), 1
forged falso(a)
 — document documento falso (*m.*)
forgery falsificación (*f.*)
forget olvidar, 18
forgive perdonar, 8
forgiveness perdón (*m.*), 8
form papeleta (*f.*), 19
fortunately por suerte, 13
foster parents padres de crianza/adoptivos (*m. pl.*)
fourth cuarto(a), 4
fraud estafa (*f.*), 14
freckle peca (*f.*), 7
freeze! ¡quieto(a)!, 3; ¡no se mueva(n)!, 6
frequently frecuentemente, 8
fresh nuevo(a), 6
friend amigo(a) (*m., f.*), 3
frightened aterrorizado(a), 18
from desde, 8
front frente
 — door puerta de la calle (*f.*), 5
 in — of frente a, 1
fur coat abrigo de piel (*m.*)
future futuro (*m.*)

G

gag mordaza (*f.*)
gang pandilla (*f.*), 3
garage garaje (*m.*)
garbage basura (*f.*), 10
garden jardín (*m.*)
gardener jardinero(a) (*m., f.*), 3
gas gas (*m.*), 19
 — station gasolinera (*f.*), estación de servicio (*f.*)
 — pedal acelerador (*m.*)
gasoline gasolina (*f.*)
gearshift cambio de velocidades (*m.*)
 — lever palanca de cambio de velocidades (*f.*)
generally generalmente, 5
gentleman señor (Sr.) (*m.*), P
get conseguir (e:i), 8
 — away alejarse
 — down bajarse
 — hold of agarrar, coger, 9
 — hurt lastimarse, 13

© 2017 Cengage Learning

— **in (a car, etc.)** subir, 3
— **off** bajarse, 9
— **on one's knees** ponerse de rodillas
— **out** salir, 5; bajarse, 9
— **up** levantarse, 13
— **worse** agravarse, 15
girl muchacha (*f.*), 2
girlfriend novia (*f.*), 15
give dar, 3; entregar, 11
— **CPR** dar respiración artificial
— **a gift** regalar, 15
— **a ticket** imponer una multa, 12
— **notice** avisar de, 1
gladly! ¡cómo no!, 7
glass vidrio (*m.*)
— **cutter** cortavidrios (*m.*)
— **eye** ojo de vidrio (*m.*)
glove guante (*m.*)
— **compartment** guantera (*f.*), 7; portaguantes (*m.*)
go ir, 3
— **away** irse, 10
— **in** entrar, 4
— **out (with)** salir (con), 17
— **through a red light** pasarse la luz roja, 12
— **with** acompañar, 7
goddaughter ahijada (*f.*)
godfather padrino (*m.*)
godmother madrina (*f.*)
godson ahijado (*m.*)
gold oro (*m.*), 16
good bueno(a)
— **afternoon** buenas tardes, P
— **evening** buenas noches, P
— **morning (day)** buenos días/ buen día, P
— **night** buenas noches, P
good-bye adiós, P
grab agarrar, coger, 9
grade school escuela primaria, escuela elemental
graffiti grafiti (*m.*)
granddaughter nieta (*f.*)
grandfather abuelo (*m.*)
grandmother abuela (*f.*)
grandson nieto (*m.*)
gray gris, 20
gray-haired canoso(a)
great gran, 14
green verde, 3
greet saludar, 15
greeting saludo (*m.*)
ground suelo (*m.*)
group grupo (*m.*), 5
guilty culpable

H

hair pelo (*m.*), 17; cabello (*m.*)
body — vello (*m.*)
hairpiece peluca (*f.*)
hairy velludo(a)
hall pasillo (*m.*)
hallucinations alucinaciones (*f. pl.*)
halt! ¡alto!, 3
hand mano (*f.*), 6
— **grenade** granada de mano (*f.*)
— **in hand** de la mano, 2
hands up! ¡manos arriba!
handcuffed esposado(a), 16
handcuffs esposas (*f. pl.*), 16
handkerchief pañuelo (*m.*), 16
handsaw sierra de mano (*f.*), serrucho de mano (*m.*)
happen pasar, suceder, 2; ocurrir
hashish hachich (*m.*), hachís (*m.*), *col.:* chocolate (*m.*), kif (*m.*), grifa (*f.*)
hat sombrero (*m.*), 4
have tener, 4
— **a good time** pasarlo bien, pasar un buen rato, 15
— **bad weather** hacer mal tiempo
— **(something) fixed** hacer arreglar, 19
— **good weather** hacer buen tiempo
— **just (done something)** acabar de (+ *inf.*)
— **on** tener puesto(a), llevar puesto(a), 17
— **the right to** tener el derecho de, 6
— **to (do something)** tener que (+ *inf.*), 4
hazard light baliza (*f.*)
head cabeza (*f.*), 9
headlight faro (*m.*), 19
health salud (*f.*)
to your —! ¡salud!
hear oír, 19
heart corazón (*m.*), 7
— **attack** ataque al corazón (*m.*), 7
heavy pesado(a), 20
heel talón (*m.*), 9
height estatura (*f.*), 20
of medium — de estatura mediana, 4
helicopter helicóptero (*m.*)
hello hola, P; (*when answering the telephone)* aló (*Puerto Rico*), bueno (*Méx.*), diga (*Cuba, España*), mande (*Méx.*), oigo (*Cuba*)
helmet casco de seguridad (*m.*), 2
help ayuda (*f.*), 1; ayudar, 5
help! ¡socorro!, ¡auxilio!, 5
her su, 3
here aquí, 1
heroin heroína (*f.*); *col.:* caballo (*m.*), chiva (*f.*), manteca (*f.*) (*Caribe*)
herself: by — por sí misma
hi hola, P
high alto(a), 12
high school escuela secundaria (*f.*), 15
highway autopista (*f.*), 12; carretera (*f.*), 13
hijack asaltar
hijacking asalto (*m.*)
him lo, 6
himself: by — por sí mismo
hip cadera (*f.*)
his su, 3
Hispanic hispano(a), 2; hispánico(a), latino(a)
hit chocar, 13; golpear, 18
hold-up asalto (*m.*)
hole agujerito (*m.*), 5
home casa (*f.*), 1
homicide homicidio (*m.*), 16
honk the horn tocar la bocina
hood capucha (*f.*); (*car*) capó (*m.*); cubierta (*f.*)
hope: I — ojalá, 17
horn bocina (*f.*)
hospital hospital (*m.*), 4
hotel hotel (*m.*)
hour hora (*f.*), 3
house casa (*f.*), 1
how? ¿cómo?, 2
— **are you?** ¿cómo está Ud.?, P
— **do you spell it?** ¿cómo se escribe?
— **long?** ¿cuánto tiempo?, 5
— **many?** ¿cuántos(as)?, 2
however sin embargo, 14
humidity humedad
humiliate humillar
hurt herido(a), 1; lastimado(a), 7; doler (o:ue), 8; perjudicar, 14; causarle daño a
husband esposo (*m.*), marido (*m.*), 4
hypodermic syringe jeringuilla (*f.*), jeringa hipodérmica (*f.*)
hysterical histérico(a)
hysterically histéricamente, 18

I

ID identificación (*f.*), documento de identidad, 3
idea idea (*f.*), 5
identification identificación (*f.*), 3
identify identificar, 5
if si, 4
I'll see you tomorrow hasta mañana, 18
immediately inmediatamente, 5
imperfection desperfecto (*m.*), 19
important importante, 5
impose a fine imponer una multa, 12
imprudently imprudentemente, 12
in en, 1; dentro (de), 6
— **charge of** a cargo de, 8
— **front of** en frente de, 1; a la vista de, 16
— **installments** a plazos, 5
— **order to** para, 5
— **the afternoon** por la tarde, P; a la tarde
— **the evening** por la noche, P; a la noche
— **the first place** en primer lugar, 5
— **the morning** por la mañana, P; a la mañana
— **the presence of** a la vista de, 16
— **self-defense** en defensa propia
— **this way** de este modo, así
— **writing** por escrito, 16
inch pulgada (*f.*), 7
index (finger) (dedo) índice (*m.*), 5
indicted procesado(a)
infiltrate infiltrar, 15
inform avisar de, notificar, 1
information información (*f.*), P
personal — dato personal (*m.*), 1

© 2017 Cengage Learning

injured herido(a), 1; lastimado(a), 7; lesionado(a), 8
injury lesión (*f.*), 8
in-laws parientes políticos (*m. pl.*)
innocent inocente, 14
inserted in metido(a), 19
inside dentro, 4; adentro, 8; metido(a), 19
install instalar, 5
installment plazo (*m.*), 11
  in —s a plazos, 10
instead of en lugar de, 8
instrument panel tablero (*cars*), 9
insured asegurado(a), 11
interlace entrelazar
interpreter intérprete (*m., f.*)
interrogate interrogar, 6
interrogation interrogatorio (*m.*), 6
intertwine entrelazar
interview entrevista (*f.*)
intoxicated intoxicado(a), 19
introduce presentar, 15
investigate investigar, 8
investigating investigador(a), 16
investigation averiguación (*f.*), 10; investigación (*f.*)
it lo, 6
  — is (+ *time*) son las (+ *time*)
  — may be puede ser, 17
item objeto (*m.*), 11

J

jack gato (*m.*), gata (*f.*) (*Costa Rica*), 20
jacket chaqueta (*f.*), chamarra (*f.*) (*Méx.*), 20; saco (*m.*)
jail cárcel (*f.*), prisión (*f.*)
jewelry joya (*f.*), 10
  — store joyería (*f.*)
job trabajo (*m.*), 8; empleo (*m.*), 11
joint (drugs) *col.:* cucaracha (*f.*), leño (*m.*), porro (*m.*)
judge juez(a), (*m., f.*), 8; juzgar, 14
jump saltar, 13
junior high school escuela secundaria (*f.*), 15
jury jurado (*m.*), 14
just: it's — that . . . es que..., 9
just in time a tiempo
juvenile juvenil
  — court tribunal de menores (*m.*)
  — delinquent delincuente juvenil (*m., f.*)
  — hall centro de reclusión de menores (*m.*)

K

keep guardar; mantener (e:ie)
  — right conserve su derecha; mantenga su derecha
  — walking seguir (e:i) caminando
key llave (*f.*), 5
kick patada (*f.*)
kidnap secuestrar, 12
kidnapper secuestrador(a), 1
kidnapping secuestro (*m.*), 5
kill matar, 8
kind clase, (*f.*), 7
kitchen cocina (*f.*), 5
knee rodilla (*f.*)
knife cuchillo (*m.*), 18
knock at the door tocar a la puerta, 8
know conocer, saber, 5

L

ladder escalera (*f.*)
  rope — escala de soga (*f.*)
  hand — escalera de mano (*f.*)
lady señora (*f.*), P
lame cojo(a)
lane carril (*m.*), 12
language lengua (*f.*)
large grande, 2
last último(a), pasado(a), 11
  at — ya, 8
  — month el mes pasado
  — name apellido (*m.*), P
  — night anoche, 10
  — week la semana pasada
  — year el año pasado
late tarde, 2
later más tarde, 2; después, 6; luego, 10
Latin latino(a), 15
law ley (*f.*), 2
lawn césped (*m.*), zacate (*m.*) (*Méx.*), 5
lawsuit demanda (*f.*)
lawyer abogado(a) (*m., f.*), 6
learn aprender, 15
leave salir, 5; irse, 10
  — behind dejar, 5
  — turned on dejar encendido(a), dejar prendido(a)
left izquierdo(a), 7
left-handed zurdo(a), 7
leg pierna (*f.*), 13
lend prestar
less than menos de, 4
let dejar, 9
  — go of soltar (o:ue)
let's (do something) vamos a (+ *inf.*)
  — go vamos, 2
  — see a ver, 6
license plate placa (*f.*), chapa (*f.*), 11
lie mentira (*f.*), 8
  — down acostarse (o:ue)
life vida (*f.*), 2
lift levantar
light luz (*f.*), 4; foco (*m.*); (*light in color*) claro(a), 11; liviano(a), 20
like como, 14; gustar, 8
  — this así, 9
limit límite (*m.*), 9
line línea (*f.*), 9
lip labio (*m.*)
liquor licor (*m.*), 20
liquor store licorería (*f.*), 7
lisp hablar con (la) zeta
list lista (*f.*), 11
lit prendido(a), 19
little (*quantity*) poco; (size) pequeño(a), 1
  a — un poco de, 1
  — finger meñique (*m.*)
live vivir, 2
living room sala (*f.*)
local local, 8
lock cerrojo (*m.*), cerradura (*f.*), 10; cerrar (e:ie) con llave, 5; seguro (*car*), 9
  — up encerrar (e:ie), 16
locked cerrado(a), 11
  — up encerrado(a), 8
lodging alojamiento (*m.*), hospedaje (*m.*)
log in registrar, fichar, 16
long largo(a)
long-sleeved de mangas largas
look mire, 6
  — at mirar, 5
  — for buscar, 2
  What does he/she/you — like? ¿cómo es?, 4
lose perder (e:ie), 6
  — one's job quedarse sin trabajo, 14
lost perdido(a), 2
low bajo(a)
LSD ácido (*m.*); *col.:* pastilla (*f.*), pegao (*m.*), sello (*m.*)

M

Ma'am señora (Sra.) (*f.*), P
machine gun ametralladora (*f.*)
Madam señora (Sra.) (*f.*), P
mail correo (*m.*), correspondencia (*f.*), 5
make hacer, 3; (*brand*) marca (*f.*)
man hombre (*m.*), 3
manage conseguir (e:i)
manslaughter homicidio (*m.*), 16
many muchos(as), 2
marijuana (*col.*), mariguana (*f.*), marihuana (*f.*), marijuana (*f.*); *col.:* juanita (*f.*), mota (*f.*), pasto (*m.*), pito (*m.*), yesca (*f.*), yerba (*f.*) zacate (*m.*)
marital status estado civil (*m.*)
mark marca (*f.*), 6; mancha (*f.*)
market mercado (*m.*), 20
  open-air — mercado al aire libre (*m.*), tianguis (*m.*) (*Méx.*)
married casado(a), P
mask máscara (*f.*)
mat felpudo (*m.*)
measure medir (e:i), 7
mechanic mecánico (*m.*)
meddle entremeterse, 8; entrometerse, 8
medication medicina (*f.*), medicamento (*m.*)
medicine medicina (*f.*), 7
medium mediano(a)
  — height de estatura mediana
meeting junta (*f.*), reunión (*f.*), congregación (*f.*), mitin (*m.*), 5
member miembro (*m., f.*), 3
mention: don't — it de nada, no hay de qué, P
message mensaje (*m.*), 7
methadone metadona (*f.*)

© 2017 Cengage Learning

middle medio (*m.*)
about the — of the month (week) a mediados de mes (semana)
— finger dedo mayor (*m.*), dedo corazón (*m.*)
midnight medianoche (*f.*), 3
mile milla (*f.*), 9
minor menor de edad (*m., f.*), 3; menor
Miranda warning advertencia Miranda (*f.*), 6
mirror espejo (*m.*)
misdemeanor delito (*m.*), 5
miss señorita (Srta.) (*f.*), P
missing desaparecido(a)
mixed race (*black and white*) mulato(a); (*any of two or more races*) mestizo(a)
model modelo (*m.*), 11
mole lunar (*m.*), 17
mom mamá (*f.*), madre (*f.*), 2
moment momento (*m.*), P
money dinero (*m.*), 8
month mes (*m.*)
a — ago hace un mes, 13
monument monumento (*m.*)
more más
— or less más o menos, 8
— . . . than más... que, 4
morgue morgue (*f.*)
morning mañana (*f.*), 10
early — madrugada (*f.*), 9
in the — por la mañana, a la mañana, 7
morphine morfina (*f.*)
most important thing lo más importante, 5
motel motel (*m.*), 15
mother madre (*f.*), mamá (*f.*), 2
— in-law suegra (*f.*)
motive motivo (*m.*)
motor motor (*m.*), 9
motorcycle motocicleta (*f.*), 13
motor-driven cycle motocicleta (*f.*)
moustache bigote (*m.*), 18
mouth boca (*f.*), 17
move moverse (o:ue), 6
don't —! ¡no se mueva(n)!, 6
movie theatre cine (*m.*), 15
movies cine (*m.*), 15
mow cortar, 5
MP3 player reproductor MP3
Mr. señor (Sr.) (*m.*), P
— and Mrs. (Ruiz) los señores (Ruiz) (*m. pl.*), 17
Mrs. señora (Sra.) (*f.*), P
much (*adv.*) mucho, 4
mud barro (*m.*), fango (*m.*), 10
muffler amortiguador (de ruido) (*m.*), silenciador (*m.*)
mug asaltar
mugging asalto (*m.*)
municipal municipal
murder asesinar; asesinato (*m.*)
murderer asesino(a) (*m., f.*); homicida (*m., f.*), 1
murmur murmurar, 20
muscular musculoso(a)
must deber, 2
mute mudo(a)
my mi, 1

N

name nombre (*m.*), P
near cercano(a), 10; (*prep.*) cerca de
nearby cercano(a), 10
necessary necesario(a), 5
neck cuello (*m.*), 13
necklace collar (*m.*), 14
need necesitar, 1; hacer falta, 8
needle aguja (*f.*), 6
neighbor vecino(a), 5
neighborhood barrio (*m.*), colonia (*f.*) (*Méx.*), 5; vecindario (*m.*), 5
— watch vigilancia del barrio (*f.*), 5
nephew sobrino (*m.*)
never nunca, 6
— before nunca antes, 11
nevertheless sin embargo, 14
new nuevo(a), 6
newspaper periódico (*m.*), diario (*m.*), 5
next próximo(a), 4; siguiente
— month (year) el mes (año) que viene, el mes (año) próximo
— week la semana que viene, la semana próxima
the — day el día siguiente
next-door (*neighbor, house*) de al lado, 10
niece sobrina (*f.*)
night noche (*f.*), 5
the — before last anteanoche, antes de anoche
no turn on red prohibido girar en rojo
nobody nadie, 8
noise ruido (*m.*)
nonsense tontería (*f.*), 10
north norte (*m.*)
northeast noreste (*m.*)
northwest noroeste (*m.*)
nose nariz (*f.*), 9
note nota (*f.*)
take — of anotar, 10
nothing nada, P
notice notar, 5
notify avisar
noun nombre (*m.*)
now ahora, 1
number número (*m.*)

O

oath juramento (*m.*)
to take an — jurar
under — bajo juramento
object objeto (*m.*), 11
obligate obligar, 18
obscenity obscenidad (*f.*), 20
observe observar, 5
occasion ocasión (*f.*), 17
occur ocurrir, 14
of de, 1
— age mayor de edad
— course desde luego, 2; claro que sí, 10
off (*light*) apagado(a), 9
offer ofrecer, 14
office oficina (*f.*), 12
officer agente (*m., f.*), P
often a menudo, 6
oh, goodness gracious! ¡ay, Dios mío!, 2
oil aceite (*m.*)
okay bueno, P
old anciano(a), 1; viejo(a), 7
older mayor, 3
oldest mayor, 3
on en, 1; a, 2; (*by way of*) por, 2; (*a light*) encendido(a), prendido(a), 5; sobre, 20
— a bike en bicicleta, 2
— foot a pie, 2
— the sides a los costados, 9
— time a tiempo
— time payments a plazos, 10
— top of sobre, 20
— vacation de vacaciones, 4
once again otra vez, 6
only sólo, solamente, 5
the — thing lo único, 8
open abierto(a), 5
opium opio (*m.*)
opportunity oportunidad (*f.*), 16
opposite opuesto(a)
in the — direction en sentido contrario, 13
or o, 3
order orden (*f.*), 8; ordenar, 20
organize organizar, 5
other otro(a), 4
the —s los (las) demás, 5
our nuestro(a), 5; nuestros (as), 15
out (*light*) apagado(a), 9
— on bail en libertad bajo fianza, 16
— on one's own recognizance en libertad bajo palabra, 16
outside fuera, 4
oven horno (*m.*), 19
over there para allá, 1
overdose sobredosis (*f.*)
owe deber, 11
owner dueño(a) (*m., f.*), 3

P

paid (for) pagado(a), 11
pants pantalón (*m.*), pantalones (*m. pl.*), 4
paramedic paramédico(a) (*m., f.*), 1
pardon perdón, 8
parents padres (*m.*), 3
park parque (*m.*)
parked estacionado(a), 11
parking lot zona de estacionamiento (*f.*), 7
part parte (*f.*)
party fiesta (*f.*), 10
pass (a car) pasar, rebasar (*Méx.*), 13
do not — no pasar; no rebasar (*Méx.*)
pass away fallecer, 11
passenger pasajero(a) (*m., f.*), 13

© 2017 Cengage Learning

patrol patrulla (*f.*), 5
  — car carro patrullero (*m.*), 1
pawn empeñar, 14
pay pagar, 6
  — attention (to) hacer caso(a), 2; prestar atención, 9
  — attention (to someone) hacerle caso a, 8
payment pago (*m.*), 11
pearl perla (*f.*), 14
  cultured — perla de cultivo (*f.*), 14
pedestrian peatón(ona) (*m., f.*)
penetration penetración (*f.*), 18
people gente (*f.*), 20
perform realizar, 18
perhaps tal vez, 28
permission permiso (*m.*), 20
permitted permitido(a), 16
person persona (*f.*), 1
  in — en persona, 1
personal data dato personal (*m.*), 1
personally en persona, 1
phone teléfono (*m.*)
  by — por teléfono, 1
  on the — por teléfono, 1
  — call llamada telefónica (*f.*), 5
  — number número de teléfono (*m.*), P
photograph fotografía (*f.*), 3; retratar, 16
pick up recoger, 5
picklock llave falsa (*f.*), ganzúa (*f.*)
pierced atravesado(a), 18
pill pastilla, píldora (*f.*), 19
pimple grano (*m.*)
pinstriped de rayas
pistol pistola (*f.*), 4
place lugar (*m.*), 5; colocar
  to — nearby arrimar, 9
plaid de cuadros
plan (to do something) pensar (e:ie) (+ *inf.*), 5
please por favor, P
pocket bolsillo (*m.*), 6
point (a gun) apuntar, 20
poison veneno (*m.*), 19
police (force) policía (*f.*), 1
  — officer policía (*m., f.*), 1
  — station comisaría (*f.*), estación de policía (*f.*), jefatura de policía (*f.*), P
polka dot de lunares
porch portal (*m.*), 5
pornographic pornográfico(a)
portly grueso(a)
possible posible, 5
post office oficina de correos (*f.*), correo (*m.*), 2
pound libra (*f.*), 20
practice practicar
precaution precaución (*f.*), 13
prefer preferir (e:ie), 5
pregnant embarazada
preliminary preliminar, 16
premium prima (*f.*), 16
present (*adj.*) presente, 6
prevent prevenir, 5
preventive preventivo(a), 16
print estampado(a)
prison cárcel (*f.*), prisión (*f.*)
private privado(a)
  — property propiedad privada
problem problema (*m.*), 3
program programa (*m.*), 5
prohibited prohibido(a)
promise prometer, 20
property propiedad (*f.*), 11
prosecutor fiscal (*m., f.*), 16
prostitute prostituto(a) (*m., f.*)
prostitution prostitución (*f.*)
protect proteger, 5
protest protestar, 3
pull over (a car) arrimar, 9
punch trompada (*f.*), puñetazo (*m.*)
punish castigar, 8
purse cartera (*f.*), bolsa (*f.*), bolso (*m.*), 17
push empujar, 18
put poner, 9; colocar
  — away guardado(a), 10
  — on ponerse, 18
  — one's hands against the wall poner las manos en la pared
  — out (a fire) apagar, 13

Q

question interrogar, 6; pregunta (*f.*)
questioning interrogatorio (*m.*), 6
quick(ly) rápido, 5
quiet callado(a), 6; quieto(a), 13
quite bastante, 8

R

race raza (*f.*), 18
railroad ferrocarril (*m.*)
rain llover (o:ue); lluvia (*f.*)
raincoat impermeable (*m.*)
ransom rescate (*m.*)
rape violar, 18; violación (*f.*), 18
rapist violador(a), 1
rather más bien, medio, 7; bastante, 8
razor navaja (*f.*), 8
reach llegar (a), 2
read leer, 6
ready listo(a), 19
realize darse cuenta (de), 13
reason por qué (*m.*), 8
receive recibir, 4
recent reciente, 17
recently recientemente
recite recitar, 9
recklessly imprudentemente, 12
recognize reconocer, 7
recommend recomendar (e:ie), 16
recover recobrar, 11
red rojo(a), 4
red-haired pelirrojo(a), 7
refuse to negarse (e:ie) a, 6
register matricularse, 15
registered registrado(a), 11
registration registro (*m.*), 6
rehab rehabilitación (*f.*), 19
relative pariente (*m., f.*)
remain permanecer, 6
remaining ones los (las) demás, 10
remember recordar (o:ue), 6; acordarse (o:ue) (de), 10
report reporte (*m.*), informe (*m.*), 1; (*of a crime*) denuncia (*f.*); (*a crime*) denunciar, 1; avisar de, notificar, 1
represent representar
rescue rescatar
resident parking estacionamiento para residentes
residential residencial, 9
resist hacer resistencia, 18
resisting arrest resistencia a la autoridad (*f.*)
respond responder, 15
rest: the — lo demás, 6
restaurant restaurante (*m.*)
return regresar, 2; volver (o:ue), 6
review revisar, 10
revolver revólver (*m.*), 4
rich rico(a)
rifle rifle (*m.*)
right derecho (*m.*), 6; (*adj.*) derecho(a), 13
  — ? ¿verdad?, 2
  — away enseguida, 1
  — hand side a la derecha (*f.*), 16
right-handed diestro(a), 7
ring anillo (*m.*), 17
  — finger anular (*m.*)
risk riesgo (*m.*), 11
road camino (*m.*), 13
rob robar, 10
robbery robo (*m.*), 1
rock (*col.* **crack cocaine**) piedra (*f.*), 15
roof techo (*m.*)
room cuarto (*m.*), habitación (*f.*), 10
rope soga (*f.*)
run correr, 7
  — away escaparse, fugarse, 17
  — into chocar, 13

S

safe seguro(a)
safety seguridad (*f.*)
  — belt cinturón de seguridad (*m.*)
  — (bike) helmet casco de seguridad (*m.*), 2
same mismo(a), 9
sandal sandalia (*f.*), 17
save salvar, 2
saved guardado(a), 10
say decir (e:i), 7
scar cicatriz (*f.*), 17
school escuela (*f.*), 7
  — crossing cruce de niños (*m.*)
scream gritar, 18
sealed sellado(a), 16
seat asiento (*m.*)
secret secreto(a), 15
section sección (*f.*), división (*f.*), 1
sedative calmante (*m.*), sedante (*m.*), sedativo (*m.*), 19

© 2017 Cengage Learning

see ver, 2
— **you later** hasta luego, P
— **you tomorrow** hasta mañana, P
seem parecer, 4
seen visto(a)
self-defense: in — en defensa propia
sell vender, 3
semiautomatic semiautomático(a), 20
send enviar, mandar, 1
sentence dictar sentencia, sentenciar; sentencia (*f.*), condena (*f.*)
sentimental sentimental, 14
separate separar
sergeant sargento (*m., f.*), P
serial number número de serie (*m.*), 10
series serie (*f.*), 10
serious grave, 1; serio(a), 13
serve servir (e:i)
service servicio (*m.*), 15
set on fire incendiar
several varios(as), 5
sex sexo (*m.*), 15
sexual sexual, 18
shake temblar (e:ie), 13
shave afeitarse, 20
shirt camisa (*f.*), 4
shiver temblar (e:ie), 13
shock absorber amortiguador de choque (*m.*)
shoe zapato (*m.*)
shoelace cordón (del zapato) (*m.*), 16
shoot disparar, 3; tirar, dar un tiro, dar un balazo, pegar un tiro, pegar un balazo
— **up** pullar (*col.*) (*Caribe*)
shopping mall centro comercial (*m.*), 2
short (*in height*) bajo(a), bajito(a) (*Cuba*), chaparro(a) (*Méx.*), 4; (*in length*) corto(a)
shorts shorts, pantalones cortos (*m. pl.*), 4
short-sleeved de mangas cortas
shot balazo (m.)
shotgun escopeta (*f.*)
should deber, 2
shoulder hombro (*m.*)
shout gritar, 18
show mostrar (o:ue), enseñar, 7
shower ducharse
shut up! ¡cállese!, 20
side lado (*m.*), 13
sidewalk acera (*f.*), banqueta (*f.*) (*Méx.*), 9
sign firmar, 12
silent callado(a), 6
silver plata (*f.*), 11
silverware cubiertos (*m. pl.*), 11
sincerely sinceramente, 14
single soltero(a), P
sir señor (Sr.) (*m.*), P
sister hermana (*f.*)
— **in-law** cuñada (*f.*)
sit-down sentar(se) (e:ie)
sit down tome asiento, siéntese, 8
situation situación (*f.*)
size tamaño (*m.*)
skeleton key llave falsa (*f.*), ganzúa (*f.*)
skin piel (*f.*)
skinny flaco(a)
skirt falda, pollera (*f.*), 17
slap bofetada (*f.*), galleta (*f.*) (*Cuba y Puerto Rico*)
— **on the buttocks** nalgada (*f.*)
sleep dormir (o:ue), 6
sleeveless sin mangas
slow despacio
slowly despacio, 1
small pequeño(a), 1
smell olor (*m.*), 19
— **of** olor a, 19
smoke humo (*m.*), 5; fumar, 7
smuggle contrabandear
smuggler contrabandista (*m., f.*), 1
smuggling contrabando (*m.*)
snort (cocaine) darse un pase
snow nevar (e:ie); nieve (*f.*)
so tan, 12; por lo tanto, 20
— **long** hasta luego, P
— **that** para que
sobriety test prueba del alcohol (*f.*), 9
Social Security Seguro Social, 7
solicit solicitar, 15
some algún, alguno(a), 6
someone alguien, 4
something algo, 5
sometimes a veces, 2
son hijo (*m.*)
— **in-law** yerno (*m.*)
soon pronto, 4
sorry: I'm — lo siento, 6
south sur (*m.*)
southeast sureste (*m.*)
southwest suroeste (*m.*)
Spanish (language) español (*m.*), 1
spanking nalgada (*f.*)
sparkplug bujía (*f.*)
speak hablar, 1
special especial
speed velocidad (*f.*), 9; (drugs) clavo (*m.*) (*col.*)
— **limit** límite de velocidad (*m.*), velocidad máxima (*f.*), 9
spell deletrear, 1
spirits licor, 20
sports car carro deportivo (*m.*)
spot mancha (*f.*)
spread extender (e:ie), 9
— **one's feet** separar los pies
spreadeagle abrir las piernas y los brazos
spring primavera (*f.*), 10
— **break** descanso de primavera (*m.*), vacaciones de primavera (*f. pl.*), 10
stab dar una puñalada
stand pararse, 16
— **up!** ¡póngase de pie!
standing parado(a), 7
start (a car) arrancar
starter arranque (*m.*), motor de arranque (*m.*)
state estado (*m.*), 2; (*adj.*) estatal, 9
statue estatua (*f.*)
stay permanecer, 6; quedarse, 10
steal (from) robar, 10; llevarse, 11
steering wheel volante (*m.*), timón (*m.*) (*Cuba*)
stenographer taquígrafo(a) (*m., f.*)
stepbrother hermanastro (*m.*)
stepdaughter hijastra (*f.*)
stepfather padrastro (*m.*), 3
stepmother madrastra (*f.*), 3
stepsister hermanastra (*f.*)
stepson hijastro (*m.*)
still (*adv.*) todavía, 2; (*adj.*) quieto(a), 13
stolen robado(a), 10
stomach estómago (*m.*)
stone piedra (*f.*)
stop suspender, 5; detener, 6; parar, 12
— **!** ¡alto!, 3; ¡párese!, ¡pare!
— **mail (newspaper) delivery** suspender la entrega del periódico (de la correspondencia)
— **(doing something)** dejar de (+ *inf.*), 6
— **line** línea de parada (*f.*), 12
store tienda (*f.*)
straight (*hair*) lacio(a)
to go — ahead seguir (e:i) derecho, 2
strange extraño(a), 4
stranger extraño(a) (*m., f.*), 5; desconocido(a) (*m., f.*)
street calle (*f.*), 1
step paso (*m.*), 9
stretch out extender (e:ie), 9
stretcher camilla (*f.*)
strike golpear, 18
struggle luchar, 18
student estudiante (*m., f.*), 7
study estudiar, 17
stutter tartamudear
stutterer tartamudo(a) (*m., f.*)
submit (oneself) to someterse a, 9
succeed in (doing something) llegar a (+ *inf.*), 18
such a thing tal cosa, 19
sue demandar
sufficient suficiente, 15
suffocate ahorcar, 8; sofocar, 8
suggest sugerir (e:ie), 16
summer verano (*m.*)
supermarket mercado (*m.*), supermercado (*m.*)
support apoyo (*m.*)
supreme court tribunal supremo (*m.*)
sure! ¡cómo no!, 7
surname apellido (*m.*), P
suspect sospechar, 7
suspicion sospecha (*f.*), 8
suspicious sospechoso(a), 5
swear jurar
sweater suéter (*m.*), 17
swimming pool alberca (*f.*) (*Méx.*), piscina (*f.*)
swindle estafar, 14; estafa (*f.*), 14
switchblade navaja (*f.*), 8
system sistema (*m.*), 5

© 2017 Cengage Learning

T

take llevar, 2; tomar, 6
— a drug darse un pase
— a seat tomar asiento, P
— a step dar un paso, 9
— away quitar, 8
— care of cuidar, 5
— drugs endrogarse
— measures tomar medidas, 5
— off (clothing) quitarse, 16
— out sacar, 6
talk hablar, 1; conversar
tall alto(a), 4
tank tanque (*m.*)
tape recorder grabadora (*f.*), 11
tattoo tatuaje (*m.*), 7
teacher maestro(a) (*m., f.*)
technician técnico(a) (*m., f.*), 10
teenager adolescente (*m., f.*), jovencito(a) (*m., f.*), 17
telephone teléfono (*m.*), 1; telefónico(a), 4
— book guía de teléfonos (*f.*), 16
— call llamada teléfonica (*f.*), 5
— number número de teléfono (*m.*), P
— operator telefonista (*m., f.*), 1
television set televisor (*m.*), 10
tell decir (e:i), 7; contar (o:ue), 18
temperature temperatura (*f.*), 12
tennis shoe zapato de tenis (*m.*); zapatilla
tenth décimo(a), P
tequila tequila (*f.*), 15
terrace terraza (*f.*)
terrified aterrorizado(a), 18
test prueba (*f.*), 9
thank you (very much) (muchas) gracias, P
that que, 3; eso (*m.*), 5; aquel, aquello(a), 18
— is to say . . . es decir..., 18
— one ése(a), 8
then entonces, 4
there para allá, 1; allá, allí, 2; ahí, 16
— is (are) hay, 1
— was (were) hubo, 11
therefore por lo tanto, 20
these estos(as), 6
thief ladrón(ona) (*m., f.*), 3
thin delgado(a), 7; flaco(a)
thing cosa (*f.*), 6; artículo (*m.*), 14
think creer, 4; pensar (e:ie), 5
to — so creer que sí, 7
third tercero(a), 8
this este(a), 2
— one éste(a) (*m., f.*), 8
— time esta vez, 8
threat amenaza (*f.*), 20
threaten amenazar, 18
through por, 2
throw echar
— away tirar, 10
thumb pulgar (*m.*)
ticket multa (*f.*), 6
tie atar
tie corbata (*f.*)
tile roof techo de tejas (*m.*)
tilt one's head back echar la cabeza hacia atrás, 9
time hora (*f.*), 3; tiempo (*m.*), 5; vez (*f.*), 8
just in — a tiempo, 13
on — a tiempo, 13
tip punta (*f.*), 9
tire llanta (*f.*) (*Méx.*), goma (*f.*) (*Cuba*), neumático (*m.*), 20
tired cansado(a), 8
title título (*m.*)
to a, 2; hacia; para, 5
— the al, 3; del, 3
— the left (right) a la izquierda (derecha), 2
today hoy, P
toe dedo del pie (*m.*)
together juntos(as), 9
tomorrow mañana
tongue lengua (*f.*)
tonight esta noche, 5
too también, 5
— much demasiado(a), 12
tooth diente (*m.*)
top quality de primera calidad, 14
totally totalmente, 11
touch tocar, 9
tow zone zona de grúa
toward hacia, 7
town pueblo (*m.*), 10
toy juguete (*m.*)
— store juguetería (*f.*)
traffic tráfico (*m.*); tránsito (*m.*)
slow — tránsito lento (*m.*)
— light semáforo (*m.*), 12
— sign señal de tránsito (*f.*)
— violation infracción de tránsito (*f.*), 6
trained entrenado(a), 4
trash basura (*f.*), 10
treat tratar, 8
tremble temblar (e:ie), 13
trespassing: no — prohibido pasar
trial juicio (*m.*)
trim bushes (trees) podar arbustos (árboles)
trip viaje (*m.*)
trousers pantalón (*m.*), pantalones (*m. pl.*), 4
truck camión (*m.*), 13
true? ¿verdad?, 2
trunk (of a car) maletero (*m.*), cajuela (*f.*) (*Méx.*), baúl (*m.*) (*Puerto Rico*), 20; portaequipajes (*m.*)
truth verdad (*f.*), 11
try (to) tratar (de), 4
T-shirt camiseta, (*f.*)
turn doblar, 2; girar, 13
— around darse vuelta, voltearse, (*Méx.*), virarse, 2
— off apagar, 9
— on (a light) prender, 4; encender (e:ie), 5
— over (something to someone) entregarle a, 11
— signal luz de giro (*m.*)
twice dos veces, 17
two-way traffic doble circulación (*f.*), doble vía (*f.*)
type clase (*f.*), 7

U

uncle tío (*m.*), 5
uncomfortable incómodo(a), 2
unconscious desmayado(a), 13
under debajo (de), 13
— the influence (of) bajo los efectos (de), 6
undercover police policía secreta (*f.*), 15
underneath debajo de, 13
understand entender (e:ie), 6; comprender, 18
underwear ropa interior
united unido(a), 5
unless a menos que, 19
until hasta, 2; hasta que, 19
unusual no usual, 5
up to . . . hasta el/la...
up-to-date al día, 11
upholstery tapicería (*f.*)
urgent urgente, 4
urgently urgentemente, 14
urine orina (*f.*), 9
use uso, 2; usar, 4
can be used puede usarse, 6
will be used se usará, 6
used usado(a)
usual usual, 5
usually generalmente, 17

V

vacant desocupado(a), 3
vacation vacaciones (*f. pl.*); descanso (*m.*)
valid válido(a), 12
value valor (*m.*), 11
vandalism vandalismo (*m.*), 6
vehicle vehículo (*m.*), 13
venereal disease enfermedad venérea (*f.*), 18
verb verbo (*m.*)
verdict fallo (*m.*), veredicto (*m.*)
very muy, P
— much muchísimo, 15
veterinarian veterinario(a)
victim víctima (*f.*), 17
video camera cámara de vídeo (*f.*), videocámara (*f.*), 10
videogame videojuego
violent violento(a), 8
visible visible, 5
vocabulary vocabulario (*m.*)
voluntarily voluntariamente, 20

W

waist cintura (*f.*), 13
— high a nivel de la cintura
wait (for) esperar, 7

© 2017 Cengage Learning

walk caminar, 2
wall pared (*f.*), 6
wallet cartera (*f.*), billetera (*f.*), 16
want desear, 1; querer (e:ie), 5
warning advertencia, 12
warrant orden (*f.*), 8; permiso (*m.*), 20
wart verruga (*f.*)
waste perder (e:ie), 6
watch reloj (*m.*), 16; mirar
watching mirando
water agua (*f. but* el agua)
  — pump bomba de agua (*f.*)
watering riego (*m.*), 5
way manera (*f.*), modo (*m.*), 5 forma (*f.*), 8
weapon arma (*f. but* el arma), 8
wear llevar, llevar puesto(a), 2; tener puesto(a), 17
week semana (*f.*), 4
  a — ago hace una semana, 14
weigh pesar, 20
weight peso (*m.*)
welcome: you're — de nada, no hay de qué, P
well bien, P
west oeste (*m.*)
what lo que, 8
what? ¿qué?, 1; ¿cuál?, 4
  — can I (we) do for you? ¿en qué puedo (podemos) servirle?, ¿qué se le ofrece?, P
  — else? ¿qué más?, 7
  — time was (is) it? ¿qué hora era (es)?, 18
  — 's new? ¿qué hay de nuevo?, P
  — 's wrong? ¿qué tiene(s)?, 7
wheel rueda (*f.*)
wheelchair silla de ruedas (*f.*)
when cuando, 6
when? ¿cuándo?, 4
where? ¿dónde?, 1
  — to ¿adónde?, adonde, 5
whereabouts paradero (*m.*)
which? ¿cuál?, 4
while mientras, 20
white blanco(a), 4
who? ¿quién?, 1; ¿qué?, 2
whole todo(a), 8
  the — . . . todo(a) el (la)...
whose cuyo(a), 15
why? ¿por qué?, 2
widow(er) viudo(a) (*m., f.*)
wife esposa (*f.*), mujer (*f.*)
wig peluca (*f.*)
will voluntad (*f.*), 17
willing dispuesto(a), 8
window ventana (*f.*), 5; (*in a car*) ventanilla
  — with bars con rejas, 5
windshield parabrisas (*m.*)
  — wiper limpiaparabrisas (*m.*)
wine vino (*m.*), 20
winter invierno (*m.*)
wish desear, 1; querer (e:ie), 5
with con, P
  — (black) hair de pelo (negro), 17
  — blue eyes de ojos azules, 7
  — her con ella; consigo
  — him con él, 6; consigo
  — me conmigo, 6
  — you contigo (*informal*), 15; con usted (*formal*)
within dentro de, 6
without sin, 3, 9
  — fail sin falta, 19
witness testigo (*m., f.*), 14
woman mujer (*f.*), 1
word palabra (*f.*)
work trabajo (*m.*), 8
working: not — descompuesto(a), 19
wrist muñeca (*f.*)
write escribir, 6
  — down anotar, 10

X

X-ray radiografía (*f.*), 13

Y

yard patio (*m.*), 3
year año (*m.*), 11
yellow amarillo(a), 7
yes sí, 1
yesterday ayer, 8
yet todavía, 2
You are under arrest! íQueda arrestado(a)!
young joven, 4
  — boy (girl) chico(a) (*m., f.*), chamaco(a) (*m., f.*) (*Méx.*), 13
  — lady señorita (Srta.) (*f.*), P
  — man (woman) joven (*m., f.*), 6
younger menor, 4
your su, 1; tu, 2
yours suyo(a), tuyo(a)
yourself sí mismo(a)

Z

zone zona (*f.*), 9

© 2017 Cengage Learning

Hispanos en Estados Unidos

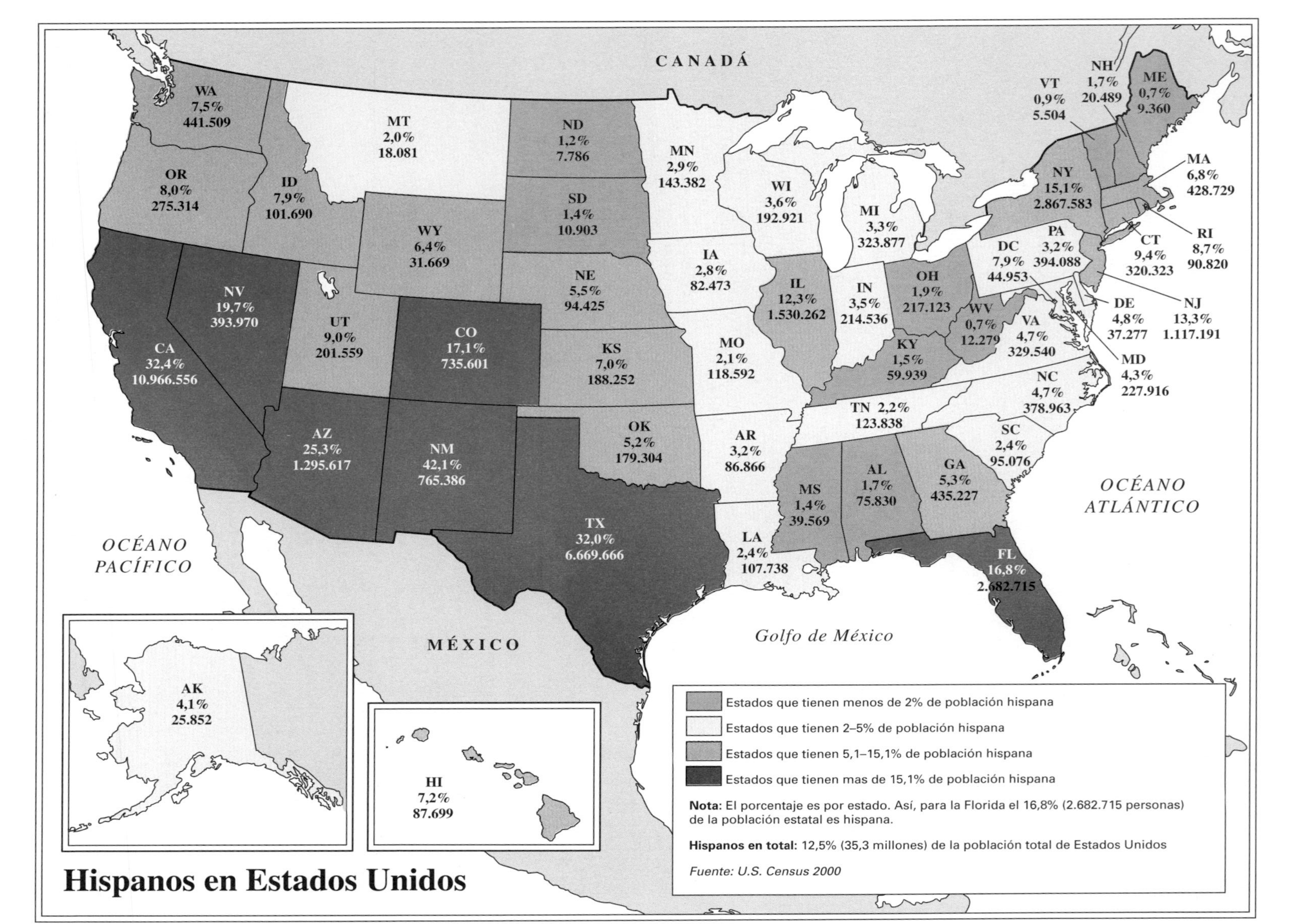

Mar Caribe
OCÉANO ATLÁNTICO
OCÉANO PACÍFICO
TRINIDAD Y TOBAGO
Puerto España
Barranquilla
Cartagena
Maracaibo
Caracas
La Guaira
San Carlos
Ciudad Bolívar
VENEZUELA
Río Orinoco
Georgetown
Paramaribo
Cayena
Salto Ángel
GUYANA
SURINAM
GUAYANA FRANCESA
Medellín
Río Magdalena
Zipaquirá
Bogotá
Cali
COLOMBIA
Popayán
San Agustín
Otavalo
Pichincha
Santo Domingo de los Colorados
Quito
ECUADOR
Chimborazo
Guayaquil
CORDILLERA DE LOS ANDES
Ecuador
Río Negro
Río Amazonas
Manaos
Belén
Iquitos
Río Madeira
Sipán
Trujillo
BRASIL
Recife
PERÚ
Machu Picchu
Callao
Lima
Cuzco
Lago Titicaca
Puno
La Paz
Cochabamba
Arequipa
Tiahuanaco
Río Paraguay
Brasilia
Salvador
BOLIVIA
Arica
Sucre
Potosí
Iquique
Bello Horizonte
Río Paraná
Filadelfia
PARAGUAY
Asunción
Río de Janeiro
San Pablo
Santos
Trópico de Capricornio
Antofagasta
Salta
San Miguel de Tucumán
Puerto Iguazú
Resistencia
CHILE
Río Uruguay
Puerto Alegre
Córdoba
Aconcagua
Mendoza
Viña del Mar
Valparaíso
Santiago
Rosario
URUGUAY
Montevideo
Buenos Aires
La Plata
Punta del Este
ARGENTINA
Río de la Plata
Concepción
Mar del Plata
Río Colorado
Bahía Blanca
Bariloche
Puerto Montt
PATAGONIA
Estrecho de Magallanes
Islas Malvinas
Punta Arenas
TIERRA DEL FUEGO
Cabo de Hornos
ISLAS GALÁPAGOS
San Salvador
Santa Cruz
San Cristóbal
Isabela
ECUADOR
América del Sur
0 250 500 Km.
0 250 500 Mi.

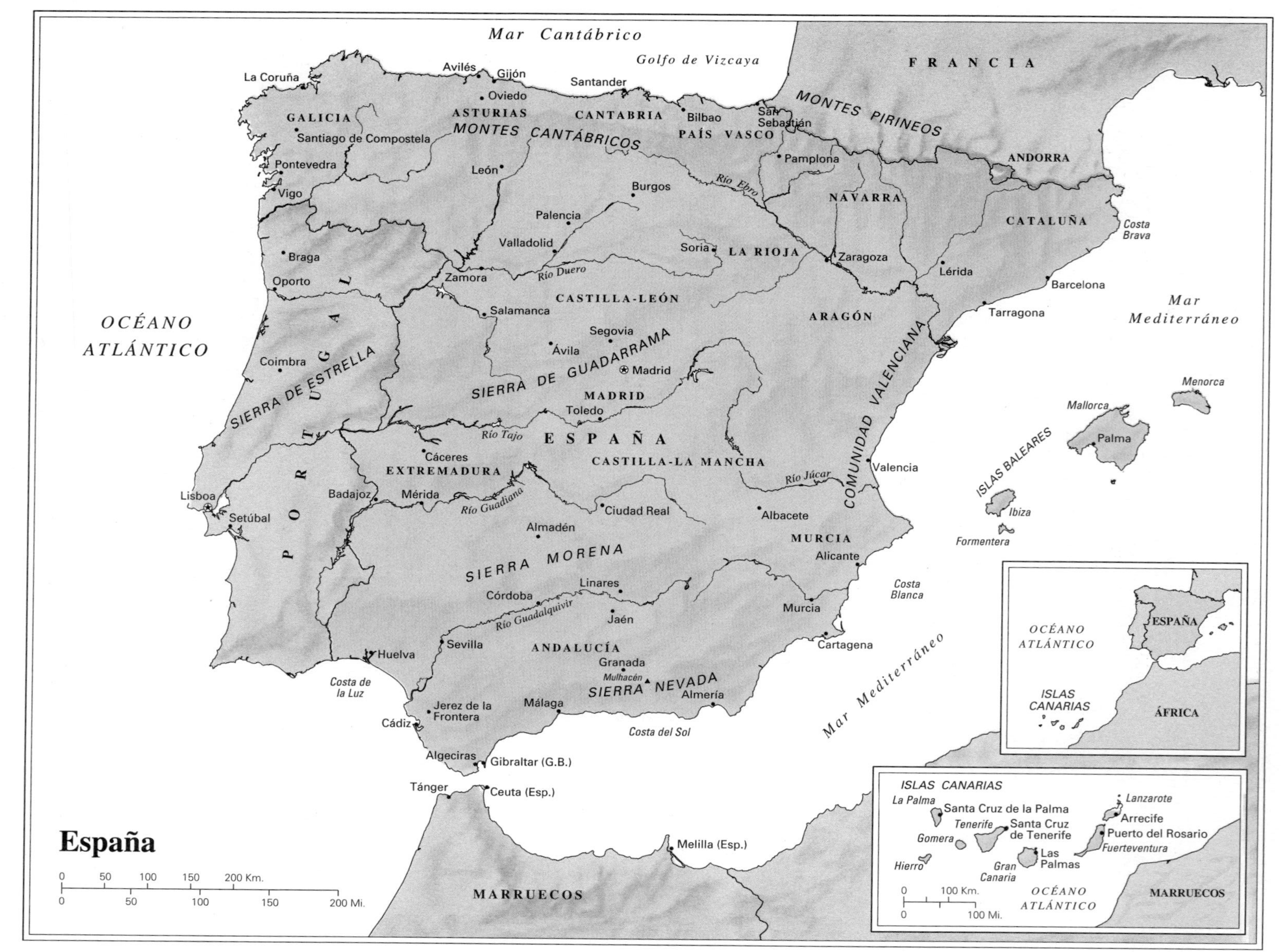
España
Mar Cantábrico
Golfo de Vizcaya
FRANCIA
MONTES PIRINEOS
ANDORRA
OCÉANO ATLÁNTICO
Mar Mediterráneo
La Coruña
Avilés
Gijón
Oviedo
Santander
Bilbao
San Sebastián
GALICIA
Santiago de Compostela
ASTURIAS
MONTES CANTÁBRICOS
CANTABRIA
PAÍS VASCO
Pamplona
Pontevedra
Vigo
León
Burgos
Río Ebro
NAVARRA
CATALUÑA
Costa Brava
Palencia
Valladolid
Soria
LA RIOJA
Zaragoza
Lérida
Barcelona
Braga
Oporto
Zamora
Río Duero
Tarragona
CASTILLA-LEÓN
Salamanca
ARAGÓN
Segovia
Ávila
SIERRA DE GUADARRAMA
Madrid
MADRID
Toledo
Coimbra
SIERRA DE ESTRELLA
PORTUGAL
COMUNIDAD VALENCIANA
Río Tajo
ESPAÑA
Cáceres
EXTREMADURA
CASTILLA-LA MANCHA
Valencia
Río Júcar
Lisboa
Setúbal
Badajoz
Mérida
Río Guadiana
Ciudad Real
Albacete
Almadén
MURCIA
Alicante
SIERRA MORENA
Linares
Córdoba
Río Guadalquivir
Jaén
Murcia
Costa Blanca
Cartagena
Sevilla
ANDALUCÍA
Huelva
Granada
Mulhacén
SIERRA NEVADA
Almería
Costa de la Luz
Jerez de la Frontera
Málaga
Cádiz
Costa del Sol
Algeciras
Gibraltar (G.B.)
Tánger
Ceuta (Esp.)
Melilla (Esp.)
MARRUECOS
ISLAS BALEARES
Menorca
Mallorca
Palma
Ibiza
Formentera
ESPAÑA
ÁFRICA
ISLAS CANARIAS
ISLAS CANARIAS
La Palma
Santa Cruz de la Palma
Tenerife
Santa Cruz de Tenerife
Gomera
Hierro
Gran Canaria
Las Palmas
Lanzarote
Arrecife
Puerto del Rosario
Fuerteventura
MARRUECOS
0 100 Km.
0 100 Mi.
0 50 100 150 200 Km.
0 50 100 150 200 Mi.